ISBN 978-1-330-45547-0
PIBN 10064727

1 MONTH OF
FREE
READING

at

www.ForgottenBooks.com

By purchasing this book you are eligible for one month membership to ForgottenBooks.com, giving you unlimited access to our entire collection of over 700,000 titles via our web site and mobile apps.

To claim your free month visit:
www.forgottenbooks.com/free64727

English
Français
Deutsche
Italiano
Español
Português

www.forgottenbooks.com

Mythology Photography **Fiction**
Fishing Christianity **Art** Cooking
Essays Buddhism Freemasonry
Medicine **Biology** Music **Ancient
Egypt** Evolution Carpentry Physics
Dance Geology **Mathematics** Fitness
Shakespeare **Folklore** Yoga Marketing
Confidence Immortality Biographies
Poetry **Psychology** Witchcraft
Electronics Chemistry History **Law**
Accounting **Philosophy** Anthropology
Alchemy Drama Quantum Mechanics
Atheism Sexual Health **Ancient History**
Entrepreneurship Languages Sport
Paleontology Needlework Islam
Metaphysics Investment Archaeology
Parenting Statistics Criminology
Motivational

ENGLISH PHILOSOPHERS.

Though not issued in chronological order, the series will, when complete, constitute a comprehensive history of English Philosophy. Two Volumes will be issued simultaneously at brief intervals.

The following are already arranged :—

BACON.
> Professor FOWLER, Professor of Logic in Oxford.

BERKELEY.
> Professor T. H. GREEN, Professor of Moral Philosophy, Oxford.

HAMILTON.
> Professor MONK, Professor of Moral Philosophy, Dublin.

J. S. MILL.
> Miss HELEN TAYLOR, Editor of the " Works of Buckle," &c.

MANSEL.
> Rev. J. H. HUCKIN, D.D., Head Master of Repton.

ADAM SMITH.
> Mr. J. FARRER, M.A., Author of "Primitive Manners and Customs."

HOBBES.
> Mr. A. H. GOSSET, B.A., Fellow of New College, Oxford.

BENTHAM.
> Mr. G. E. BUCKLE, M.A., Fellow of All Souls', Oxford.

AUSTIN.
> Mr. HARRY JOHNSON, B.A., late Scholar of Queen's College, Oxford.

HARTLEY.   JAMES MILL.
> Mr. E. S. BOWER, B.A., late Scholar of New College, Oxford.

Preparing for Publication, in Monthly Volumes, a Series of

ILLUSTRATED TEXT-BOOKS

OF

ART-EDUCATION.

Edited by **EDWARD J. POYNTER, R.A.,**

DIRECTOR FOR ART, SCIENCE AND ART DEPARTMENT.

———————

he First Series of ILLUSTRATED TEXT-BOOKS OF ART-EDUCATION
will be issued in the following Divisions :—

PAINTING.

CLASSIC AND ITALIAN.
GERMAN, FLEMISH, AND DUTCH.
FRENCH AND SPANISH.
ENGLISH AND AMERICAN.

ARCHITECTURE.

CLASSIC AND EARLY CHRISTIAN.
GOTHIC AND RENAISSANCE.

SCULPTURE.

ANTIQUE: EGYPTIAN AND GREEK.
RENAISSANCE AND MODERN.

ORNAMENT.

DECORATION IN COLOUR.
ARCHITECTURAL ORNAMENT.

Each Volume will contain from Fifty to Sixty Illustrations, large crown 8vo,
will be strongly bound for the use of Students. The price will be 5*s*.

SWEDEN AND NORWAY.

LONDON :
PRINTED BY GILBERT AND RIVINGTON, LIMITED,
ST. JOHN'S SQUARE.

DL
9
. W89

GUSTAF ADOLF.

[Frontispiece.

GUSTAF AI

WAY.

DS, B.D.

.GE, OXFORD.

 _USTRATIONS.

London:

MARSTON, SEARLE,

BUILDINGS, 188, FLEET ST.

1882.

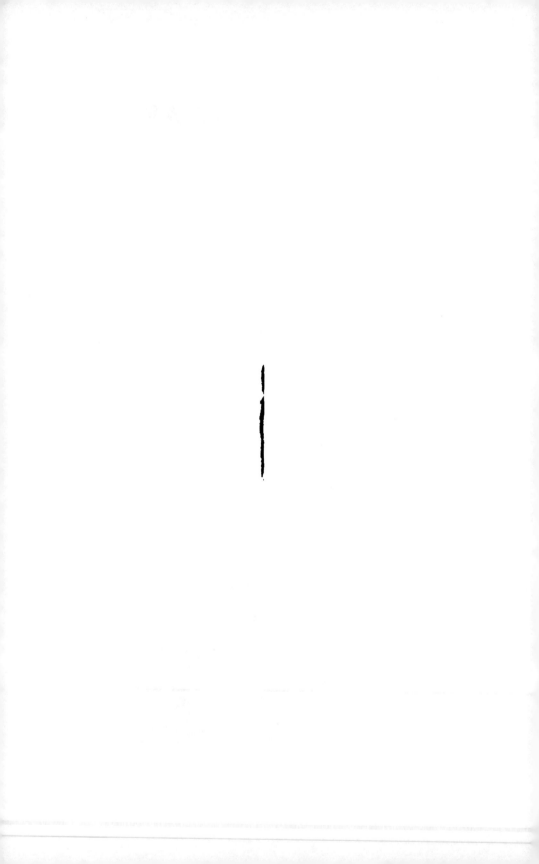

SWEDEN AND NORWAY.

BY THE

REV. F. H. WOODS, B.D.

FELLOW OF ST. JOHN'S COLLEGE, OXFORD.

WITH ILLUSTRATIONS.

London:

SAMPSON LOW, MARSTON, SEARLE, & RIVINGTON,

CROWN BUILDINGS, 188, FLEET STREET.

1882.

PREFACE.

THE interest felt by different classes of minds in a foreign country admits of a boundless variety. Some care for little but natural scenery and adventure. With the eye of an artist, or the enthusiasm of an explorer, they will travel hundreds of miles to visit some novel picture of natural beauty, or attempt some untried and dangerous exploit. To others, the great charm of a country is its natural history. It is chiefly interesting to them in proportion as its animals and plants, or the rocks of which it is composed, open out new fields for scientific inquiry. The interest of many, on the other hand, is entirely engrossed by the inhabitants. They wish to learn all that concerns the present condition of the people, or its past history ; they seek, perhaps, to discover what contributions it has made, or is making, towards European civilization in general and special branches of culture.

In preparing this book, I have tried to keep

these different classes in view; but, on the whole, the work is designed for the general reader rather than the specialist. The latter can hardly expect to be satisfied, without consulting some special work on his favourite theme. I have added in Appendix D, at the end of the volume, all the books from which I have obtained any substantial information. I have attempted as far as possible to give throughout my own impressions of the country and the people, correcting them and enlarging them, where it seemed necessary, by a comparison with the most trustworthy sources which were within my reach. On all statements of a statistical character I have taken the greatest pains to get accurate information. That the work in other respects is full of imperfections, I am only too painfully aware.

Perhaps some special apology is due for having devoted so much of my limited space to the historical part of the subject. I did this advisedly; it seemed to me that the interest attaching to this people lay more in their past history than in their present condition. In thinking of Scandinavia, we are naturally reminded of the time when "the hardy Norseman" was the terror of all the coasts of Europe, or that in which a Gustaf Adolf or a Karl XII. made an indelible impression on European history. If some considerable space is devoted to such kings as Olaf Tryggvason and

Gustaf Vasa, it is because to the energy and power of such men the Norwegian and Swedish nations may be almost said to owe their existence.

The spelling of foreign names has proverbial difficulties. In the case of Scandinavia these are more than usually great, on account of the different methods employed, not only by Swedish and Danish writers respectively, but even by individual writers in either country. My chief aim has been to be consistent, even at the risk of seeming pedantic. I have studiously avoided all attempts to Anglicize Scandinavian names or words, a practice which often only increases the confusion. In modern Swedish words, I have adopted the official spelling employed in Government reports, &c. The Danish orthography I have only altered where a different symbol is employed to express what is philologically and phonetically precisely the same letter. Thus I have always used *k* to express the hard *c* and hard *ch* in both languages ; and have altered the crossed *o* and double *a* of the Danish to the corresponding *ö* and *å* of Swedish. On the same principle I have represented the other double vowels of Danish by simple vowels.[1] This method is on the lines of the recommendations made by the commission for the reform of spelling, which met at Stockholm in 1869. It is obvious that in a work

---

[1] Especially in describing Norway, where Danish is the language used, see pp. 113—117.

describing the two kingdoms in close connexion, the adoption of some such plan was almost necessary. Otherwise the same words must have been differently spelt, as they happened, often accidentally, to be used of one or the other kingdom, and anything like a comparison between the two languages would have been extremely perplexing to those unacquainted with either. The reader is reminded that *j* always has the sound of consonantal *y*. The letter *v* has been used in this work wherever the English *v* sound was intended, as in such words as Vener, Vetter, which are always so pronounced; on the other hand, *w* is intended to have its ordinary English pronunciation.

I beg to take this opportunity of thanking all those who have in one way or another helped me in preparing this work. I feel especially grateful to Mr. York Powell, Law Lecturer at Christ Church, Oxford, and Dr. Vigfusson, to whose help in early Scandinavian studies I owe very much. Above all, I wish to express my best thanks to Dr. Wickberg, Docent at Lund University, who has helped me not only by much valuable information about the state of education in Sweden, but also by many useful suggestions and corrections of inaccuracies throughout the work. At the same time I wish to acknowledge my obligations to all those writers whose works I have consulted in preparing this work (see Appendix D).

CONTENTS.

~~~~~~

a

CHAPTER VIII.

CHAPTER IX.

CHAPTER X.

LIST OF ILLUSTRATIONS.

0 2 4 6 8 10 12 14 16 18 20 22

70 68 66

N A

O

LOROTEN

C

Swedish Län.

1. Stockholm, Bro & Södermanland & Upland.
2. Upsala, Upland.
3. Södermanland, Södermanland.
4. Östergötland, Östergötland.
5. Dalsborge,
6. Kronoborg, } Smaland.
7. Kalmar,
8. Gotland, Gotland.
9. Blekinge, Blekinge.
10. Kristianstad, } Skåne.
11. Malmöhus,
12. Halland, Halland.
13. Göteborg & Bohus, Bohus.
14. Elfsborge, } Dal. & Vestergötland.
15. Skaraborge,
16. Vermlands, Vermland.
17. Örebro, Nerike & Vestmanland.
18. Vestmanland, Vestmanland.
19. Kopparborge, Dalarne.
20. Gefleborge, Helsingland & Gestrikland.
21. Vesternorrland, Angermanland.
22. Jemtlands, Jemtland.
23. Vesterbotten, } Lapland.
24. Norrbotten,

Norwegian Amts.

1. Smaalenene.
2. Akershus.
3. Jarlsberg & Laurvik.
4. Buskerud.
5. Kristians.
6. Hedemark.
7. Bratsberg.
8. Nedenäs.
9. Lister & Mandal.
10. Stavanger.
11. S. Bergenhus.
12. N. Bergenhus.
13. Romsdal.
14. S. Trondhjem.
15. N. Trondhjem.
16. Nordland.
17. Finmark.

SWEDEN AND NORWAY.

CHAPTER I.

GEOGRAPHICAL DESCRIPTION.

THE Peninsula of Scandinavia is the most northerly land of the European Continent. Its most distant points are 71° 10′ and 55° 20′ north latitude, and 5° and 31° east longitude.

In shape it may be described as an oblong, with two bulging excresences, one on the west and south-west, the other, which is longer and narrower, on the south. The length from the North Cape, the furthest point on the north, to Lindesnäs, or, as it is usually called, the Naze, the most southerly point of the western excrescence, is 1030 miles; while to Sandhammar, the most southerly point of all, it is 1160. In breadth it varies between about 250 miles in its northern half, and 450 miles (between Hardanger Fjord on the west, and Björkö on the east) at its broadest part towards the south. On the north this peninsula is washed by the Arctic Ocean ; on the west by the North Atlantic and the North Sea ; on the south-west by the Skager Rak ; and, further south, by the Kattegat ; below which it is separated from Denmark by the Sound, a

B

strait about four miles broad. On the south and south-east it is bounded by the Baltic, and on the east by the Gulf of Bothnia, which separates it from Finland. On the north-east it is contiguous to Russian Lapland, from which it is divided mainly by the Tana, Muonio, and Torne rivers. The northern and western parts consist of a mass of gneiss rock, which rises here and there in lofty peaks on the western side, but gradually slopes down into the flatter country on the east and south. This is intersected by many large rivers and lakes.

The northern part of the country for about 300 miles from the North Cape lies within the Arctic Circle. Within this limit the sun goes round the horizon in the north without setting, for a period varying from one day at the southern boundary to nearly three months (i. e., from the 11th of May to the 1st of August) at the North Cape.

From the time when the inhabitants of Scandinavia first had what may be called an historical existence, down to the present day, this country has comprised two kingdoms, Sweden and Norway. Since 1814 they have had a king in common, but in almost all other respects the kingdoms are distinct. The limits of these kingdoms have varied considerably at different times, and have not been marked by any natural boundaries; but as a whole Norway has been confined to the mountain land of the west, while Sweden has comprised the lower land on the east and south. At present the boundary between the two kingdoms lies along the mountain summits of the northern peninsula, at an average of about fifty miles from the western coast, but afterwards diverges in a nearly southerly direction at about an equal distance of 150 to 225 miles from either coast. This boundary is marked throughout by a clearing in the forest of an average road's breadth with stones at regular intervals.

Both kingdoms are divided into a number of provinces, now called in Sweden *läns*, and in Norway *amts*. These are usually based on very ancient divisions, called in Sweden landships (*landskap*), and are, in Norway especially, decided by the physical features of the country. A list of both will be found on the political map at the beginning of this volume.

Besides these there are in Sweden larger divisions, which have arisen mainly out of the historical circumstances of the people, and (though traces of them still remain in the distribution of the courts of justice, and of certain military corps[1]), can hardly be said to constitute political divisions of the country. Thus we have the name Svealand sometimes applied to the country round the Mälar Lake, and some way to the north and west, as being the land of the Svear or Swear, an ancient tribe who settled there, and in course of time, as we shall see, gave their name to *Sweden*. South of Svealand the country is sometimes called Götaland (originally Gautland), as being the land where the Gauts first settled. This name still appears in the Östergötland and Vestergötland landships. It does not properly include the extreme southern *läns*, which till the seventeenth century belonged to Denmark, and are in the title of the Swedish king, and the divisions of the artillery referred to under the name Vende.[2] The country to the north of Svea-

---

[1] See pp. 186, 199.
[2] The official title is *Sveriges, Norges, Gotes och Vendes Konung.*

land is still called Norrland or " Northern Land." In ancient times it was little inhabited, and regarded as almost beyond the pale of civilization. Strictly speaking it is included in Svealand. Further north still, in the mountains, the parts inhabited by the Lapps are conveniently distinguished as Lappmark.

The name *Scandinavia* first occurs in the writings of the elder Pliny (A.D. 79), who describes it as an enormous island. In another passage he calls it *Scandia*. These words are the Latin forms of the word *Scandey*, the island of the Scands, probably an early tribe who settled in the extreme south, where the landship is still called Skåne. Pliny mistook it for the name of the whole peninsula, which he thought was an island. In modern times the term is occasionally, on philological and ethnological grounds, made to include Denmark, and even Iceland.

The word *Norway* exactly corresponds to the old name of the country. The earliest passage in which the name occurs is in the work of the elder Pliny. There can be little doubt that the form *Nerigon* which he uses is a corruption of *Norweg*, still preserved in our English word, and in the French *Norvége*. The *w* was afterwards dropped, whence in old Norse the form became *Noreg*. The transposition of the last two letters in the modern *Norge* probably arose from a false derivation of the word from *rige* "a kingdom," analogous to the formation of *Sve-rige*. The word *Norweg* or *Nordweg*, "north way," was probably given to the

The word Vende was originally applied to the Vendish provinces south of the Baltic, acquired by Gustaf Adolf, and lost in the beginning of this century. The title was retained, but its meaning altered.

country by the early seamen of Sweden as being the land of northern travel, on the same principle that the Baltic in the east was called by them *Osterveg*, or the " east way."

The key to getting a clear knowledge of the main features of a country like Scandinavia is to understand the character of its mountains. The extreme north of the country and the whole of the west may be regarded as consisting of an elevated mass of gneiss rock, declining gradually towards the south-east, but sloping by more abrupt terrace-like declivities towards the west. In this rock have been chiselled on its western side, probably by the action of glaciers, deep and narrow valleys, cut far deeper than the sea level. These being filled with the sea form those sea-arms or *fjords* which penetrate in some cases for 100 miles or more into the heart of the country, and give the coast that extremely irregular appearance which it presents on the map. The word *fjord* is the modern form of the old Norse *fjörð*, plural *firðir*, which we still find, as given by the northmen, in the *firths* or *friths* of the north and east of Scotland. It is connected with the English " fare," in the old sense of "travel " (as in " farewell"), and probably meant any water which, from its sheltered position, made navigation safe. Hence we find it not unfrequently applied to the larger inland lakes of Norway, as for example Rands Fjord in the south-west, and to sounds, as e.g. that between the Lofoten Islands and the mainland, which is called Vestfjord.

The smaller bays are called *viks* (originally *wik*). Traces of this word also have been left by the Northmen on our own coasts in such words as Harwich and Sandwich. A point or headland is called *näs* or *nes*, an old Norse word meaning properly "nose," which is also frequent in such names as Caithness, Shoeburyness, and others, given by the Northmen to places on our shores.

- The mountains, as though by way of retaliating on the invasion of their dominion by the sea, not only stretch out in what may be called descending terraces into the water, but still show their tops in the form of islands—at first lofty and large, but gradually diminishing till they become sunken rocks, making navigation extremely difficult and dangerous.

A larger island is called *ö* or *öland*, which are merely different forms of the old English words *ey* (from which were named such places as Anglesey, Selsey) and *eyland* (which came to be written *island*, because believed to be connected with the word *isle*). Small islands are called *holms*, a name which has been left by the Northmen on the *holms* of the Bristol Channel and elsewhere. Another very striking feature is the absence of tide, or of enough tide to affect the appearance of the coast, especially in the south.[3] It appears even less than it really is, from the way in which the rock or mountain slopes down abruptly into the sea, without a beach, or bank, or even cliff. So that, in some places, the wild flowers grow only just above the seaweed.

Outside, among the islands, the scenery is desolate, and yet tame. As we enter the fjords the outlook is at once richer and grander. The blue-green sea, often as smooth as glass, looks like some enormous flood slowly creeping up the sides of the mountains, which rise on either side in gigantic

[3] See p. 53.

but far from perpendicular precipices, to the height of 4000 or even 5000 feet. There is not a single feature in common with the coast scenery of an English shore.

About two-thirds down the western side of the coast, and just above what has been called the western excrescence, is a narrow fjord which penetrates south-west for seventy miles, and, after making a sharp bend, extends for 120 miles towards the north-east. The name Trondhjem, which was originally given to the whole district, is now used both for the fjord and the ancient capital, built on the south of the bend. North and south of this point, there is a considerable difference in the character of the country. To the north, the mountain mass is long and comparatively narrow, nowhere exceeding 100 miles or so in breadth. In some parts it has something of the character of a ridge, whence the name *Kölen*, " the keel," sometimes applied to it. The intersecting valleys are deeper than those to the south, and the mountain summits more peaked and regular. The same peaked character is preserved in the islands, which are nothing more nor less than mountains with their roots under water. This gives a wild and beautiful effect to the coast scenery of the north.

To the south of Trondhjem the mountain expands into a wide plateau, averaging from three to four thousand feet, sloping down gradually on the Swedish side, but descending more abruptly by what may be called peaked terraces towards the west. The highest elevation of this mountain mass is about 120 miles distant from the western coast. From the top of the plateau there rise several higher peaks or groups of peaks, but in an irregular way, and not so as to form any definite chains. The highest of these are about 8000 feet high. In Norway the word *fjäld* or *fjeld* is generally used to express a group of peaks, or any part of the mountain plateau, which is divided off by natural boundaries from the rest; whereas the word *bjerg* usually signifies a single hill or mountain summit. The modern Danish *fjeld* or *fjäld* is a corrupt spelling of the old word *fjäll*, signifying "mountain," which is still used in Sweden, and was also applied by the Northmen to the *fells* of Cumberland. The Icelandic form is *fjall*.

As in all mountains of sufficiently high elevation or latitude, the higher summits of the range are covered with perpetual snow. The snow-line, as it is usually termed, i.e. the lowest limit at which snow remains unmelted during the summer, depends chiefly on two conditions, viz., the latitude of the mountain, and its distance from the sea, the sea having the effect of modifying the summer heat and so preserving the snow. The line, therefore, varies very considerably in different parts of the country, but is lower in the north and west, higher in the east and south. Thus, in the mountains north of Trondhjem the average height of the snow-line is about 3000 feet, in those south of Trondhjem it is about 5000. The most important of the snow mountains in this part lie to the west of the highest peaks; and in some cases, as in the famous Folgefond, quite close to the sea. The snow-line on this mountain averages not more than 1632 feet.

The character of the snow depends very much on the shape of the mountains. That falling on the flat-table lands disappears in spring and summer, except a few patches here and there which, from

their depth or sheltered position, are able to pro-
tract their ebbing existence till reinforced by the
fresh snows of August and September. On the
single tower-shaped peaks rising here and there out
of the flat wilderness of rock, the snow forms a
convex cap, from which streams of water descend
through the clifts chiselled in the sides. But far
more frequently we find a group of smaller peaks
rising out of a common base, and enclosing a large
hollow, which becomes filled with a convex mass of
ice and snow called a *fond*. These *fonds* frequently
rise far above the surrounding peaks, and sometimes extend for many miles, as e.g. the Jostedal
Fond, which is over ninety miles in length. Down
the valleys, which descend more or less abruptly
between the peaks, the ice, formed by the alternate
process of melting and freezing, is pressed down by
the weight of snow and ice above into numerous
glaciers, which sometimes extend several miles in
length, occasionally even reaching to the sea. The
usual modern word for glacier is *brä;* but the term
is often applied in a wider sense to a *fond* or any
snow-covered summit. The old Norse word for
glacier was *jökull*, which in the later form *jökel*
frequently appears as an appellative, as in Halling
Jökel.

The rivers which drain the mountain mass may
be divided into three classes. (1) Those which
issue from the mountain bogs or tarns supplied by
the summer rains, which collect wherever there is
a sufficient depression in the surface. (2) Those
which are fed by the constant melting of the summer snow. (3) Those which flow from the ends
of the glaciers.

The depth, velocity, and other characteristics of

the rivers, vary much in different parts of their course, according to the nature of the valley by which they find an outlet. On the mountain plateau above, they move so sluggishly that it is not always an easy matter to see which way they are flowing, and frequently expand into broad and shallow marshes and pools. As they leave the upper level they change their character, sometimes with a surprising suddenness. The river, which just now was almost motionless, becomes seized as with a fit of madness, and dashes down over rocks and boulders, roaring, and splashing, and hissing, in endless cascades and waterfalls. As it reaches the lower level of the fjord, it almost as suddenly collects itself again, and becomes a broad deep sober river. In many cases it expands once more into a long lake, properly called a *lo*,[4] which is divided from the fjord by a narrow piece of land called a *täng* or "tongue," said to have been formed by the moraine of an ancient glacier. Sometimes the rivers are still more violent in their behaviour, and throw themselves down headlong from the table-land above into some deep gorge below, or tumble in a succession of cascades down the sloping sides of the rocky mountain valleys. The immense and numerous waterfalls are perhaps, next to the fjords, the most characteristic feature of Scandinavian scenery. In Norway a waterfall is called a *fos*, the modern Danish form of the old Norse word *fors* which still exists in Sweden, though *vattenfall* is the more usual word. Like *fjäll*, the word *fors* was brought to our shores by the Northmen, and is still retained in the northern counties. The spell-

---

[4] As in Oslo, the ancient town near which Kristiania was built.

ing "force" has arisen from the supposed identity of the word with that meaning " power."

On the eastern side the landscape is far less bold. The courses of the rivers are longer and less steep. The valleys are broader, and the hills or ridges between narrower. The rivers expand constantly into long lakes, till they reach the uneven, rocky, but low line of the sea coast. The islands are numerous, but not marked, like those on the western coast, by any regular gradation towards the mainland ; as a rule, too, they are more wooded and peaked.

In the north the rivers have a remarkably straight and nearly parallel course from north-west to south-east ; but those which rise in the mountains opposite Trondhjem southwards, begin to deflect down to the south, till by degrees they empty themselves into those large and beautiful lakes which form almost as striking a feature of the south of Sweden as the fjords do of the Norwegian coast. Those that rise a little further south take an almost southerly course, and flow into the Skager Rak. This is especially the case with the great Glommen river, the largest in the whole of Scandinavia. The change in the direction of the rivers is mainly due to the broken mountain chain, which descends from the Norwegian mountain land in a south-easterly direction, passing between the Vener and Vetter lakes. There is a tolerably regular radiation of the rivers round the south coasts both of Sweden and Norway.

Though the eastern side of Scandinavia is far less elevated than the mountain land of the west, it is far from being strictly speaking a flat country. If we except the extreme southern *läns*, there are

very few flat plains or fens of any extent. For
the greater part the country is divided by
rocky hills, not much unlike, though much lower
than the mountains of the west. They are in fact
a continuation of the spurs of these mountains.
There are, besides these, other hills much resembling them in shape and, like them, covered
usually with pines, but composed of gravel and
sand, and often running in a different direction.
These will be spoken of again in connexion with
the geology of the country. Even the alluvial
soil has in many parts been washed into broad
undulating ground, in general contour much like
the eastern side of the Cotswolds in England.

The most striking feature in the south of Sweden
is the enormous number of lakes. Besides the
larger inland "seas," which we shall have to mention in detail, the rivers often form, for a large part
of their course, continuous chains of little lakes,
too small to be marked on the map. The rivers,
though numerous, are small, and not very deep.
They are generally slow in their course, so that
the lakes, unlike the clear deep tarns of the Norwegian mountains, are apt to be shallow and
muddy, and not unfrequently degenerate into
marshes. The hills in this part of the country are
comparatively low, and in no case much exceed
1000 feet.

We will now mention more in detail those
features of the country which, from their size or
other reasons, specially claim our attention. In
this description we will follow, as far as possible,
the general direction of the Scandinavian mountains from north to south.

On the extreme north-east of the peninsula, and

all but dividing Norway from Finland, is the
Varanger, a fjord of considerable size, but, owing
to its inaccessibility, except by a long circuitous
voyage, seldom visited. To the west the coast is
indented by three large fjords—the Tana, Laxe,
and Porsanger. The first of these is the mouth of
the Tana, a river about 250 miles in length, which,
for three parts of its course, forms the division
between Scandinavia and Russian Lapland. The
Porsanger Fjord extends inland for eighty miles.
A little to the west of its mouth lies the island
Magerö. At its northern extremity is the Nordkap (North Cape). This cape is not itself very
imposing, as compared with many parts of Norway, the highest point in the hill being not more
than 935 feet high. Its chief interest lies in its
being the most northern point in the country,
and hence the spot from which the midnight sun
may be seen at its greatest height and for the
longest time. Every summer, therefore, it is
visited for this object by crowds of pleasure-
seekers from all parts of the world. About 230
miles north of Nordkap is Bear Island. Its name
is derived from the polar bears, which cross over
from Spitzbergen on the ice in large numbers
during the winter season. For the purpose of
hunting these and the walrus, which also abounds
here, parties of Norwegians often take up their
winter quarters in the island; but in some cases,
whether from cold or scurvy or drink, or these
causes combined, have all been cut off. The
island is chiefly composed of coal, which, however,
is, from its sulphurous character, of little use for
fuel.

The most remarkable mountain in the north is

Jökels Fjeld, a large snow mountain near a small fjord which bears its name. The glaciers of the Kvenangstinder opposite are said to be the only glaciers in Norway which actually touch the sea.[5] For 300 miles from the North Cape the coast is completely girded by a band of islands, many of them of a considerable size, and containing lofty mountains. These terminate at last in the famous Lofoten group. The scenery of these islands is extremely beautiful. Out of a flat grassy surface rise mountains with the most fantastic peaks of all shapes and sizes, very different from the round-headed mountains of the south. To the Norwegians these islands are better known in connexion with the great cod fisheries[6] and eider preserves. The largest of them is Hindö, about seventy miles long by twenty-eight in the broadest part. The sound between this island and the shore is called Vestfjord. Near the southernmost extremity of the group, between the islands Värö and Moskenäs, is the world-famed current of Malström, now generally known as Mörköström. The terrors of this gulf are often much exaggerated. It is in fact nothing more than a rapid current, caused by the return of the tide through a narrow and shallow strait, and is only really dangerous at spring-tides, especially when the ebb is met by a gale from the north-west. In ordinary cases it is quite safe for navigation, and fishermen allow themselves to be drifted by its waters in their small boats without fear of danger.

Further south the mountains become higher, till

[5] See Forbes, pp. 78, 79.
[6] See below, pp. 162, 163.

they culminate in Sulitelma, at the head of the
Salten Fjord. This mountain is 6200 feet, and
the highest of the so-called Kölen range. On the
south of Salten Fjord the great Svartisen begins.
This mountain is covered by one of the most extensive *fonds* in the whole country. It is said to
be a mass of ice and snow forty miles long, and
covering an extent of 400 square miles ; but as the
mountains of the north of Scandinavia have not
as yet been perfectly surveyed, no great reliance
can be placed on these figures. This mountain
is very near the sea coast, and its glaciers descend
within a short distance of the sea level.

A little to the south of the extremity of
Svartisen is the quaintly-shaped island called
Hestmandö, or " Horseman Island." It is so called
from its supposed resemblance to a mounted horse.
There is a curious old legend connecting it with
the island Lekö, some 150 miles further down the
coast. It is said that while the horseman was
pursuing Lekömö, the fair "maid of Lekö," they
were both at her prayer transfixed by a sun-
beam and turned into stone. The custom has not
yet died out of taking off the hat to *Lekömö* on
passing the island. Some eighty miles south of
Hestmandö is the no less singular island of Torget.
This contains a granite hat-shaped hill called
Torghatten, about 800 feet high, and pierced right
through by a natural tunnel from east to west.
This cave is 400 feet from the ground, and on its
western side 240 feet high, but diminishes to sixty-
four feet on the east.

About forty-five miles to the east of Torghatten
is a large snow-mountain, over 4000 feet in height,
called Store Börgetjeld. It is, from its position,

however, difficult of access, and not often visited.
A little to the south of Lekö is the group of the
Vigten Isles.

Two rivers only of any considerable size empty
themselves into the sea on the north, the Tana
and the Alten. The former has been already described ; the latter, whose sources rise a little to
the west of the Tana, after a course of 130 miles
flows into the Alten Fjord. As the mountains of
this part of the country lie mostly near the sea, the
rivers which flow to the west have generally a short
and rapid course, and are many of them without
tributaries. To this rule the river Nam forms the
one remarkable exception. Rising in Nams Vand,
a lake to the south of Börgefjeld, it flows after a
course of about ninety miles into a small fjord
below the Vigten Isles, to which it as usual gives
its name. For the reasons above given there are
but few lakes on the western side of the mountain
range. The chief exception is Rös Vand, a lake
about twenty-eight miles long by twelve broad,
which lies not far south of the Svartisen. On
the east, on the contrary, are several large and
rapid rivers. Furthest north is the Torne, which
empties itself into the northern extremity of the
Gulf of Bothnia. This river, with its tributary the
Muonio, forms part of the boundary between the
Russian and Swedish dominions, and gives its name
to the Torne Träsk, the lake from which it rises,
and to the now Russian town of Torneå [7] at its
mouth. The town opposite to it on the Swedish
side is Haparanda. Almost parallel with the
Torne is the Kalix, with its tributary the Lina.

---

[7] The å in the words Torneå, Luleå, &c., means "river."

Further south are the two branches of the Lule, the Great (Stora) and Little (Lilla) Lule, which give their names to the waters through which they flow (Stora Lule Vatten and Lilla Lula Vatten), and to the town of Luleå at the river's mouth. In the same way the Pite and Skelefte give their names to towns at their mouths. Through the lakes Stor Vindeln and Stor Uman flow the Vindel and Ume rivers, which unite about twenty-seven miles from the coast, where lies the town of Umeå. The Ume has the reputation of being the swiftest river of Scandinavia. But by far the largest river in this part is the Ångerman, which stretches into a long fjord-like mouth, in some places as much as two miles broad. This river is navigable for thirty-eight miles. The scenery at its mouth is wild and rocky, much resembling, though in miniature, the fjord scenery of the west. It thus stands in marked contrast to the more southern rivers.

Towards Trondhjem the mountain mass becomes more broken, and is divided by several easy passes. Perhaps the most celebrated of these is that between the Skjäker valley on the west, and the Indal on the south-east. It was by this pass that Olaf the Saint descended with his army into Norway before the fatal battle of Stiklestad. The river Indal flows through a chain of lakes to that which from its size is called Stor Sjön, " the great sea ;" and after being joined by another large tributary, Ammer, finds its way into the gulf, some thirty miles to the south of the Ångerman. To the south of this pass, nearly opposite Trondhjem, are the Syl and Helags fjelds, mountains about 5000 feet high, and just within the Swedish boundary. The mountain spur which descends south-east from these heights, is divided from the western fjeld by the great Glommen river.

In order to get at all a clear idea of the character of the mountains south of Trondhjem, it is most important to get rid of the misleading notions of distinct chains running either north and south or east and west. The whole is one raised convex mass, out of which peaks rise in almost every direction. At the same time it is often necessary, for the sake of classification, to give the peaks which lie near together some common name. We shall have to mention some of the chief of these groups, and the more prominent peaks.

To the south-west of Trondhjem the mountain is called Dovre Fjeld. This plateau, or rather this part of the great plateau, does not exceed an average height of 4000 feet; but from it rise some of the highest peaks in the whole peninsula. The largest of these is Snehätten, "the snow hat," about 7600 feet high, and eighty miles distant from Trondhjem; but the peaks Sorelhö and Gjelthö to the west of it are nearly as large. The Svartås and the Rundane mountains are continuations of the Dovre Fjeld, on the east and south-east. The Dovre Fjeld is drained on the north by the Orkla river, and its numerous tributaries. This river flows through the Orkedal into one of the many branches of the Trondhjem Fjord. To the north-west the fjeld is drained by the Driva, or the Sundals river as it is more usually called from the valley it flows through, which also gives its name to the fjord. On the east and south-east the fjeld is drained by the great river Glommen, and its almost equally large tributary the Lågen; on the west by the northern tributaries of the Rauma. The Glommen

TROLTINDERNE, IN ROMSDAL.

Page 19.

is the largest river in Scandinavia. Its course,
about 352 miles long, is mainly from north to south.
It discharges itself into the Skager Rak at Frederikshald, sixty miles south of Kristiania. It is navigable
at intervals for about 150 miles, interruptions being
caused by frequent falls and rapids. The Rauma
and the Lågen flow out of the same lake, the
Lesje Vand, and so together form a continued
watercourse across the country. The Lesje Vand
is a long, narrow mountain pool, some twelve miles
in length. It lies in a valley which cuts into the
mountain plateau, so that its elevation is not more
than 2000 feet above the level of the sea. Thus the
Dovre Fjeld is to a certain extent divided off from
the mountain-land to the south-west. The Rauma
and Lågen valleys, best known as Romsdal and
Gudbrandsdal, are the most remarkable valleys in
Scandinavia, and are each quite typical of the
character of the rivers on the west and south-east
of the mountain-land. The Rauma is very rapid,
full of cataracts and waterfalls, till it reaches the
lower level, where it glides through a broad valley,
shut in by mountain precipices, whose dark, tower-
ing, snow-crested forms stand out in bold contrast
with the quiet scenery of the valley from which
they rise. The most imposing of these are the
jagged peaks called Troltinderne, "the goblin peaks,"
on the one side, and the thumb-shaped summit of
Romsdalhorn on the other. The Lågen river is
far more peaceable, and only once or twice varies
its comparatively staid pace. At Lillehammer,
some 120 miles from Kristiania, it spreads itself
into the Mjösen Lake, the largest in Norway, being
sixty miles long, by twelve in its broadest part.
At the southern extremity it narrows again into a

broad and deep river ; about twenty miles further
south it flows into the Glommen.   The great
interest of Gudbrandsdal lies in its historical associations.   In ancient times, as at present, it formed
one of the readiest means of communication between north and south, and is constantly alluded
to in the Sagas.   Gudbrand himself, who gave his
name to the valley, was a franklin, contemporary
with Olaf Tryggvason, and grandfather of Olaf
the Saint.   It was also in this valley that the
former pursued the luckless Earl Hakon, when he
hid himself in the pig-stye, and was betrayed by
his faithless thrall.   It was here, too, that Olaf the
Saint is said to have cut down the great image of
Thor, and to have disclosed the rats and mice
which devoured the offerings of his worshippers.
Eidsvold, at the south of the Mjösen Lake, is a
place which recalls very pleasant memories to a
patriotic Norwegian.   It was here that the Constitution was drawn up which guaranteed to the people
their long-lost freedom and independence.

Immediately south-west of Romsdal are " the
Long Mountains " (Langfjeldene), a name sometimes rather vaguely used to include all the mountains south of Dovre Fjeld.   These mountains are
low compared to many in this part of Norway, and
many of them do not rise above the snow level.
Among their roots twist the arms of the beautiful
Stor Fjord.   One of these, the Geiranger, forms
one of the grandest pieces of fjord scenery in the
whole country.   It is about ten miles long, and in
reality a mile broad ; but the mountains which rise
on either side to the height of from 4000 to 5000
feet give it quite the appearance of a narrow
channel.   On the north side of the fjord is a curious

group of waterfalls called the "Seven Sisters," and opposite to these a frowning black precipice, looking like a man's face, which has given rise to many a curious old legend. This fjord ends in a round basin of blue transparent water, surrounded by mountains cut by the silver threads of distant cascades. From the Long Mountains, towards the south-west, stretches the great Jostedal Fond, like in character to Svartisen, but much longer. It is a great mass of snow and ice, over ninety miles in length, and covering an extent of 550 square miles; at its greatest elevation it is 6495 feet in height. Numerous glaciers descend from it on both sides. On its western side, and penetrating almost to its very foot, is the long and narrow Indvik Fjord, chiefly remarkable for the Näsdal and Brixdal glaciers, to which it forms the readiest approach. To the east of Jostedal lie the Jotun—"giant" mountains. The highest of these is Galdhöpiggen, 8161 feet. This is the loftiest mountain in Scandinavia. The summit consists of a conical peak rising out of a snow *névé*, from which several small glaciers descend. A little further south are the Skagastölstinder and Horungtinder peaks. To the very foot of these extends the great Sogne Fjord, which is both in length and breadth by far the largest fjord in Norway, and has many branches. Of the latter the Lyster extends 120 miles from the coast, and is extremely grand. But as a whole, and especially in its straight western part, the very breadth of the fjord makes the barren mountains on either side look small and unimposing.

The chief branches of the Sogne to the north are those of Fjärland and Sogndal. The former leads up to two of the most beautiful of the Jostedal glaciers, Bojums and Suphellens Brä. The whole view up the Fjärland Fjord, with the snow-line of the Jostedal broken by the double peaks of the Skejde mountain, is one of the grandest in Scandinavia. Bojums Brä is about a quarter of a mile broad, and is united by a rough, in-accessible ascent of ice, with the snow fjeld above. In its lower part it is nearly flat, with a silky-looking, waved surface, and cut by a great number of longitudinal crevasses. The termination of the glacier is extremely beautiful—an abrupt cliff of blue and white ice, with the most picturesque peaks, some 500 feet in height, and pierced with dark, hollow caverns, from which flow several glacier streams, enhancing the beauty of the scene, but discomforting the beholder. Suphellens Brä is less beautiful, but remarkable as being completely broken off from the ice above. There is a con-siderable interval of rock between, and in sunny weather avalanches may be seen shooting across. The lowest part of this glacier is only 157 feet above the sea level, and hardly four miles from the end of the fjord. The most important glaciers of the Jostedal Fond, besides those already mentioned, are the glaciers in Daledal or Jostedal valley, which extend for several miles along the eastern side of the mountain. Of these the most striking are the Krondal, Lodal, and Nigård. The latter is especially remarkable for its tortuous shape. The Lodal, which heads the valley, is seven miles long —the largest true glacier in Norway.

On the west of the Sogne Fjord are the Årdal and Lärdal branches. The former leads to the beautiful Årdals Vand, and after some distance to the Morka or Vettis Fos, a great fall of about 1000

VÖRING FOS.

Page 23.

feet, magnificent in early summer, but in the later months deficient in volume. From the Lärdal valley there is a mountain pass over the Fille Fjeld to Kristiania. On the south of the Sogne Fjord there is only one branch of any importance, viz. the double-forked Närodal. Up the magnificent Närodal valley there is a pass across the mountain to the Hardanger Fjord. Between the two forks of the Närodal rises the Stegenåse mountain, and on either side are several snow-capped peaks, of which Blåskarl on the east, and Fresviks Brä on the west, are the most conspicuous. South of Fille Fjeld is the great Halling or Hardanger Fjeld. The highest summit is Halling Jökel, a not very imposing snow mountain, 6350 feet high, at the extremity of the Hardanger Fjord. To the south, Haukelid, Uglefot, and several other summits, varying from 5000 to 6000 feet, continue to rise out of the mountain mass, till at about eighty miles from the coast they begin to descend in the usual terraced fashion towards the sea.

The Hardanger Fjord, in size second only to the Sogne, has, unlike the latter, only two branches of any considerable size. One extends to the east to the foot of the Halling Fjeld, near the source of the river Vöring. The Vöring Fos, the fall which this river makes, is grand beyond description. The river throws a volume of water about as large as that of the Thames at Oxford over a precipice of 968 feet, into a narrow gorge, from which the spray, boiling and frothing like a gigantic cauldron, is dashed up and carried across the fjeld for many miles. The Sör branch turns from the main fjord at a very sharp angle, thus cutting off the Folge-fond from the main fjeld. It is this mountain which adds a special charm to the most beautiful of the Norwegian fjords, combining as it does throughout the most lovely contrast of verdure, wildness, and grandeur. The Folgefond is a great snow *névé*, thirty miles long, and covering an extent of about 100 square miles. On both sides several glaciers descend, of which the most striking are Bondhus and Buerbrä. The former, which is the largest, lies above the Mauranger Fjord, a branch on the west side of the mountain; the latter lies nearly opposite to it on the south, above a little lake, Sandvens Vand, which forms the southern extension of the Sör branch. This beautiful little blue glacier is remarkably interesting to the physiographist, from the fact that it is not, like most glaciers in Norway, receding, but is gradually encroaching on the Jordal valley below, and doing constant injury to the land by the immense boulders it brings down with it. On the east side of the Sör branch, up the Tyssedal valley, is the Ringedals (or Skjæggedals) Fos a broken waterfall of great magnificence; and above, on the fjeld, is a remarkable mountain summit called Hårteigen, a snow-capped tower, which rises out of a wilderness of barren rocks. In the Sandven valley, at the south of the fjord, is a remarkable series of waterfalls, of which Hildals and Låte Fos are most worthy of notice.

The only considerable fjord on the south coast of Norway is that of Kristiania, which, after extending for about sixteen miles at a nearly even breadth of ten miles, suddenly expands to double its breadth, and four miles further north is divided into two narrow channels, that on the east extending into the wide bay of Kristiania, that on the west continuing its narrow course to the town of Drammen.

On the south-east of Norway, the largest valleys are Valders Dal, Halling Dal, and Numedal. The river of Valders Dal, the most northerly of these, drains the Fille Fjeld near the eastern extremity of the Sogne Fjord. Its course is marked by several small lakes. Further down it is joined by Rands River, which flows out of the lake called Rands Fjord, long celebrated for its beauty. A little below is the Hönefos, a fall remarkable for its great breadth and volume. Here the river expands into another large lake called Tyris Fjord. A little further south it unites with the Halling Dal River, which drains the eastern side of Halling Fjeld. The united stream, now called Drammens River, at last finds an outlet at Drammen. Almost parallel with the Halling Dal River is that of Numedal, a river which drains the southern portion of the Halling Fjeld, and at last finds an outlet in the Kattegat near the modern town of Laurvik, a little to the west of Kristiania Fjord.

In the district of Telemark, to the south-west of these valleys, the mountain-land presents very singular features. There is no longer that gradual sloping towards the south-east which occurs elsewhere so universally, but a strange confusion of rivers, lakes, and mountains, in no regular order. It is this which contributes so much to the beauty of the district, and makes it a magnificent exception to the comparative tameness of the eastern side of the fjeld. The most striking object is Gausta Fjeld, a snow peak, or rather ridge, of some 6000 feet, quite cut off from the mountains of the western fjeld by a group of lakes. Out of these flow, eastward and southward respectively, two rivers, the Tin (or Mån), and the Songa, which afterwards curve round and meet in Nordsjöen, a curious double-forked lake in the south. The Tin, which unites the Mjös Vand and Tin Sjöen, flows close by the Gausta Fjeld, after having a little above formed the magnificent double fall of Rjukan Fos, the "Smoking Fall," one of the finest in the country, and well deserving its name.

It still remains to notice the most important geographical details of the south of Sweden, i. e. the part of the country south of the Indal. The Syl Fjeld is drained on the south-east by the sources of the Ljusne, which flows into the Gulf of Bothnia, some seventy-five miles below the mouth of the Indal. By far the most celebrated rivers in this part of the country are the Eastern and Western Dal, which drain the northern part of the ridge separating Sweden from the Glommen valley. These rivers, after a tolerably parallel course, meet a little above the modern Falun, and at length expand into a long narrow lake, from two to three miles broad, which still retains the name of the river. After again narrowing to half a mile's breadth, it joins the gulf a little below the town of Gefle. The eastern branch flows through the Siljan, and near the Runn, lakes, which, though small in size, are memorable for the stories of Gustaf Vasa's early adventures when fleeing from the Danes.[8] Almost parallel with these is the Klar River, which flows out of the Fämund Lake near Rörås, on the Norwegian Fjeld, into the great Vener Lake. The Norwegian part of the river is called Trysil.

[8] See p. 92.

The Vener is by far the largest lake in Scandinavia, being no less than eighty miles long by forty broad. Its oval shape is only broken by the long projecting point, called By Näs, on its north-western side. The country round lies for the most part very low, and from some points in the centre land cannot be seen, except on a very clear day. The surface of the lake is 147 feet above the level of the Baltic. In the south-east, especially, it is full of islands and rocks, which render its navigation difficult and dangerous. At its southern extremity, the lake finds an outlet in the Göta River, which joins the Kattegat at Göteborg, about fifty miles further south. Some ten miles south of the lake are the Trollhätta Falls, a succession of cascades, of no considerable size, but beautifully situated, and made famous by the great Trollhätta Canal. The whole height of the falls taken together is about 120 feet. To the west of the Vener are the Hjelmar and the Mälar lakes. The latter is long and narrow, stretching for sixty miles from west to east, with innumerable smaller branches, and studded with pretty fir-clad islets. It forms one of the most beautiful districts in Sweden. At Stockholm the lake converges into a narrow neck, almost closed by a group of holms, on which, as well as on the two sides, the city is built. To the east of the city the lake continues till it joins the Baltic. This continuation is called "the Salt Sea" (Saltsjön). The two parts are in reality one long fjord, though the water of the Mälar is fresh, because, from the absence of tide, the flow is always seaward. South-west of the Hjelmar, and almost parallel to the Vener, is the almost equally celebrated Vetter. Its direction is from north-east to south-west. Its length is eighty miles, and average breadth twelve, so that it is in point of size the second lake in Scandinavia, and more subject to squalls than any other. The chief outlet is the Motala, a river which joins the Baltic by a little chain of lakes.

The chief hills in the south of Sweden lie in the neighbourhood of the Vetter. The highest is Taberg, 1030 feet high, a little to the south of the lake ; near it is the Husqvarna waterfall. These hills are drained on the west by the Laga, Nissa, and Ätra, the only considerable rivers in the south of Sweden.

The Swedish coast like that of Norway, is bounded by a chain of islands and holms, called the *Skärgård*. There are only two islands of any considerable size. These both lie in the Baltic. The largest, Gotland, is situated about fifty miles from the coast, south-east of Stockholm. Including the island Fårö, which is only separated from it in the north by a sound eleven feet broad, it is eighty-four miles long by twenty broad. In almost every respect it is unlike the rest of Scandinavia. It is surrounded by cliffs, averaging 120 feet ; and consists of a slightly undulating table-land, which never rises to more than 255 feet. It has several extensive marshes, called *träsks*, but no large lakes or rivers. Öland lies parallel with the coast, about forty miles south-west of Gotland, the nearest point being about four miles distant from the shore. It consists of a narrow strip of land, eighty miles long, with a slightly elevated backbone or ridge running the greater part of its length. For the most part it is very dry and barren. A bleak and stony foreground, with a row of windmills in

the back, gives perhaps the best idea of the .
present character of this desolate island. The
interest of both islands lies not in their scenery,
but in their architecture, and historical relics of
all kinds.

CHAPTER II.

FAUNA AND FLORA, GEOLOGY, ETC.

THE fauna of Scandinavia is very similar to what that of our British Isles must have been before the more dangerous animals were exterminated. The largest and most striking animal is the elk (*Alces palmatus*). This noble creature is tolerably abundant in the border forests of Sweden and Norway, where it feeds on the mountain ashes and willows. It is now preserved by stringent laws. Besides the elk there are two species of the deer tribe, the reindeer and the red deer. The former are very abundant on the fjelds, where they collect in large herds in summer, and in winter descend regularly towards the Baltic. They subsist mainly on reindeer moss, which grows abundantly on the otherwise barren rocks ; they are rather darker in colour than those reared by the Lapps.[1] The red deer are now found almost exclusively on a few islands to the southwest of Trondhjem, and are likely before very long to become extinct.

Of carnivorous animals the most remarkable are bears, wolves, gluttons, lynxes, and foxes. The brown bear (*Ursus arctos*) is rapidly diminishing

---

[1] Vide Chapter X.

through the efforts of the Swedish and Norwegian governments, who offer a reward of twenty *kronor* (about 1*l*. 2*s*. 6*d*.) for every one of these animals killed. They are still, however, pretty abundant, especially in the pine forests of Norway, and about 150 on an average are shot annually in this country alone. Great damage is occasionally done to the cattle in a district where one of these formidable animals takes up its quarters. They are found chiefly in the north and west of the country, but occasionally in the south. There is in the Natural History Museum at Stockholm a large stuffed bear, which was shot as far south as Trollhätta. The polar bear is found only on Bear Island.[2] Wolves are also becoming much scarcer, but when the winter is unusually severe they descend in large numbers from the north and do great damage. Two species of glutton are met with, the *Gulo Linnai* and *Gulo borealis*, which chiefly frequent the Norwegian fjelds. Several species of lynx occur, which are often trapped for their skins. There are several kinds of fox; the most prized for its fur is the Arctic or Polar species, which turns white when exposed to severe cold.

Of sea animals, the walrus is found only about Bear Island. Whales are not infrequent in many parts, especially towards the north. The commonest species is the Greenland whale (*Balæna mysticetus*), which is captured in great quantities for the sake of the oil and whalebone. An enormous specimen, caught near the mouth of the Göta River, is pre-served in the museum at Göteborg. Porpoises are very abundant, and are sometimes found in crowds together. There are at least two kinds of seal—the

[2] See p. 13.

spotted seal (*Phoca vitulina*), which is abundant
all along the coast; and the bearded seal (*Phoca
barbata*), which is confined chiefly to the north of
Norway.

Of freshwater animals the otter is very common,
and proves exceedingly destructive to the numerous
species of fish. The beaver is now almost, if not
entirely, extinct; it is certainly not found except in
some of the larger rivers in Norway.

Among other land animals we may mention
hares, badgers, and squirrels. Hares are of two
kinds, the ordinary English brown hare, and the
"blue hare" of the northern counties. These
animals are found for the most part in Sweden.
Badgers are also confined chiefly to this country:
they are frequent on some parts of the west coast,
especially about Göteborg. Squirrels are not very
common, and are necessarily confined to those parts
of the south of Sweden where oaks and beeches
are plentiful.

Of small animals there is a large variety.
Several species of weasel occur. Among these the
ermine (*Mustela erminea*) is highly prized for its
fur. There are many sorts of rodents. What is
now known as the common English rat, is said to
have been brought to our shores in Norwegian
vessels.[3] The most interesting of the rodents is
the lemming (*Hypudæus norvegicus*).[4] It is much
the shape and size of the mole, but longer and
rounder; its colour is a golden buff, with a large
black spot on its neck; its head is rather flat, and
it has often a ring of longer hairs, forming a sort of

[3] However, the Old Norse name, *Mýss Valkar*, "Welsh or foreign
mice," disclaims the animal altogether.
[4] The *Mus lemmus* of Linnæus.

ruff, round its neck. The habitat of this animal is believed to be the mountains of Lapland. From this country great swarms of these creatures emigrate about every ten years. They make their way southward along the Norwegian fjelds, where numbers of them fall victims to birds of prey. Even the reindeer are said to stamp upon them with their feet, and devour their stomachs. Still more are drowned in the rivers and streams which they attempt to cross. The reckless way in which they climb rocks, swim over streams, and even plunge into fjords they can never cross, has given rise to many strange traditions. The commonest of these is to the effect that the army of lemmings used to make their way to some land once united to the country, but now separated by the sea ; that governed by long inherited instincts, and ignorant of the altered condition of things, they still try to follow their old custom, but are invariably drowned in the attempt. The true explanation of these emigrations is probably that these are swarms of young lemmings driven out by the older and stronger on account of the scarcity of food.

The species here described is peculiar to Scandinavia ; but there is one other smaller kind, found only in Siberia. Reptiles occur in the greatest abundance. As might be expected, frogs are extremely common ; toads are quite exceptional. There is a great variety of lizards and newts. Snakes are not very common, but both the common English snake and the adder occur in Sweden.

The birds of Scandinavia are very interesting to a naturalist. There are a great many species of sea and freshwater birds. Curlews, cormorants, ospreys, oyster-catchers, sandpipers, guillemots, and gulls of many kinds, abound among the islands, especially in the north. Among others are found the wild swan, the grey goose, and the great northern diver (*Colymbus glacialis*), and the greater and lesser grebe (*Podiceps minor*). The latter is the bird from which ladies' muffs are often made : it is exceedingly common in all parts of the country. But perhaps the most useful bird to the people is the eider duck. These birds abound to the north of Trondhjem, especially on the Lofoten Islands, where they are carefully preserved, and have become almost domesticated. The eggs are largely used as an article of food, while the down is collected from their nests, and sold for quilts, &c. The birds show a remarkable degree of forbearance, and continue to lay when their nest has been thus doubly spoiled. The great auk (*Alca impennis*) was formerly very abundant, and even a common article of food, but has now become quite extinct ; the little auk (*Alca torda*) is still frequent. Freshwater birds are almost as numerous. The mountain tarns of Norway, and lakes and marshes of Sweden, are particularly suited to the habits of these animals. We may mention among others the red-shanks (*Totanus calidis*) which is very common, and distinguished at once by its lanky red legs and long bill; the green-shanks' (*Totanus glottis*), the red-necked diver (*Colymbus arcticus*), and a large variety of snipe and wild duck.

Of land-birds the predatory kinds are best represented. Several species of eagle occur. Among others the great golden eagle (*Aquila chrysaetos*), which in the north is often very destructive to the young lambs. Owls of all kinds abound ; the most beautiful is the great snowy owl (*Syrnia nyctea*).

Ravens, falcons of several kinds, and nightjars are also frequent. The commonest bird in the country is the magpie. In Norway especially, these are seen everywhere in the valleys and along the fjords. As in England, they are the subject of numberless superstitions. The people think they bring good luck, and, though the Government offer ten *skillings* ($1\frac{1}{2}d$.) apiece for every one killed, will not shoot them. They are allowed to hop about unmolested at the very doors of the houses, and hardly condescend to move out of the way of the passer-by. They sit sometimes a dozen together on the hay rails or on the walls, and form almost as invariable an accompaniment of Norwegian scenery as the birches or pine trees themselves. Another very common bird both in Sweden and Norway is the saddle-backed crow (*Corvus cornix*). The *kråka*, as it is there called, is about as common as the rook in England. It is at once distinguished by its grey back, which gives it a curious appearance. In Scotland it is more frequent. It is not uncommon in the eastern counties of England, where it occurs only in the winter months, and is known as the Royston crow. Fieldfares are also abundant; they feed especially on the berries of the rowan, or mountain-ash.

Of game birds, including snipe and wild duck, there is a large variety. Among these the great capercailzie (*Tetrao urogallus*) deserves the first place. The male of this bird is nearly as large as a turkey, but the hen is much smaller. They were once indigenous in Scotland, but have since been exterminated, and have lately been reintroduced. The black cock (*Tetrao tetrix*) and hazel grouse (*Bonasia europœa*) are very frequent; and in Sweden and some parts of Norway the partridge has become naturalized. But by far the most frequent of game birds is the ptarmigan, known by Swedes and Norwegians as *ripa* or *rype*. These birds are trapped by thousands in the winter months, when they are brought down from the north in sledges, and form a staple article of food. There are several species of this bird in Scandinavia; the most frequent are the *Lagopus saliceti*, and the *Lagopus mutus.* The former is confined to the valleys, the latter is the mountain bird. Like the polar fox, it always turns white in winter or when it lives among the snow of the fjelds. This species is frequent in the highlands of Scotland.

Most of our familiar species are found, especially in the south of Sweden, but are less abundant as a rule than in England. Of these may be mentioned the cuckoo, the greater and less woodpecker, greater whitethroat, missel-thrush, skylark, wood-lark, robin, starling, and sparrow, besides several species of linnet and tit, and many others. The commonest of small birds is the water-wagtail which is met with almost everywhere both in Sweden and Norway.

Of fish there are very many kinds. Those only will be here mentioned which are used for food, or otherwise connected with the industries of the people. The most important by far are the herring and the cod. The former are found all along the west coast, but principally in the north. They visit the coast in the late summer and early autumn in search of smaller prey. The cod abounds, more than anywhere else, near the Lofoten Islands, and is taken in great numbers, chiefly in the spring months. There is besides a large quantity of ling, coal-fish (*Merlangus carbonarius*), as well as the

Greenland shark (*Scymus glacialis*), all of which are found useful as supplying the market with "pure cod-liver oil." Several kinds of flounders, turbot, brill, and other flat fish are numerous, especially on the south coast; as also mackerel, the fisheries of which are next in importance to those of the cod and herring. Another common fish is the halibut, which also finds its way to the English market. The coasts of the Baltic are frequented by a fish called *strömming*, which is much like a herring. The *strömming* fisheries are almost as important to the inhabitants of these parts as the herring fisheries to those on the western side of the fjeld.

Of crustaceæ the most important are the lobsters, which swarm in the deep water of the coasts, especially about Bergen and the south, and are largely exported to England. Besides the common lobster there is an attenuated species, found chiefly about the south-west coasts of Norway and Sweden, called by Linnæus *Nephrops norvegicus*.

The coast teems with all kinds of star-fish, jelly-fish, and sea-urchins. Of shell-fish there are comparatively few, excepting mussels, which are everywhere abundant, and oysters, which are plentiful in some parts, especially in the south.

Of freshwater fish the most abundant are trout and salmon. Of both of these there are several species; but salmon is becoming far scarcer than it was, through the zeal of sportsmen, who visit the country every summer for the sake of fishing.

The right of fishing in very many of the rivers has been let by the peasant farmers to Englishmen, Scotchmen, and even Americans; and some of the most famous salmon rivers are now nearly destitute of fish. Probably, also, too little care is taken to enforce the laws intended to insure the preservation of the fish in the winter months. Grayling and char are to be found in many parts.

In the less rapid rivers of Sweden eels and pike are very common. The Mälar Lake has a fish peculiar to itself, known in Sweden as *gös*. It has a head like a pike, but fins and spines like a perch. Its scientific name is *Lucioperca sandra.*

It is obvious to any one who considers the great variety of latitude of the different parts of Scandinavia that it must possess an extensive flora. Such is really the case; and yet the country cannot claim to be a land of flowers. The number of species is large, no doubt, but, as a whole, flowers grow sparingly. This is due to the nature of the country. The surface of the greater part consists of rock, either quite barren, or covered with reindeer moss (*Lichen rangiferinus*) and some of the coarser kinds of grass. It is only in the valleys that vegetation to any large extent is found. Still there is much to make the flora peculiarly interesting. No one who has any taste for botany can help feeling some enthusiasm for flowers in the land which produced Linnæus. The great and peculiar variety of natural features in different parts of the country illustrates in a most remarkable manner the conditions required for the growth of various species.

Arctic and Alpine flowers abound, especially in Norway and the north of Sweden. Glacial flowers are frequent, though not so much so as in Switzerland. The moraines of glaciers of themselves present the most interesting botanical study. As the ice recedes in summer the plants beneath quickly spring up and bloom, so that within a few yards the same species may be seen in all its successive stages of growth, and spring and summer flowers are found blooming close together.

The most celebrated place for the study of Arctic plants is the Dovre Fjeld. Some of the most beautiful of this class are the blue gentians and primulæ, which blossom almost beneath the snow. One of the most frequent of mountain plants is the *Salix herbacea*, a most striking little species of willow. The whole plant is usually not more than a few inches in size. It only becomes conspicuous towards the end of July, when it seeds, and the whole ground is covered with large patches of white down.

Below the snow level there is a great variety of mountain plants. Of stonecrops and saxifrages, especially, there are several species. The most beautiful of the latter is the *Saxifraga aizoon*, which grows in lower situations than many of its kind, chiefly on dripping rocks, or by the sides of waterfalls. The leaves form a regular rosette some eight inches in diameter, from which a flower-stalk shoots up in spring to the height of two to three feet, with a feathery mass of whitish flowers. A less imposing species is the *Aizoides*, so well known to Alpine botanists. It has beautiful little orange flowers with red spots. The *Stellaris*, which is very abundant on all the higher mountains, is not unlike its cultivated sister the London pride. Of rock-loving plants, one of the most frequent is the *Silene rupestris*. The *acaulis*, a favourite Alpine flower, is, on the other hand, chiefly confined to the fjeld. One of the most interesting, and in Norway most abundant, of mountain plants is the cloudberry (*Rubus Chamæ-morus*), which abounds on all the mountain bogs, beginning at an altitude of about 2000 feet. This plant is in reality a species of blackberry, though unlike any of the commoner varieties. The main stem grows buried in moss or peat, and from it spring rough ivy-shaped leaves, and a stalk with a single raspberry-like flower. The fruit is at first bright red, but turns as it ripens into a pale yellow. It has a pleasant aromatic taste, and is quite one of the natural delicacies of the country. The *Rubus arcticus*, a species with large red flowers, is confined to the mountains of the north.

A very characteristic plant of the Norwegian valleys is the wolf'sbane (*Aconitum leucoctonum*). It is a paler and much more emaciated form of aconite than the ordinary *Napellus* of our old-fashioned gardens. The hood has become so attenuated as to resemble the spur of its first cousin, the larkspur, for which it is constantly mistaken. The only true Scandinavian larkspur is a common weed among the Swedish cornfields. The aconite is hardly found in Sweden, but abounds in the rocky valleys of Norway. Notwithstanding its specific name, " wolf-killing," it is far more harmless than its kindred species ; and in the extreme north wolves are said to eat it without harm.[5]

Of the flowers of the heath family there are, as might be expected in a mountainous country, a very large number, especially in the valleys of Norway and forests and moorlands of Sweden ; though, oddly enough, neither heath nor ling them-

---

[5] I am indebted for this statement to a curious old book in Upsala Library, of which I do not remember the name.

selves are very abundant. Perhaps the two most interesting plants of this order are the *Phyllodoce* (*Menziesia*) *cærulea* and the *Ledum palustre.* The former, which a reckless botanical zeal has almost succeeded in eradicating from its last habitat in Great Britain, is still fairly common in the valleys of the higher mountains of Norway and Sweden. The flowers are of a blue-purple colour, in shape much like those of a heath, but growing on upright pedicels, and forming a symmetrical group round the flower-stalk.

The *Ledum palustre* abounds in the forest bogs of Sweden. The whole plant is very remarkable. In size and texture it is almost a small bush. The stalks are covered with a velvety coat of brown hairs ; the crowded narrow leaves have a sweet aromatic scent, while the flowers in white terminal masses form a striking object when the plants grow, as is often the case, thick together. Several species of pyrola—including the single-flowered (*uniflora*)—are found, and all kinds of whortleberry and other mountain berries are abundant. From the north the cranberry is largely exported to England and other countries.

Among the most characteristic flowers of the valleys and forests are the lily-of-the-valley and the so-called French willow (*Epilobium angustifolium*). The latter, though not uncommon in Great Britain in its wild state, is most familiar to us as an old-fashioned garden plant, which, like many others, is gradually making way for geraniums and calceolarias. In Norway and Sweden it grows to a great height, often forming large red clusters, in beautiful contrast to the dark purple rocks, or green cornfields, where it is sometimes quite a troublesome weed. No less striking than either of these is the *Cornus suecica*, a diminutive species of cornel, conspicuous for its bright red berries among the undergrowth of the forest. It has small white flowers, and is in every respect unlike its larger relative, the common cornel. Another interesting flower, very rare in England, but in Norway quite common, is the *Trientalis europœa*, which is remarkable as being the only flower of the old Linnæan order *Heptandria*. Curiously enough the number of each part of the flower—leaves, sepals, petals, and stamens—is usually seven; but all have a tendency to vary. One of the commonest flowers in the forests of Sweden and the south of Norway is the little blue hepatica, so common with us as a garden spring flower, though we never find it wild. But the most worthy of notice of all the spring flowers is the *Linnæa borealis*, which has been adopted as the emblem of the great botanist. Its low trailing habit and late bloom are considered as typical of Linnæus' humble origin and late fame. It is a long creeping plant, with small nearly round opposite leaves, and two tiny pinkish flowers hanging together from an upright stalk, and blossoms in July. Excepting some few localities in Scotland, it is hardly known in Great Britain, but it is exceedingly abundant in Norway and in parts of Sweden, where it grows in the pine forests.

In the northern forests of Sweden the lady's-slipper (*Cypripedium Calceolus*) is sometimes found, but it is quite a rare plant. The country is also rich in other kinds of orchids. One, the *Orchis ustulata*, is confined to the island of Gotland. Another very striking plant, found both in Sweden and Norway, is the wild balsam (*Noli-me-tangere*), which, though nowhere abundant, is fairly distributed, growing generally by banks of streams or moist woods. Its Latin name is derived from the Vulgate of St. John xx. 17, and alludes to the habit the pods have (in common with those of other balsams) of splitting and dropping the seeds when touched. The flowers are curiously shaped, with very long curly spurs hanging from the fleshy stalk by long filiform pedicels. In England this plant is very rare. Another very remarkable flower, quite peculiar to Sweden, is the *Pedicularis Sceptrum carolinum.* This name was given to the plant by Rudbeck, in honour of Charles XI. It is a very large species of lousewort, with handsome yellow and purple flowers. It is found almost exclusively in Norrland and Dalarne.

The meadow plants of the south of Sweden and Norway are much the same as those of England (especially of the northern counties) and Wales. There are a very large number of roses, especially varieties of *canina* and *villosa.* Of brambles there are very few species. The most striking are the *Rubus saxatilis*, a low-growing plant with few-seeded red berries ; and *suberectus,* a large, almost upright plant, with singularly acrid, claret-coloured fruit. The wild raspberry is very abundant. Perhaps the most frequent flowers of all are the common harebell and small blue pansy.

As is natural from the marshy character of parts of the country, Sweden abounds in species of fresh-water plants. Water-lilies, both yellow and white, are very abundant. The latter are frequent also on the Norwegian tarns. Another very common plant in Sweden, but unknown in England, is the *Calla palustris,* which is closely allied to the common cuckoo-pint. The flowering rush (*Butomus umbellatus*) is extremely common. Sweden is also very rich in liliacious plants. Solomon's seal (*Polygonatum verticillatum*) and the beautiful little *Smilacina bifolia,* both rare in England, are there abundant.

Strangely enough, when we consider the enormous size of its seaboard, Scandinavia is extremely deficient in sea plants. A large proportion of those belonging to our shores are, it is true, represented, but they occur only at wide intervals. This is to be accounted for by the little variation of tide and the rocky character of the coast, and consequent absence of tidal deposit impregnated with salt. The few flowers which grow by the fjords are mostly fresh-water plants, such as the grass of Parnassus, the large yellow loosestrife (*Lysimachia vulgaris*), and the common skull-cap. What marine plants there are, are chiefly confined to the mouths of the rivers in the south of Sweden. The most common are the sea-aster (*Aster Tripolium*) and the sea-pimpernel (*Glaux maritima*). On the other hand, the scurvy-grass (*Cochlearia anglica*) only occurs in Norway.

As in England, a large number of plants are practically confined to the corn-fields. This is especially the case in the south of Sweden, where a considerable part of the country is now laid under cultivation. It is quite impossible to say how far any of these can claim to be indigenous, but they have, most of them at least, as much right to be considered wild as our common English poppy, and form quite a striking feature of Swedish corn-fields. Besides the blue corn-flower, the wild chicory, and corn-cockle, and many others common in England, there are two at least quite common in Sweden, which in our country are very rare, and almost certainly naturalized. One is the *Delphinum Consolida*, which has been already referred to, a small annual species of larkspur; and the other the *Anchusa officinalis*, a fine velvety purple alkanet, which abounds in the south of Sweden.

As might naturally be supposed from the differ-ence of geological and physical features, the flora of Gotland differs considerably from that of the rest of Sweden; and there are several flowers which occur only in that island; others which occur only there and in the southern provinces, in-cluding Öland. Among the former class may be noticed the *Orchis ustulata* and *Coronilla Emerus*, a striking leguminous plant with single yellow flowers; of the latter class, the *Allium Schœno-prasum*, and many others.

Notwithstanding the large extent of the Scan-dinavian flora, of which the account above given is extremely scanty,[6] there are not a few plants which an Englishman greatly misses. Such common flowers as the primrose and the wild hyacinth are not to be found in Scandinavia at all; while others, such as the sweet violet, dog's mercury, and common ivy, are only found here and there in the south. Linnæus' descendants still point to a quantity of dog's mercury which the great botanist planted among his pet flowers at Hammarby. Ivy in Norway is very commonly grown as a pot plant, and trained along the inner walls of the houses.

[6] A larger list of plants likely to interest the reader is given in Appendix A. at the end of the volume.

Even the common daisy is quite a rare plant, and is not unfrequently grown as an edging for borders.

Compared with England the trees of Scandinavia present little variety. The two trees which abound everywhere throughout the whole length and breadth of the peninsula are the Scotch fir (*Pinus sylvestris*) and white birch (*Betula alba*). The first of these is the typical tree of the country. In Norway it grows chiefly in the valleys, where it often grows at an elevation up to 2000 or 3000 feet. In Sweden it forms those enormous forests which extend almost unbroken for hundreds of miles in the north. By the sides of the fjords it is sometimes to be seen growing, samphire fashion, out of the crevices of the rocks. The wonder is how its roots can find moisture enough to grow. About the inner branches of the Hardanger Fjord especially it is very abundant. In a large part of Sweden, and on the borders of large rivers and other more accessible places in Norway, these trees are constantly cut down for timber; but in very many districts, where, through the absence of means of conveyance, the value of the timber does not repay the cost, they are allowed to grow in their natural wildness, forming with the old decayed trees masses almost impenetrable except for the wild animals which haunt them. The birch-trees are far more sparing in their growth, generally growing in patches on the rocks or swards which line the Norwegian rivers, or mixing themselves here and there among the pines. About as common as either of these, but more confined in its range, is the common spruce (*Pinus Abies*). This is very abundant in a large part of Sweden and the south of Norway; but, like other forest trees in

Sweden, is rapidly giving way before the increase of agriculture. Another very frequent tree is the aspen (Swedish *asp*) which abounds especially in Sweden. The rowan, or mountain ash (*Pyrus Aucuparia*), and bird-cherry (*Prunus Padus*) are also of frequent occurrence.

In the south the trees are more like those of England. In the southern provinces oaks grow to a great size. There were once large forests of these trees, which were gradually destroyed in the Danish wars. They are now preserved by Government. Even as far north as the Sogne Fjord a few scattered oaks are to be found, but they are usually small. Beeches grow only in the south of Sweden, the most northerly being those which grow near Alvastra Monastery, on the east side of the Vetter Lake. A fairly common tree is the so-called Norwegian maple (*Acer platanoides*), a tree resembling, but not identical with, the English sycamore; it is now often planted, but it is undoubtedly indigenous. Elms have been planted, and flourish, in many parts of the south. Only the wych elm is really wild.

Of shrubs, the most characteristic of the country is the dwarf birch (*Betula nana*), a dark species, which grows on the higher mountains, and forms a pretty regular belt between the pines and the coarse grass of the mountain plateau; others, such as the elder, blackthorn, hawthorn, hazel, and many more, are confined chiefly to the south.

Several kinds of cryptogamous plants occur, particularly in Norway, where the moisture of the air, and the natural watering and drainage of the rocky valleys, are specially suited to their growth. Of Lycopodiums there is a very large

variety. Of ferns the actual number of species is
rather less than with us, the climate being of course
too cold to allow of the growth of such delicate
kinds as the maidenhair and the film ferns.
Almost every other British sort is found. By far
the most common species (hardly excepting the
bracken and male fern) are the lady, beech, and oak
ferns. The first of these is often found at a great
height, where the cold snow winds sometimes tinge
the leaves with bright scarlet. The beech fern
grows in almost every conceivable situation, and
sometimes so covers the moist hillside meadows as
to form the main part of a hay crop. The parsley
fern is exceedingly abundant among the mountain
rocks ; the holly fern is less frequent. Perhaps the
two most interesting ferns to an English botanist
are the *Asplenium septentrionale,* and the *Woodsia
ilvensis.* These are both very rare in Great Britain,
and grow almost entirely in nearly inaccessible
places. In Norway they are both, but the latter
especially, very abundant, and grow among the
rocks, chiefly in the lower valleys. The *Asplenium
Germanicum* is more rare. The *Osmunda regalis*
is found only in the extreme south, and is quite a
rare plant. A more complete list of Scandinavian
ferns is given in Appendix A., at the end of the
volume.

The interest of Scandinavian geology does not
arise, as in England, so much from the variety of
strata—these are comparatively few—as from the
way in which it illustrates the recently discovered
theories of the action of ice, in its various forms,
on the surface of the earth.

The whole of the Scandinavian range consists
entirely of metamorphic and palæozoic rocks.

The great mass is almost entirely composed of gneiss, here and there mingled with granite, porphyry, and serpentine. This was originally covered by a stratum of slate, which appears in many parts of Norway. The slate is often variegated by parallel lines of quartz of a crystalline character. The Silurian and Devonian strata, which were once above the slate, have now been worn away, except in some of the more southern parts of Norway, as about Kristiania and the centre of Sweden, where they form an interrupted line from Norrland southwards. In Dalarne especially this system is very extensive.

Between the Devonian rocks and the Tertiary formations no strata are found, i.e. if we except the island of Gotland and the extreme south of Sweden. This is all the more striking, because it is to the interval between the Devonian and the glacial periods that the formation of by far the larger part of Europe belongs. Gotland consists of a rock called *encrinite* limestone, from the number of those fossils it contains. This formation lies between the upper and lower trias: in Germany it is called *muschelkalk;* it is not found in England. In the extreme south of the island there is a little red sandstone. In the south of Sweden there are small quantities of mountain limestone, and even later formations ; so that, geologically, this part of the country belongs rather to Denmark than to the rest of Scandinavia. In parts of Skåne, near Helsingborg, some coal-fields have been lately discovered. The coal is in character much like the Welsh coal, but is not extensive, and as yet hardly repays the cost of working.

The diluvial and alluvial deposits of Scandinavia

E

are very rich. The former are due to the action of ice, which has worn away the original rocks. In Norway the most striking phenomena belonging to this formation are the sandhills, which occur in very great frequency in all the larger valleys. They still shift about a great deal, being bare on the side most exposed to the wind, and covered with vegetation only on the top and more sheltered sides. In many parts the valleys are sprinkled with rocks, which have been brought down by glaciers, or fallen from the precipices above. Rocks are frequently still brought down from the sides of the valleys by the action of the winter frosts. The wide valleys of Sweden, as they would otherwise be, which lie between the roots of the Scandinavian range, are as a fact filled up to a large extent with deposits of various kinds. They have been all brought down in one form or another from the Norwegian fjeld. We will now speak of the most important of them.

The *Krosstenar*, " cross stones," and *Krosstengrus*, " cross-stone gravel," are cornered, sharp-pointed stones found in beds of fine dust or gravel, which is highly valued for agricultural purposes. These are very different from the *rullstenar*, " rolled-stones," which are large or small round stones of gneiss, granite, hornblende, feltspar, &c., which have evidently been rolled a long way by the action of water. The hills, in which these lie—usually near the bottom, but sometimes, as especially in Dalarne, exposed to view—are called *åsar*. They are composed of yellow sand and gravel, called *rullstengrus*, " rolled-stone-gravel," which is largely used in the manufacture of roads. The hills have given rise to much discussion. The now most commonly received explanation, as given by Erdmann and others, is that they were brought down by glaciers at a time when the east of the present country was all under water, and were deposited as the sea receded. This would explain the fact that the highest hills are those which lie furthest from the sea. The most curious phenomenon connected with the *åsar* is that they lie, not in the direction of the rivers and lakes, but usually from north to south, sometimes even from north-east to south-west. In many cases they are abruptly divided by a river or lake. This would seem to show that the *Åsar* belong to a different and much earlier glacial period than that to which the system of lakes and rivers belongs. Besides these there are here and there large single rocks of gneiss, called *erratiska block,* "erratic blocks." These are believed to have been brought down and deposited in their present position by icebergs. They occur also on Gotland, and again on the lands south of the Baltic, where there is no gneiss *in situ*, and they must therefore have found their way thither from the Scandinavian mountains. Another deposit is the red and white sand, known as *finmo*, which occurs chiefly to the north of the Mälar Lake, especially in Dalarne, but also in some parts of east and west Götaland. It is formed by the abrasure of the Silurian rocks. Besides these are found the stratified marl, distinguished by its red, black, and white lines, which is formed from the Silurian dust acted upon by water, and is very fertile; the black clay, which often lies at the margin of lakes and rivers; and the regular beds of upper and lower clay.

There are besides a large number of alluvial de-

E 2

posits, consisting of various kinds of clay, sand,
peat, &c. From this period is dated the gradual
rise of the Scandinavian coast. The whole of the
coast, as far as Kalmar, has from this period been
sensibly rising. The average rate in the century is
three to four feet in the north, becoming gradually
less towards the south, till below Kalmar the coast
begins to sink in the same proportion. Both on
the western and eastern sides beds of shells have
been discovered, some at 100 feet or more above
the level of the sea, showing the old limits of the
coast. In some cases towns once on the sea, such
as the old Hudiksvall, Sundsvall, and many more,
have been left at some distance from the sea-line,
where new towns in each case have taken their
place.

The temperature of Scandinavia varies enormously in different parts of the country. It
depends in each locality chiefly on three conditions, viz. the latitude, altitude, and, above all,
the distance from the sea. The sea being far
warmer than the air in winter, and far colder than
the air in summer, has the effect of keeping the
coast lands at a much more even temperature than
those of the interior. Thus, while the Mälar Lake
and Kristiania Fjord are frozen over every winter,
and not unfrequently the Sound also—as in the
January of the present year, 1881—the Alten and
Porsanger fjords, in the extreme north, are open
the whole winter. The average temperature in
July (night and day) varies in the south of Sweden
between 61° and 63° Fahr.; in the north between 57°
and 61°; on the Norwegian coast it averages 57°; on
the Norwegian fjelds only 50°. The average temperature in January is, on the fjelds of Finmark, 3°;

in the south of Sweden, 23° to 25°; while on the extreme west coast of Norway it is actually a little above the freezing-point. The highest annual temperature is 86° in the south of Sweden, round Kristiania, in Finmark, and in Swedish Lapland; while the lowest annual temperature varies between 14° above zero on the coast, and 58° below zero on the Finmark Fjeld. The mean temperature throughout the year varies between 45° along the west coast and the extreme south of Sweden, and 28° on the Finmark Fjeld. It has been calculated that nearly a fifth part of the country, and that containing 16,000 inhabitants, has an average temperature at or under the freezing-point. The great influence of the sea on the temperature is in a large measure due to the Gulf Stream. It is estimated that the average temperature of the coast of Norway is thirty-six degrees higher than that of other countries of the same degrees of latitude.

The rainfall varies chiefly with the distance from the sea. It is greatest on the west coast, especially from Sogne to the Stor Fjord. Here it reaches 79 inches. Bergen has a bad reputation, but the rainfall here is not really quite so great, being reckoned at 73 inches. Round Kristiania it is 21 inches, at Stockholm 17 inches, at Rörås only 13 inches. It will be seen from this that Sweden is far drier than Norway.

In the north, where the sea is most affected by the Atlantic wave, there is the greatest variation of tide. At Hammerfest it is as much as 9 ft. 10 in. Further south it gradually diminishes. At Bergen it is 4 ft. 3 in., in Kristiania Fjord it is only 4 in., while in the Sound and in the Baltic it becomes imperceptible.

The climate of Scandinavia—Norway especially —is as a whole remarkably healthy. There is one disease which in the Middle Ages was more or less common to all European countries, but is now restricted to the coast lands of Norway. Leprosy of two kinds (technically known as *elephantiasis tuberculosa* and *anæsthetica*) here prevails. It is especially common in Nordre Bergenhus Amt. Though in most cases hereditary, the disease is largely fostered by a poor diet, consisting too much of fish, and by dirty living. Great pains have been taken by the Government to grapple with the evil, and special leper-houses have been established at Bergen and elsewhere. The results are very satisfactory, and leprosy is rapidly decreasing. In 1856 there were as many as 2858 lepers in the kingdom, whereas in 1878 they had steadily diminished to 1681 ; so that probably it will not be long before the disease quite dies out.

CHAPTER III.

ORIGIN OF THE SCANDINAVIAN KINGDOMS.

THE first peopling of Scandinavia involves questions of great uncertainty. For a long time it was regarded as a settled conclusion that from prehistoric times the whole country was inhabited by Lapps. These, at a time—variously given—between 400 B.C. and 400 A.D., were supposed to have begun to recede before the immigration of a mighty Teutonic people called Goths, identical with those who, in the fifth century, overwhelmed the Roman Empire. This idea had much to commend it. The Swedish historian Geijer shows that the Lapps—or, as they were anciently called, "*Finnar*,"[1]—occupied even in historical times a far larger part of the country than they do at present: and we are able to trace the steps by which they have diminished, while the Teutonic nations have increased. It is now, however, agreed that this view must be given up, or at least greatly modified. The change of opinion is due chiefly to the great light which has been thrown on the subject by the archæological discoveries of the last fifty years. A careful investigation of the ancient graves, weapons, utensils, and other antiquities of all kinds—which in Scandinavia are very

---

[1] See Chapter X.

abundant—has tended to prove the following
results. (1) That at a period at least 2000 years B.C.
(some put it 1000 years earlier), Denmark and the
southern coasts of Sweden were inhabited by a race
in some respects even more civilized than the Lapps
of the present day. (2) That the large majority
of the skulls of this period are of a similar type
to those of the modern Danes, and belong clearly
to an Aryan, probably a Teutonic people. (3) The
steps of civilization through which this semi-
barbarous people passed are precisely similar to
those which are found in the progress of every other
nation. It is true that even at the period of
which we are speaking, known by archæologists as
the later Stone Age, there are several skulls of a
Lappish type; and as we go farther back they
preponderate, till in the earliest Stone Age—the
earliest period of which we have any relics preserved—they appear to be universal. This would
seem to show that the earliest inhabitants of the
Peninsula were a race *akin* to the Lapps; but they
do not appear to have any direct historical connexion with the modern inhabitants of Lapland.
The latter are shown, it is true, by ancient remains
in Norrland, to have passed through somewhat
similar stages of development; but the relics
belonging to them in each Age exhibit distinctive
features, and are believed by archæologists to prove
a more recent date. The real aborigines appear to
have been gradually absorbed, rather than expelled,
by the Teutonic races which continually immigrated
to the shores from the south.

The antiquities discovered not only prove a
gradual progress in the arts of civilization—especially in the use of metals—but also point out the

direction in which the population spread. The earliest graves are found almost entirely by the coast of the sea and the margins of the larger lakes, showing that the earliest races gained their livelihood chiefly by fishing. They are met with in all the south and west coasts of Sweden, especially in the landships of Skåne, Halland and Bohuslän, while comparatively very few are found in the south of Norway, the east coasts of Sweden, and the islands of the Baltic. The graves of the Bronze Age, placed by Montelius at least a thousand years before Christ, and by others still earlier, point to a gradual extension of the population. Skåne was still the most thickly populated district; but graves are found continuously as far west as the south coast of Norway, round the east coast of Sweden, and as far north as the Mälar Lake, on the islands of Gotland and Öland, and along the larger lakes of the south.

In the beginning of the Iron Age, which in Sweden was about contemporary with the beginning of the Christian era, the population appears to have extended to the sea coasts and valleys of Norway, as far as the old province of Trondhjem, and in Sweden as far north as the Dal rivers. It is probable that the Lapps also may have already found their way into the north by this time.

The great number of Roman coins, belonging chiefly to the second century, found in Gotland, Öland, and the eastern coast of Sweden, seem to point to the immigration to these parts of a people from the very first far surpassing their neighbours in that commercial enterprise which continued to characterize the Gotlanders to the end of the middle ages.

It is also exceedingly probable that another still
more important immigration took place into
Sweden in the fourth century A.D.   A comparison
of ancient relics found in Upland with those found
on the east and south coasts of the Baltic, would
seem to show that the people in question came
from the latter districts, and settled to the north of
the Mälar Lake.   Here, in the so-called Svealand
or Upland, they formed the nucleus of the Swedes
properly so called, and were long distinguished from
the Gauts or Göts in the south.[2]   One of the most
ancient towns belonging to this settlement, as
appears both from Sagas and recent archæological
discoveries, was Bjorkey (now Björkö), " Birch
Island," which lies in the Mälar Lake, not far from
Stockholm.

Thus by A.D. 400 it appears that three distinct
tribes had established themselves upon the old
strata of population.   The Svear or Swear, round
—but chiefly to the north of—the Mälar Lake,
the Gauts on the west and south, and the Guts on
the islands of the Baltic and the neighbouring
Swedish coast.   It is very doubtful whether either
of the two last names has any philological connexion either with the Juts (or Jutes) of Jutland
or the Gots (or Goths) of Central Europe.

A large number of interesting relics found in
Scandinavia prove the very great influence of Rome
on the early civilization of the country.   Not that
the Romans themselves had any direct intercourse with the inhabitants.   They show in their
scanty notices, profound ignorance of the north ;
and very few works of art found in the country
seem to have come from Rome itself.   But while

[2] See Sveriges Hist. Mont. i. p. 238.

the relics discovered bear traces in their design and ornamentation of Roman influence, they exhibit other characteristics peculiar to Scandinavia and the lands immediately south of the Baltic. The lines of country in which the coins have been discovered, show that by means of the Oder and Vistula rivers an active trade was carried on between the people of Gotland and the south-east coasts and the races inhabiting the tracts north of the Alps. The most important article which Scandinavia at this time produced was amber, a thing much coveted by the fashionable world of Rome. These relations appear to have continued with great vigour during the second, third, and fourth centuries, but to have gradually diminished with the decline of the Roman Empire.

But as the intercourse with old Rome decreased, the Scandinavians were brought more and more into contact with the eastern division of the empire, and its new capital, Constantinople. It was again mainly by means of the Vistula that the amber and furs were brought which were exchanged for Byzantine coins wrung by the Goths and Huns from the eastern emperors. That these coins also are chiefly found in Gotland and Öland again shows the great commercial importance of the inhabitants of these islands. They belong almost entirely to the latter half of the fifth century : after which time the trade in question appears to have gradually declined. We shall have further on to mention a second great era of commercial activity between these parts and Constantinople.

Much light is thrown on the language and ethnology of the later immigrants into Scandinavia by a study of ancient runes found in this country and in other parts of Europe. This method of writing appears to have been introduced into Scandinavia about the end of the third century, and to have been the only one then known, until the Roman alphabet came in with Christianity in the tenth. Runes were almost confined to inscriptions on jewels, wooden implements, weapons, and stones, and (beyond funeral inscriptions in verse, a fragment of an heroic poem, and a few curious numerical or mnemonic sentences) were never made the vehicle of anything deserving the name of literature.[3]

These inscriptions seem to show that in the fourth and fifth centuries, the period to which most of the early synchronous runes belong, the inhabitants of the southern parts of Sweden, Norway, as well as of Denmark, and the south coasts of the Baltic, used substantially the same language. It would appear from this that the newly immigrated people had so much influence that their language was accepted, for official purposes at any rate, by all the tribes of the wide-spreading area. A conclusion which is also borne out by an investigation of the written remains of a later date. The custom of having skalds or bards to recite the deeds of heroes, &c., at their great festivals, which seems to have been once common to all Scandinavian people, must have done much to preserve this language unaltered. A comparison of the runic inscriptions and the Icelandic literature of the

[3] It is, on the whole, most probable that the forms of the runes are derived from a corruption of the Greek alphabet. The reasons for the order of the runic letters F, U, Ð, O, R, K, G, W: H, N, I, J, EO, P, Z, S : T, B, E, NG, D, L, M, O, Á, A, Y, EA, has never been explained.

twelfth and following centuries, with the earliest remains of Anglo-Saxon, Saxon, and Frisian, points to a near relationship between the languages of Scandinavia and those of England and the Teutonic races of the north-west of Europe ; while a study of the Moeso-Gothic fragment of Ulphilas points to a still closer relationship between the ancient language of Scandinavia and that of the Gothic invaders of the Roman Empire. For a more exact view of the mutual affinities of these languages, we must refer the reader to Appendix B., at the end of the volume.

In early times the Northmen were little known to the rest of Europe. Their boats, such as that discovered at Nydams Moss, in Denmark,[4] and believed to be as old as 300 A.D., appear to have been row-boats intended for trading in the Baltic. Yet among a semi-barbarous people the trader and the pirate were not so easily distinguishable, and one might easily grow out of the other. It was about the end of the eighth century that the *wikings* first made their presence felt in distant lands. The name *wiking* has been variously explained : most probably it means the people of the *Wik* or "Bay," as the district round the Kristiania Fjord was then called. Across the North Sea, round the British Isles, on all the coasts of Western Europe, Germany, France, Spain, Italy, and even Greece, up the courses of the larger rivers, swarmed bands of pirates, destroying and pillaging men and women, lands and buildings, with a reckless ferocity. At first their attacks were few and desultory—mere raids of adventurers, instead of organized expeditions. But

[4] See Sveriges Hist. Mont. vol. i. p. 201.

by degrees these increased both in frequency and
strength. They were no longer content to carry
off their spoil, and depart; but began to make
settlements in the countries they ravaged. By the
close of the ninth century they had succeeded in
possessing themselves of the northern half of
England (the Denelaga, or "land of the Danes," as

WIKING'S SHIP, FROM TAPESTRY AT BAYEUX.

it came to be called), the Orkneys and Shetland,
besides the Hebrides and the Isle of Man. In
Ireland, their kings ruled at Dublin, Waterford,
Wexford, and Limerick. In France, a large part
of the north had fallen into their power. They had
twice attacked and virtually taken Paris. With
equal activity in the East, they had gained a per-

manent footing both at Novgorod, and Kiev, and the Swedish Rus had already formed the nucleus of the Russian Empire.[5] Through Russia, communications—first of a peaceful, afterwards of a warlike character—were established between the Northmen and the East, and many Kufish coins are still found in Scandinavia, pointing to a traffic, which must at one time have been enormous. At Constantinople, the battle-axed Northmen had twice appeared as enemies, and left an awful impression on the Greek mind. Afterwards they entered the Emperor's service as a special body-guard, long known by the name of *Wäringar*, which in process of time proved a fashionable opening for the enterprising spirits of England and other countries.

Savage and desperate pirates as the *wikings* showed themselves, they were far from being such uncivilized barbarians as the accounts of their enemies describe them. By studying their ancient poems and sagas, which, though coloured no doubt by feelings of patriotism, bear many internal evidences of truth, we are able to look at these *wikings* from a different point of view. We there find that loyalty to the king's person, a strong attachment to their family, a love of hospitality, were among the most striking of the gentler features of a Northman's character. Revenge for a friend or brother's death was a duty never omitted, and often led to family feuds, lasting for many generations. Deeds of savage treachery, disloyalty,

[5] On the connexion of the Swedes with the Russian Empire, see Thomsen's Ancient Russia. He connects the word *Rus*, the ancient name of the people, with *Ruotsi*, the modern Finnish word for Sweden, which he would derive from *Rodskarlar*, or some equivalent word 'meaning "rowers," and applied originally to the Swedish pirates.

breaches of hospitality, of course occur, as when Sigrid the Haughty burnt her two importunate suitors in the guest-chamber; but such acts were looked upon as disgraceful. Open robbery or manslaughter was little regarded; the slayer rather gloried in being surnamed the "bane" of his victim; but theft, or deceit of any kind, brought infamy on those who practised them. Wager of battle among those mortally offended was frequent, and originally the dispute was decided on some distant holm, whence such a contest was called a *holmgang*, or "going to the holm."

The views with which a *wiking's* life was regarded underwent important changes as a gentler spirit prevailed. Originally a violent death was sought after by all. When there was no chance of dying in battle, an old or sick warrior would sometimes end his life by throwing himself from some high cliff into the sea. But in course of time piracy came to be looked upon as the education rather than the business of life; and an earl or king who had gained respect and wealth in his early vocation, would settle down to the more peaceful duties of government. The confusion about the succession to a throne often made it necessary for the rejected claimant to devote himself to piracy; and it sometimes so happened that he thus gained sufficient wealth and power to enable him to return and eject his more favoured rival. The arts of agriculture and pasturage had been long known, and it was a common practice for a *wiking* to sow his crops in the spring before making his unwelcome visits, and return in the autumn to reap.

The antiquities discovered from this age, such as

sickles, ploughshares, instruments connected with spinning and weaving, and domestic utensils of all kinds, seem to show that the domestic and social life of all classes at this time was much like that of the peasants of Dalarne and Norrland at the present day. The skill required to make such instruments, or such boats as e.g. the famous Long Serpent of Olaf Tryggvason, points to a high development of art. Much in this respect was derived no doubt from the lands they pillaged, especially from Ireland ; yet a careful examination of ancient relics seems to favour the conclusion that the Scandinavian art, even of the *wiking* era, was not purely foreign. It did not result from the adoption of a new and borrowed style, but from the incorporation of new ideas into the old style and forms.[6] It is very remarkable that very few of the weapons, &c., found in Scandinavia of this date are actually foreign ; while those made in the country are very numerous.

Closely connected with the life and character of the northern *wikings* are their religious beliefs. Their religion in its most important elements seems to have been common to all Teutonic peoples. Their mythology, even as it appears in their older poems, is much confused. It appears to be a mixture of two distinct religious systems, a nature worship and a hero worship. The greatest god of the first system, Thor or " Thunder," is the friend of man, who with his thunderbolt-hammer (*mjolner*) and gloves of strength, is ever slaying the giants of the rocky gorges. The arrow heads of the stone age are believed to be his bolts, and are worn as amulets by the superstitious, even to the present

[6] Vide Aarböge for Nordisk Oldkyndighed, 1880, pp. 292—324.

F

day. The battles with the giants of frost and snow
are probably an imaginative embodiment of the
groans and crashes of the frozen mountains, with
their huge glaciers reaching down to the sea. The
belief in dwarfs is probably a relic of the memory
of the Arctic races which once covered the north of
Europe. The chief of the other nature deities are
Njord, the god of wind and sea ; Frey, the god of
fruits ; and Freya, the goddess of love. Most beautiful of the legends of Scandinavia is that which
describes the death of Balder, the loved favourite
of the gods. This probably represents the absorp-
tion of the light and heat of summer in the cold
darkness of winter, a phenomenon which must have
deeply impressed the imagination of northern
races. In the marriage of the sea-god Njord with
the daughter of the giants, we may possibly see a
personification of the fjords, which leave their
natural home to court the mountains.

Woden, or (as he was afterwards called in Scandinavia) Odin, was, on the other hand, the great hero
god. He was the god of war, who first brought the
people from Asia to their Scandinavian home. From
him are derived the royal lines of Denmark, Sweden,
and Norway. He favours his devotees in battle,
and welcomes those who fall to the Walhall, to
spend their days in fighting and their nights in
revelry ; while all the rest must go beneath the
earth, and be under the government of Hell.
Woden is attended by wolves and ravens, the
emblems of warfare. In later times we begin to
see the influence of Christianity affecting the
northern mythology. Woden is now the god of
wisdom. The ravens lose their warlike character,
and become the messengers between him and the

earth. He is even represented as the ancestor of Thor; and in Snorri's-Edda[7] he has the title of "All-father;" but this is an idea probably directly derived from Christianity.

In the north, sacrificial worship was confined in ordinary cases to Thor, Woden, and Frey. Of these Frey had the chief place in Sweden, Thor in Norway. One of the chief centres of religious worship was at old Upsala. Here every nine years there was a great festival, at which human as well as other sacrifices were offered. Besides this there were three regular annual feasts, those of May Day, Harvest, and above all the great mid-winter feast of Jul (Yule). These all had their origin probably in nature worship, and having outlived all changes in the religion of the people, are still occasions for popular mirth and gaiety. The word *Jul*, which survives with us in our yule-log, yule-cakes, &c., is still the only word used for Christmas, and many more heathen customs have survived among the country people than with ourselves.

Much light is thrown by the sagas upon the social and political condition of the early Scandinavian peoples. A comparison with other Teutonic languages seems to show that originally their society consisted of two classes, *earls* and *carls* (the *eorls* and *ceorls* of England). At the time when the sagas were written, neither word had retained its original meaning. The free class are called *oðalsmenn*, "franklins;" while the word *karl* had come to signify "man" in the sense of *homo;* the *earl* or *jarl* (as it is now usually spelt), the petty prince of the small community. The

---

[7] See p. 120.

king, who became necessary as the people banded together for offence and defence, was the head of the community of franklins. By them he was elected king, after having sworn to protect them in war. In return for this they swore that they would render him personal service in war, and provide him with hospitality and means of conveyance when he passed through their land. Each kingship had its own *thing* or *moot* for administrative purposes, and its own laws. These were handed down, and were expounded by the "lawman" (*lagman*), an officer who played an important part in later Swedish constitutions. The lowest class consisted of thralls or slaves, either foreigners, or in some cases perhaps the aborigines of the country. These had no political rights, which belonged exclusively to the king and franklins as possessors of the land.

While the success of the *wikings* was due in a large measure to the divided state of the lands they attacked, it is to the gradual amalgamation of the petty kingdoms in Scandinavia that we have to attribute some of the most important of their expeditions. The lowest unit of organization was the *härad* or "hundred." Several *härads* made up one district. Each *härad* had its own *thing;* but the larger questions were reserved for the *landsthing*, or *thing* of the district, which continued to exist long after the Scandinavian kingdoms had grown up. These *things* were held under the presidency of the king, who travelled about in each *haräd* for the purpose, having been acknowledged in each as king. Gradually the further stages by which the tribal or folk-kingdoms were united into national kingdoms were reached. The king or earl gaining the surrounding landships, claimed the land as his property, and gave away feoffs to his favourites, while he exacted scot (*skatt*) or rent from the whole as his due. Hence arose a system of taxation based upon a feudal system. This change, however unjust in principle, was often very beneficial to the people ; and it is to this centralization of power and resources that law and order, and in fact a really national existence, became possible.

It is in Norway alone that history affords us any detailed account of this union and its effects. The king to whom its completion was due was Harald Fairhair. It is said in the kings' sagas, that while only king of the single province of Vestfold he paid court to the beautiful but haughty Gyda, who, though a franklin's daughter, would have nothing to say to one who was less than king of all Norway. Whereon he made a vow that he would not cut his hair till he had conquered the whole land. One after another he subdued the smaller kings, till at Hafursfjord, near Stavanger, he gained his last victory over the *wikings* who came to help them. He then married Gyda, and had his hair cut. The reforms made by Harald when possessed of power were not pleasing to the hitherto independent small kings, who had not only held their lands free of *skatt*, but made themselves still richer by plundering their neighbours. Many malcontents left the country, and with their followers settled in the Scottish isles and elsewhere, where they and their descendants were long a thorn in Norway's side. Rolf the Walker (so called because too ponderous for a Norwegian steed), an incurable pirate, had to take refuge in the old Danish settlement of Normandy, where he wrung the recognition of his claims from Charles the Simple, and became the ancestor of our Norman kings. Similar settlements were made in Iceland, Greenland, and for a time in America itself.

In Sweden the union of the folk-kingdoms appears to have been completed even earlier, probably in the ninth century; but the whole history is much confused, and accounts often disagree both with themselves and each other. Snorri Sturluson speaks of an Ivar or Ingwar as king of Denmark, Sweden, the south coast lands of the Baltic, and the fifth part of England. Later, Sigurd Ring appears, after the battle of Brâvalla, to have made himself master of Denmark and Sweden; but in the days of Björn, a later king, they appear to be again distinct.

The Sweden of this date was of much smaller dimensions than that of the present day. All the south and south-west coasts belonged to Denmark. The landships called Bleking, Halland, and Skaney (or Skandey) [8] were a constant bone of dispute between the two kingdoms. The north was only inhabited to any extent as far as Dalarne. The strip of land in the west between the Vener, the Göta, and the coast, the modern Bohuslän, belonged to Norway; while for a long time Dal and Vermland were debatable ground between Sweden and Norway.

[8] Now Skåne.

CHAPTER IV.

HISTORICAL SKETCH OF SWEDEN AND NORWAY.

WE endeavoured to show in the last chapter how the kingdoms of Sweden and Norway gradually grew out of a number of small settlements made from time to time in Scandinavia. In this chapter we propose giving a slight sketch of these two kingdoms, showing how from time to time they became united, and afterwards again separated. The most important result of the *wiking* expeditions was the introduction of Christianity. Already, as early as the beginning of the ninth century, there were many Christians settled in Sweden who had received baptism in other countries. It is said that for the benefit of these, the monks Ansgar and Witmar were sent from the monastery of Corvey, in Westphalia, at the invitation of king Björn. Though a church was built on Björk Island, the mission met as a whole with little success. The first landships where Christianity gained a firm footing were Vestergötland and the Danish Skaney. This was about the end of the tenth century. Olaf Skötkonung [1] was the first Swedish king who voluntarily received baptism, in 1008. This king found himself obliged to leave old Upsala, the centre of

---

[1] According to tradition the "lap-king"; but the word *skot* probably = *skatt*, "tribute."

paganism, and set up his court in Skara, in Vester-
götland, which he made the first episcopal see.
The great missionary bishop of this period was
Sigfrid, who is said to have been Archbishop of
York, but in all probability really came from
Germany.

The eleventh century marks the great struggles
of Christianity with paganism in the eastern provinces ; and even in the next, the zeal of Inge to
crush out the old faith brought back for a time a
terrible reaction.   He was himself driven out of the
thing for refusing to restore the old religious customs,
and his successor Blot-Swain, "Sacrifice Swain," restored the ancient faith, amidst great rejoicings.
Swain was afterwards treacherously murdered by
his nephew, and Christianity gradually made way
through the country.   In 1144 the first monastery
was founded at Alvastra.   It lies at the southern
foot of Omberget, a pretty wooded hill on the east
of the Vetter Lake, and its ruins still form a very
picturesque object.   The next year the cathedral
of Lund was completed, and the Swedish church
placed under its jurisdiction.   Twenty years later
old Upsala was made an archbishopric, but still
under the primacy of Lund.   The rivalry between
these two sees proved a long-lasting element of
discord between Sweden and Denmark.

The twelfth century was the great age of Crusades.   These were conducted against the Finnish
and Esthonian tribes on the east and south coasts
of the Baltic, who as pagans still continued the
piratical practices which Christianity had put an
end to in Sweden and Norway.   And yet the
savage methods adopted to force the people to the
new faith show that the *wiking* spirit had not yet

died out. The most celebrated of these crusades is that of the Swedish Erik the Saint, about 1160, whose success in compelling the Finns to receive baptism, gained him the honour of being regarded the patron saint of Sweden; while his English bishop, Henry, who was murdered by a newly-converted Finn, received the same distinction in Finland.

The struggles of Christianity in Sweden were connected also with political disturbances. Rival kings often appear to have taken up the one or the other religion from political motives. The loss of prestige which old Upsala incurred was made all the more serious as the Christian Vestergötland rose to compete with it. Thus for a time Christianity tended to be instrumental in breaking up the unity of the country. A period of continual discord and civil war followed, lasting from 1060 to 1135, of which the accounts are both meagre and contradictory. After this was a period of comparative peace and order, in which the kingly office alternated between the rival families of Erik and Sverker. During this time the title of *earl* (*jarl*) came first to have a new meaning. Originally belonging to a whole class of society, it had come to mean, as we have already seen, a small king, and the name was often still retained, when the smaller, or folkkingdoms, had been absorbed in the larger or national. Now, however, we find *earls* exercising an office much like that of a prince, and in this capacity drawing to themselves not only the business, but the power of the king. This office was all along confined chiefly to one family, the Folkungar. This family, by frequent marriages with the royal families of Sweden and Norway, gained a para-

mount influence, until, after the death of King
Erik Läspe,[2] the kingdom passed into their
hands.

The last and greatest of these *jarls* was Birger,
who acted in this capacity, first to Erik, and afterwards to his own son Valdemar, who had during
his father's life the empty name of king. Birger
was a great lawgiver and reformer. One of his laws
forbade *våldgästning*, or the practice which prevailed among the rich of extorting from yeomen
by violence the rights of hospitality which belonged
to the king only. All others were now by law required to purchase food, lodging, and conveyance,
at a fixed tariff—a provision which has remained in
force up to the present day. Birger also did much
to encourage commerce, by making the first treaties
with the newly-formed Hanseatic League, and for-
tifying and enlarging the little trading-town of
Stockholm. The most disastrous act of his reign
was the division of the kingdom at his death
among his sons. The two youngest of them,
Magnus and Erik, now received the new title of
hertig, or duke, probably as a check against the
foolish and dissolute Valdemar, who still remained
nominally king. This indefinite division of power and
wealth brought about a strife, which soon plunged
the land in civil war. After a long and tedious
struggle Magnus Ladulås displaced his brother,
in 1279, but afterwards proved himself nevertheless
one of the ablest kings Sweden ever had. Civil
and domestic peace were again restored. The
laws of Birger were confirmed, and expanded by
the addition of what was called the " king's peace,"
which required that every one should abstain from

[2] I. e. "The Lisping."

all acts of violence fourteen days before and after,
as well as during, the king's residence in any landship. His object seems to have been to increase
the royal prestige, for which purpose he also held
a magnificent court. To him is due the introduction of chivalry in the country, and knights
disported themselves in tournaments, and tilting-
matches, and all kinds of martial exercise. To
him is also ascribed the first foundation of the distinction between the "free" (*frälse*) and "unfree"
(*ofrälse*) land, which has exercised up to the present day a most important influence on the social
and political history of the people.[3] He ordered that
all those who provided a horse ready equipped for
battle, or served as knights in the king's court,
should be free of all *skatt*. The work of Magnus
was carried on after his death by the regent Tor-
gils, under the title of *marsk*, or "marshal." He
gained renown abroad by the brilliant victories in
Finland and Carelia which first brought Sweden
into hostile relations with Russia, and prepared
the way for a general law-code by ordering the
lagman Birger Persson to draw up a single code to
comprise all the districts of Upland. The majority
of King Birger Magnusson was followed once more
by feuds between himself and his brothers. Their
mutual cruelty and deceit reached a climax when Birger invited his brothers to a banquet at Nyköping,
and ordered them to be seized, and after a long confinement, murdered.[4] The horrible story that he
threw the keys into the moat, and then left his
brothers to starve, is inconsistent in many points,
and is probably, in detail at least, the fabrication of

[3] See pp. 200—202.
[4] This event is known as Nyköpings Gästabud.

Erik's partisans. The exasperation of the people at Birger's cruelty caused his own expulsion, and the appointment of Erik's infant son, Magnus.

During the minority of Magnus, we find the *Råd*, "Council," first becoming an important body in the state. It had long been customary for the king in matters of emergency to consult the most influential members of the kingdom ; but not till about the end of the thirteenth century do we find such a body beginning to have a recognized political status, and exercising a power which did much to check the evils of party strife. As yet, it is true, they had only a consultative voice in the deliberations of the king; but the minority of Magnus gave them an opportunity of coming to the front, of which they gladly availed themselves. This body was elected by the king out of the court, lords, and knights, while every bishop was an *ex officio* member. At their head was an officer who was called either *drotsete* or *marsk*, titles which in later times existed together as distinct offices. The election of Magnus is also important in the constitutional history, as being the first occasion on which representatives of the yeomen or *bonde* class, were summoned to the *riksmöte*, or parliament. The burghers as yet were not a body of sufficient importance to form a distinct class.

The late quarrels of the brothers brought about curious political relations with Denmark and Norway. Each party strove to strengthen its cause by matrimonial alliances with the royal families of either kingdom. For this purpose the ambitious Erik had married the infant Ingeborg, the only child of Håkon V. of Norway; so that his son Magnus Smek became at the same time King of Sweden by election, and King of Norway by inheritance.

We must now go back to trace the history of the sister kingdom, from the introduction of Christianity to the reign of Magnus. If Germany can claim the honour of sending the first missionaries to Sweden, we can certainly boast that the conversion of Norway was due to Englishmen. There was also a difference in the manner in which Christianity was introduced. In Sweden it was the work of foreigners, acting sometimes with, sometimes without, the consent of the kings, who at last agreed to receive Christian baptism at their hands. In Norway the most influential missionaries were the kings themselves. Baptized in England while fugitive *wikings,* they returned to their country as kings, and pressed the claims of Christianity on their subjects. The two great missionary kings of this type were Anlaf or Olaf Tryggvason, and Anlaf or Olaf Haraldsson, usually known as the Saint. Even before these, Håkon the Good, the foster-son of the English Athelstane, had made some efforts to introduce Christianity, but had yielded to the indignation of his subjects. The work was still more completely undone by the political feuds which followed his death, and the hostility of Earl Håkon ; and when Olaf landed in Trondhjem, in 995, after his life of early adventure in foreign lands, he found the country as pagan as ever. Olaf himself had been baptized in the Scilly Isles, and after he had made himself master of the several petty kingdoms, he set about the work of conversion with untiring zeal. The later accounts of his cruelty, which we get in the present

form of many of the sagas, have been foisted into
the earlier documents by ecclesiastical scribes, who
thought that they were adding to the glory of their
hero by ascribing to him methods of torture in behalf of Christianity as ludicrous and as cruel as
those related of the early persecutors of the Christians.   In the whole account of Olaf there is only
one authentic instance of a man put to death for
refusing to accept Christianity, and that only after
turbulent acts of violence ; whereas we have, on
the other hand, some examples of very great for-
bearance towards those who clung passionately to
their old faith.

But the conversion of Norway was not Olaf's only
ambition.   The great naval equipments of which
Snorri gives us such a detailed account in the
Heimskringla, were no doubt designed with a
view to foreign conquests, probably in Denmark
and Sweden.   His return from Pomerania, where
he had gone ostensibly to secure possessions long
acquired by marriage, was cut off by the ships of
the kings of Denmark and Sweden, and the heathen
Earls of Norway.   The battle of Svold which
followed, near the island of Rügen, is one of the
most celebrated in *wiking* history.   Olaf's great
ship, the Long Serpent, was surrounded by the
enemies' ships, and after a long and desperate
struggle he and his men were all either cut down
or threw themselves overboard.

Norway was obliged to cede large parts of its
territory to Denmark and Sweden ; the rest was
split up into factions among the earls ; and the
cause of religion suffered greatly, so that when
Olaf Haraldsson came to the country, fifteen years
later, the religious and political work of his prede-

cessors had to be done over again. Though equally zealous, Olaf Haraldsson had neither the presence nor the power of his great namesake. Finding in many cases persuasion useless, he had recourse to measures of violence, and even cruelty of the harshest kind. It is to be feared that the representations of Olaf as they often appear in Scandinavian churches,[5] with a battle-axe in the right hand and a chalice in the left, form no caricature of the character and policy he displayed. Yet it must be mentioned to his praise, that he did not content himself, like many Scandinavian kings, with baptizing his willing or unwilling converts, but took care to provide for their religious instruction ; and his very intolerance was clearly the result of an untempered zeal rather than the bigotry of petty and selfish motives. Whatever his faults were, he had to pay for them dearly. Driven out of his country by the effects of popular irritation and foreign intrigue, he sought refuge with Jarislav, King of Russia, and only returned to fall a victim, after a desperate struggle, to an army of franklins, roused almost to madness by the bribed partisans of Cnut the Great. This battle was fought at Stiklestad, a hamlet near Levanger on the Trondhjem Fjord, in 1030. Olaf did more by his tragic death to forward the cause of Christianity than he had done in his whole lifetime.

The people soon discovered that they had been fighting for Denmark, and not for Norway, and found the rule of Swain, Cnut's regent, far more oppressive than that of Olaf. Swain was expelled and Magnus Olafsson, sent for from the

---

[5] Especially those of Gotland, whose inhabitants regard Olaf as their patron saint.

court of Jarislav. They soon forgot all Olaf's faults, and remembered and exaggerated all his virtues. Superstition worked upon their excited feelings. The sand had blown away from Olaf's grave, and the body was exposed to view ; this showed clearly that he was discontented with his resting-place. Many other wonders were reported. His corpse was moved with great rejoicings to Nidaros,[6] and his shrine became the centre round which the cathedral of Trondhjem grew. This in time came to be the Archbishopric of Norway, and included in its jurisdiction Iceland, the Orkneys, and other Norwegian colonies. Thus Olaf, who was known in his lifetime as " the Thick " (Digre), became after his death "the Saint," and Christianity gained a hold on the country which, in spite of the religious and political disturbances which followed, it never entirely lost.

The political and social phases which Norway went through from this time until her union with Sweden under Magnus Smek, are very similar to those experienced by the sister country. Though we find traces of an earlier development of social and political freedom, yet these were more completely checked by the civil wars which followed. The reign of Magnus was distinguished by the first code of written laws, which thus existed 200 years before. a similar code was known in Sweden. According to Snorri Sturluson, this king made a compact with Hadacnut, that whichever king first died the survivor should inherit his kingdom. The claims made by Magnus, when the latter died, to Denmark, though supported by a faction of the Danish people, led to a series of disputes with

[6] The ancient name of Trondhjem.

Swain Estrithsson, which ended after five years in the battle of Halsted, in 1047, and death of Magnus. The reign of his uncle and successor, Harald Hardrede "the Stern" a *wiking* of the old school, was spent in constant struggles with Denmark and England, till he was overcome and killed at the battle of Stamford Bridge, 1066, while assisting Tostig against Harold of England. He was succeeded by Olaf, surnamed Kyrre, "the Peaceful," from the long period of peace and prosperity which the country enjoyed under his rule. Very different in character was Magnus "Bareleg," who succeeded his father in 1093. He gained a great name by his harryings in the Scottish Isles and Anglesey, and an attempt, unsuccessful though it proved, to reduce the northern colony in Iceland to Norwegian rule. At the same time he incurred the contempt of his countrymen by his affectation of foreign manners. It was from his adopting the Irish plaited shirt that he obtained his surname.

About this time we first see the beginnings of those dissensions which so long disturbed the peace of the country. All three sons of Magnus were appointed to succeed him. Of these Olaf soon died; and Sigurd left the country on a great crusade to Jerusalem, which got him the name of Jorsalafari. Meanwhile Eystein reigned in peace. Soon after his brother's return he died, and with the reign of the superstitious and eccentric crusader civil war soon blazed out, which lasted for a century. Among the many parties and factions in the State which showed themselves at this time, two were especially prominent, "the Crossers" (*Baglar*) and "the Birchlegs" (*Birkibeinar*). The

G

first were so called because their first leader,
Nicolaus, was a bishop; they appear to have
represented the ecclesiastical party. The *Birkibeinar*, who derived their name from their birch
leggings, appear to have represented the demo-
cratical party. For a long time the *Baglar* seem
to have been in the ascendant. In 1162 the Archbishop of Trondhjem was able to get a law passed,
declaring the crown to be a fief of St. Olaf,
and consequently in the gift of the Pope. Ten
years later we find the *Birkibeinar* coming to
the front. Their new leader, Sverri, is the greatest
man Norway had seen since the days of Olaf
Tryggvason. His enthusiastic, half-hypocritical
zeal in behalf of his fanatical religious principles;
his tact and knowledge of human nature ; above
all, his passionate eloquence, inspired both himself
and his followers, and made him triumph over
all obstacles.[7] In 1184 he was elected king, and
at last ended a life of perpetual struggle in a
fray near Bergen, in 1202. Peace was finally
restored, in 1217, by Håkon IV., who violated the
traditions of the *Birkibeinar* by lavishing favour on
the clergy. He was thus enabled to win over or
crush out all other factions. In his reign we hear
for the first time of the title of *hertig*, or duke, an
office first held by Håkon's uncle, Skule, who
abused his power by plotting against the king, and
so lost his life. To Håkon is due the first reduction of Iceland. This was made easy by quarrels
among the aristocratic factions, which cost the
unfortunate Snorri Sturluson his life. A similar
attempt to reduce Scotland was very disastrous.

[7] See Prolegomena to Sturlunga Saga, ed. by Vigfusson, pp.
lxxi, lxxii.

Part of Håkon's army was defeated in a skirmish near Largs, in 1261. The king, already ill, died soon afterwards. His son Magnus gave up the Hebrides to Alexander, but subsequently made an alliance, confirmed by the marriage of his son Erik with the Scotch princess. The reign of Magnus is of chief importance from the great improvements made in the laws, which were now collected and revised. Hence he got the name of Laga bætir, "Law-betterer." In his reign the orders of chivalry were first introduced into Norway, though they never gained the same influence here as in Sweden. His son Erik reversed the policy of his predecessor, by adopting a hostile attitude towards the church and depriving the clergy of their immunities. Hence he was called Presta-hatari, "the Priest Hater." He also made less successful efforts to curtail the privileges of the Hanse towns, which were then beginning to monopolize the trade of the country. His marriage only brought about fresh disputes with Scotland, which ended by the sudden death of his only daughter Margrete, the "Maid of Norway," while on her way to claim her grandfather's throne. Erik was succeeded, in 1299, by his brother Håkon V., who, after an eventful reign of twenty years, left the throne, as we have already mentioned, to Magnus Smek, the infant son of his daughter Ingeborg and Duke Erik, under whose government the kingdoms of Sweden and Norway were thus for a time united.

Magnus Smek, " the favourite lover," though unable to cope successfully with the great difficulties of his position, was far from being the dissolute and weak man he is sometimes represented. Though

G 2

obliged to burden the people with taxes to pay the common debt contracted by the *råd* for the purchase of the Danish provinces in the south, he did much to improve the position of the burgher and peasant classes, whom he was the first king to summon to a *riksdag*, " parliament." He drew up a code of laws defining, and limiting in some measure, the king's privileges, especially in the matter of taxes. To him is due the first institution of three distinct judicial courts, those, viz., of the *härad*, the landship, and the king.[8] The greatest disaster of his reign was the plague known to ourselves as the black death. After ravaging the western countries of Europe, it was brought to Norway by a vessel with a crew of corpses, which drifted to the shore near Bergen. For three years the plague ravaged the country (1350—1352). It is estimated that it must have cut off at least one-third of the population, besides causing an enormous proportion of the country to remain uncultivated.

The kingdom was at this time split up into factions, all hostile to the king. The nobles were jealous of the power the Folkungar family had long exercised. The clergy were irritated at being deprived of their tithes to pay the expense of a useless, though well-intended, crusade against Finland. The Norwegian *råd*, vexed at the king's continued absence from their country, appointed his younger son King of Norway, as Håkon VI.,, in 1358; while the elder son, Junker Erik, jealous of his brother's good fortune, put himself at the head of a revolt, and succeeded in wresting from his father more than half of his dominions, and but for

---

[8] The latter, called the *Hofrätt*, is now the Court of Second Instance. See p. 186.

his untimely death in 1359 would have probably become king of the whole country. Outside, two powers—Denmark, with its wily king Valdemar, and the allied Duchies of Holstein and Mecklenburg—were contending for the spoil. The king first made a weak effort to resist Valdemar's encroachments, which only ended in the loss of the Danish provinces ; but afterwards made with him an alliance, confirmed by the marriage of his son Håkon VI. with Margaret, Valdemar's infant daughter. The exasperated nobles succeeded in imprisoning the king, and offered the crown to Albrecht of Mecklenburg, in 1365. This king irritated the people by his increased taxation, and roused the jealousy of the nobles by appointing Germans to all important offices. They heartily combined in the liberation of Magnus (who was allowed to hold the feoffs of Dal and Vermland till his death) and the appointment of Bo Johnson as Drotsete, The latter ruled the country with an iron rod, until his death in 1385. Meanwhile, in 1380, Håkon had died, and Olaf, his son, was appointed King of Norway, with his mother Margaret as regent. She was now offered the throne of Sweden by Bo Johnson's heirs. A struggle ensued between Margaret and Albrecht's party, which was not decided for two years (in 1387) when Stockholm was surrendered to Margaret in default of the sum of 60,000 *riksdaler*,[9] which Albrecht, somewhile since taken prisoner, had promised to pay for his release. This town, the stronghold of the German party, had been the scene of the most fearful atrocities, perpetrated on the Swedish burghers by a confederation called the " Hat Brothers," while a band

[9] About 3333*l.*

of pirates known as the "Victual Brothers" had, on the pretence of relieving Stockholm, been making themselves the scourge of the Baltic, pillaging all vessels which came in their way.

In this year Olaf died, and Margaret succeeded in getting Erik of Pomerania, her adopted son, proclaimed king. In 1397, a council of sixty-seven deputies, specially appointed from each kingdom, met at Kalmar. Erik was solemnly crowned King of Denmark, Sweden, and Norway. At the same time were drawn up what are known as the Articles of the Kalmar Union. The most important were to the following effect :—(1) The three kingdoms were henceforward to have one king, and never to be divided. (2) The king was to be elected by the common consent of all three kingdoms ; but if the deceased king had sons, the eldest was to succeed. (3) Each kingdom was to retain its own laws and its own jurisdiction. Many questions, such as affected materially the mutual relations of the three kingdoms, were left practically undecided. It is probable that this compact was intended by Margaret to pave the way for the creation of a united Scandinavian kingdom, which should be powerful enough to check the rising power of the Hanse towns and the German princes. Had Margaret's successors been like herself, her dreams might perhaps have been realized. As long as she lived she was both wise enough and influential enough to keep the chief power in her own hands. She made it her object to minimise the distinction between Swedes and Danes, by appointing those of either kingdom to high offices of State in the other, while by newly levied taxes she succeeded in filling the empty exchequer, and by a statute of *reduction* restored to the crown the properties lost by debt.

Notwithstanding the irritation which followed these measures among all classes, her personal influence and high talents made her universally respected, and under her the country was restored once more to peace and order.

In Norway the Union thus effected remained permanent. In spite of a few spasmodic efforts to shake off the yoke, she became by degrees an integral part of the Danish kingdom. Still it must be confessed that she gained on the whole more than she had lost by the change. She was thus enabled to enjoy a long period of comparative peace and prosperity. From Denmark she derived her religion, her culture, her literature, while at the same time she retained far greater social freedom than existed either in Sweden or even in Denmark itself. In Sweden the case was very different. The nobles, though their mutual jealousies compelled them to call in one foreign power after another, were at once too patriotic and too selfish to submit long to foreign rule. The peasants long smarted under the oppressive taxations and the cruelties they suffered from their Danish rulers, and made the most noble efforts to be free. The burghers, whose rights were often curtailed by the Danish kings, usually took the peasants' part, but seldom acted on their own account. The clergy, whose privileges were supported by the Danes, with one or two exceptions took the side of the latter, but succeeded in securing to themselves both wealth and political power. The history of the fifteenth century marks the struggles of these parties, which led at last to the final liberation of Sweden under Gustaf Vasa.

The oppressive taxation of Erik, Margaret's son, to meet the expenses of a protracted war with

Holstein, and the cruelty of his officers, brought about the first efforts to throw off what had soon become a Danish yoke. The hero of the day was Engelbrecht Engelbrechtson, who twice at the head of the spirited Dalkarlar,[10] made himself master of the country, and twice had to yield to the jealousy of the Swedish nobles, and was afterwards murdered by a private enemy on a lonely holm on the Hjelmar Lake. Here he had landed, weary and ill, on his way to Stockholm, to attend a meeting of the *råd*, in 1436.

Karl Knutsson, a noble, was now at the head of the Liberation party, and remained so till his death in 1470. During this time there was a continual alternation of native and Danish rulers; a series of struggles, intrigues, and mutual hostilities; of truces frequently made and as frequently broken; while the people had all the while to suffer from the burdens necessary to keep up the armaments required. During this period Karl was three times elected king, and twice was compelled to resign his office by the jealousy of native rivals and by foreign intrigues. During these intervals of power two Danish kings—the mean and contemptible Kristopher of Bavaria, and the extortionate Kristian of Oldenburg—were successively crowned and acknowledged in Sweden, while twice the Swedish archbishops succeeded in getting the supreme power in their own hands. To make matters worse, Erik for a long time maintained himself in Gotland, whence he continued to pillage the Swedish coasts. But Karl was very unlike Engelbrecht, and showed clearly, by efforts made to secure to himself the thrones of Norway

---

[10] The inhabitants of Dalarne are so called.

and even Denmark, that he would not have objected to the union, provided he, or at least Sweden, were at the head of it.

From the time of Karl Knutsson's death (1470), we find the Liberation party gradually gaining strength. The title of king was now changed for the new title of Administrator (*Riksförestådare*), which was held in succession by Sten Sture the elder, Svante Nilsson, and his son Sten Sture the younger. The Swedish party were greatly strengthened by a victory gained over the Danes at Brunkeberg, in 1471. The scene of this battle—considered one of the most glorious in Swedish history—is what is now the King's Park (*Kungsträgården*) in Stockholm. The victory was commemorated by a colossal figure of St. George and the Dragon, placed at first in St. Nicolaus' church, but now transferred to the lower room of the State's museum. But intrigues, hostilities, and treaties with Denmark, still continued. King Hans, who succeeded to the Danish throne in 1481, was actually recognized for three years as king in Sweden. After his expulsion no Danish king gained a permanent footing in the country. This was mainly due to the unselfish and patriotic spirit of Svante Nilsson and Sten Sture the younger. The latter was gentle to a fault. But while he thus reconciled the most reasonable of the nobles, he conceded to his worst enemies—such as especially the most despicable Archbishop Gustaf Trolle—a power which they readily turned against him. Kristian II.[11] succeeded to the Danish throne in 1514, and did his very utmost, both by intrigues and force of arms, to gain power over Sweden.

[11] Surnamed "The Tyrant."

In 1518-19, after some previous unsuccessful
struggles, the crisis came. An enormous Danish
army invaded the south, and soon gained two
great victories, at Bogesund and Tiveden. At the
former of these Sten Sture was mortally wounded.
With his death the cause of the Liberationists fell.
The *råd* offered the crown at once to Kristian. The
peasants after a short struggle came to terms.
Even Sten Sture's widow yielded to the fair promises of Kristian, that no one should be held responsible for past conduct, and surrendered Stockholm. On November 4, Kristian was crowned with
great ceremonies, lasting four days. All the nobles
were invited. Kristian would not let this opportunity for vengeance go by. In spite of his promises, by the advice of his infamous favourite,
Didrik Sloghök of Denmark, and Gustaf Trolle,
the guests were seized while in the banqueting-
hall, and the next day the streets of Stockholm
literally flowed with the blood of nobles and com-
moners, bishops and laymen, many of whom had
actually supported the Danish cause. The defence
offered for this outrageous act by Gustaf Trolle
was that though Kristian had forgiven them all
personal wrong, he was obliged to carry out the
just vengeance of the Church on those who had
aided and abetted the excommunicated Sten
Sture.

This memorable massacre, known in history as
the "Blood Bath," brought about results exactly
opposite to those intended. It produced in the
Swedish mind a horror of Danish rule which, even
to the present day, it has never quite forgotten.
At the same time it cut off many of those in
power whose jealousies and selfishness might have

effectually hindered the liberation. Happily for Sweden there was left a man of sufficient patriotism, energy and strength of will, to 'be something even more than a worthy successor of Engelbrecht and Sten Sture. Such a man was Gustaf Eriksson, better known as Gustavus Vasa.

Brought up under the influence of the Stures, he had conceived from the first a horror of the Danes, which his after-experience intensified. He had distinguished himself under Sten Sture in the early conflicts with Kristian. On one of these occasions, after the battle of Brännkyrka, in 1517, he had been, together with six other Swedish nobles, treacherously taken prisoner by Kristian, and brought to Denmark. Two years after he made his escape from the custody of Erik Baner, to whose charge he was committed. He arrived at Lübeck, where he remained for eight months. The Lübeckers, seeing in him a possible counterpoise to the dangerous power of Kristian, refused to surrender the fugitive, and so far furthered Gustaf's plans as to convey him to Sweden in a small merchant-vessel. A monument now marks the point near Kalmar where he landed. First in Kalmar itself, and then in the villages of Småland and Södermanland, Gustaf went, trying to rouse his countrymen to a spirited resistance. But they were but half-hearted at best, and all had grown tired with the long struggle. The peasants were contented with a king who gave them fair promises and salt for their fish. Gustaf was advised by his own friends to capitulate to the "kind-hearted Danish king." Despairing of success at present, he went to Räfsnäs, an old family estate near Stockholm, to await the course of events.

While here he heard of the Blood Bath and its horrors—how his own father and uncle had been murdered; his mother and sisters taken off to Denmark to a cruel confinement. He saw that the blow must be struck now or never. Leaving the cold-hearted southerners, he determined to make his way to the Dalkarlar—a people who, since the days of Engelbrecht, had ever been foremost in taking the side of Swedish liberty. Clad as a peasant, with a woodman's axe in hand, he went from village to village till he reached the neighbourhood of Falun. Many are the tales told of his hairbreadth adventures in these parts. At Ornäs, on the Runn Lake, the house is still shown where he was let down by a towel from an upper room to a stable below, by his kind hostess Barbro Stigsdotter; while her faithless husband had gone for the purpose of fetching a troop of Danish soldiers. At Utmeland near Mora, on the Siljan Lake, is shown the cellar—then covered with a vat of newly-brewed yule-ale—in which he hid himself on another occasion.[12]

It was with great caution, only here and there, that Gustaf declared himself, and made known his intentions. At last, at Rättvik and Mora, on the Siljan Lake, he got opportunities of addressing the collected people. His eloquent appeals called forth tears and acclamations, and execrations on the Danish tyrant. But their ardour was easily cooled when Danish spies came, and persuaded them that the story of the Blood Bath was a lie, and Kristian was the peasant's friend. Before long

[12] The house has been since destroyed, but over the cellar, which remains, has been built a room, hung with pictures of Gustaf's adventures.

Page 92.

HOUSE AT ORNÄS.

Gustaf was obliged to take flight, first to the Western Dal and afterwards to the Norwegian frontier. Meanwhile Gustaf's words were confirmed. Fresh accounts of cruelties, and new fugitives, arrived daily from the south. At Mora a Danish officer was slain. At Rättvik a troop of 100 Danish cavalry were besieged and taken prisoners in the church tower. Two of the swiftest snow-skaters were despatched to fetch Gustaf, while just on the point of leaving his country in despair. Gustaf soon found himself at the head of 3000 men. Daily fresh villages sent their contingents. The work now began in earnest. The first battle was fought at Brunbäck ferry, on the borders of Dalarne and Vestmanland. The Danes, who tried to prevent the Swedes from crossing the river, were nearly all either cut down or drowned in the stream.

This was the beginning of a course of almost uninterrupted success. The southern provinces, one by one, either joined Gustaf or rose up against the Danes on their own account. The castles still long remained in the enemy's hands; and these, with the continued opposition of the clergy, who saw clearly the bias of Gustaf's mind, proved the greatest hindrance to his success. In August, 1521, Gustaf was able to summon a meeting of the *riksdag*, at which he was appointed president. It was not, however, till the summer of 1523 that the fortresses of Kalmar and Stockholm were at last obliged, after a manful resistance, to capitulate.

The great causes of Gustaf's success were the regular discipline which he maintained in his army, his unselfish and generous nature which endeared him to his soldiers, and, not least, the improve-

ments in military tactics and warfare which he
introduced. Of the latter, the invention of the
long spear called *ljurangel*, calculated to resist the
charge of the Danish cavalry,[13] deserves especial
mention.

The first great ambition of Gustaf's life had now
been accomplished. The country was free from
Danish tyranny; the whole of the land, including
Finland and part of Norway, were in his power;
the great mass of the people were enthusiastic in
owning his allegiance. The second great work—
the freedom from papal authority—was still to be
accomplished. It was only with a view to carry
out this object that he very reluctantly allowed
himself to be declared king, on the 20th of April,
1523. The difficulties he had to contend against
were enormous. Outside the kingdom was Denmark, smarting with the recollection of the power
it had lost, and seeking every opportunity to regain it; the Hanse towns—Lübeck especially—
jealous of a king who soon showed his intention to
interfere with their commercial monopoly; Russia,
ever ready to make encroachments on the Swedish
possessions in Finland. In addition to all these,
the complications of European politics generally,
which might at any time involve the country in a
disastrous war. Inside the kingdom the difficulties
were still greater. Among the nobles were men
like Jönsson Roos, jealous of the king, and mean
enough to ally themselves with any enemy to get
the power into their own hands. The clergy were
as a whole, naturally enough, unwilling to consent
to the loss of their wealth and ancient privileges;
and even had it not been so, ignorance and preju-

[13] See Fryxell, part iii., p. 24.

dice prevented their seeing clearly the merits of
the great religious questions of the day. But it
was with the great mass of the people that Gustaf
had the greatest difficulties to contend against.
The Reformation meant to them a cruel wrench
from all their old associations and ideas ; and,
ignorant and simple as they were, it is hardly
strange if they clung with an almost savage perti-
nacity to the faith in which their fathers had lived
and died. Three times Gustaf had to quell an
insurrection of the Dalkarlar, who fought with the
same spirit in defending their old religious customs
as they had shown in the cause of political freedom. Through all these difficulties Gustaf steered
clear, or overcame them, by a usually patient but
always unwavering determination. The final blow
to clerical power was struck at a stormy *riksdag* at
Vesterås, in 1527, when the bishops were for ever
deprived of their wealth and privileges. In his
foreign policy Gustaf made it his aim to strengthen
the defences and develope the resources of the
country at home, and avoid all foreign warfare.
Thus he even allowed Gotland to be wrested from
him almost without a struggle.

It was not till 1554 that his labours were at an
end ; and for the last six years of his life he was
able to reign over a country at peace from enemies
within and without.

Gustaf, in spite of his greatness, had his faults.
His treatment of the bishops and monks, though
almost necessitated by the state of the times, was
yet, it must in all candour be allowed, sometimes
characterized by harshness and injustice. The
constant trials and anxieties he had to suffer
told by degrees on his constitution, and partly

account for an irritability of temper which grew upon him in later life. The most painful blot on his character is the ungrateful vengeance he took on some of the leaders of the Dalkarlar, forgetting both his own promise of pardon and the services they had rendered to him in the past. But making all allowance for these and other similar defects, we cannot help acknowledging that Gustaf Vasa has well deserved the love and praise which a patriotic people have always lavished upon him. To him is due the first real foundation of the greatness and happiness which Sweden afterwards enjoyed.

At a *riksdag* in Vesterås, in 1544, the kingdom had been declared hereditary. Erik, as the eldest son, therefore succeeded on Gustaf's death in 1560. Unfortunately Gustaf, to check the power of this weak-minded prince, had followed the example of Magnus Ladulås, and left a large part of the kingdom to his other sons—Johan, Magnus, and Karl, as dukes. The quarrels and jealousies which followed in consequence were very similar in character to those which had long disturbed the kingdom in the thirteenth century, and for a time threatened once more to undo all the good which Gustaf had done. Erik was weak and suspicious, passionately fond of display, given to violent fits of passion amounting to madness, followed by as ungovernable moods of remorse. He wasted the public funds, and gained both notoriety abroad and disrespect at home by his many and costly suits. He sued alternately, and sometimes even simultaneously, for the hand of Elizabeth of England, Mary of Scotland, and many other foreign princesses ; and after many rebuffs, at last, to the grief of his subjects, married the daughter of a common soldier. He engaged in unnecessary and tedious wars with Denmark, which, though they produced such great men as Jacob Bagge, and Klas Horn, emptied the exhausted treasury, and kept alive the ill feeling between the two countries. All the leading men of the time incurred Erik's suspicions. At the instigation of his evil genius, Göran Persson, many of them were secretly poisoned or assassinated ; while his own brother Johan was kept in close confinement at Gripsholm, a castle near Stockholm. At last his suspicions burst out in a fit of cruel frenzy against the old and noble family of Stures. They were first summoned to a *riksdag*, then seized, indicted on a charge of high treason, and condemned on weak and probably false evidence. Erik did not even await the issue, but rushed madly into the prison of their leader, Nils Sture, and himself struck the first blow. The murder of the rest shortly followed. At last, the too long-forbearing nobles were roused to indignation. A civil war broke out, which, after a sharp struggle, ended, in 1569, in the dethronement of Erik and the coronation of Johan, whom, shortly before the murder of the Stures, Erik had released from confinement. Johan at first treated his brother with some degree of for-bearance, but at last, exasperated by his continual faithlessness and folly, gave way to a most cruel revenge. Erik, hurried about from one prison to another—including Gripsholm, where Johan himself had been confined—exposed to the most cruel privations, was at last secretly poisoned, in 1577. His brother seems to have feared that the nobles, disgusted with his own unprincipled government, might seek once more to place him on the throne.

H

Johan's reign was marked by calamities of every kind. There were several undecisive wars carried on with Russia and Poland, which drained both public and private resources. There was continued jealousy between Johan and his younger brother Karl, which more than once broke out in open hostilities. The cause of the greatest civil commotion was an attempt made by Johan to restore the Roman faith, an attempt which he definitely renounced shortly before his death, in 1592. Religious difficulties soon reached a climax. Sigismund, Johan's son, who had been elected to the crown of Poland in 1587, and now succeeded to the throne of Sweden, was a Roman Catholic. Duke Karl, fearing the turn things were taking, in the capacity of regent summoned a *riksdag* at Upsala, in 1593, where, after a stormy debate, the Lutheran faith, as defined at the Council of Augsberg, was first formally accepted as the national religion. The next year Sigismund was compelled to sign a charter, allowing religious liberty to his subjects, while Karl was appointed to act as regent in his brother's absence. The attempts made by Sigismund, notwithstanding, to promote in every way the cause of Roman Catholicism, brought about a long religious war, which was finally settled, in 1614, by the expulsion of Sigismund, and the appointment of Karl as hereditary king. The policy of Karl had always been to support the interests of the peasants against the nobles. This had led already to the execution of some of the leading nobles on the charge of treason at Linköping, and a most cruel massacre of the same class at Åbo. One of the first acts of his reign was to pass laws giving a distinct position to the burghers and peasants in the *riksdag.* By this act he gained for himself the title of Bönderkonung, " peasant-king." At the same time he advanced the prosperity of his kingdom by encouraging commerce and improving the industries of the country. It was by his influence that the foundations of Karlstad and Goteborg were laid. The copper and iron mines, first set on foot by the influence of the Hanse traders in the thirteenth century, were largely extended. Successful wars were carried on in Poland and Russia. The struggle with Denmark was renewed shortly before his death. But the most important acts of his reign were his foreign alliances, made with the leading Protestant countries of Europe and France, which brought Sweden into that great religious struggle known as the thirty years' war.

Gustaf Adolf succeeded to his father in 1611, at the age of seventeen. No pains had been spared to give him the best education. He had already distinguished himself as a warrior, and was in every way suited to carry out his father's policy. His first object was to strengthen the borders of the country, and secure as far as possible command of the Baltic. Having made peace with Denmark, he first turned his attention to Russia. Their refusal to accept as emperor Gustaf's brother, Karl Philip, was made a *casus belli.* This war proved so successful that in 1617 he had entirely excluded the Russians from the Baltic. A war with his cousin Sigismund of Poland met with equal success. By 1621 he had taken Riga, and made himself master of Karelia and Livonia. He now turned his attention to Germany, whose encroachments in the north must have sooner or later interfered with Swedish interests. . He had already connected himself with the cause of the German princes by a marriage with Maria Eleanora, the sister of George William, the Elector of Brandenburg. He keenly watched the struggle between the Emperor Ferdinand and the Protestants. In 1628 he forced the Emperor's general, Wallenstein, to raise the siege of Stralsund, but did not otherwise take any active part in the war till 1630. In this year, having formally gained the unanimous consent of the *riksdag*, and appointed a council of ten to rule in his absence, he left the country. The time was favourable : Wallenstein had incurred the jealousy of the Roman Catholic princes, and had been deposed. Tilly, who now commanded both armies, was a general of the old Spanish school, and, though hitherto unrivalled on the field, proved unequal to the superior tactics of Gustaf. This disparity was clearly shown when the armies of either general first met at Breitenfeld, near Leipzig, on September 17th, 1631. Both sides fought with desperate bravery, but the unwieldy masses of Tilly's army were unable to move against the flexible lines of Gustaf. The battle marks an epoch in the history of military tactics. Tilly was for the first time in his life defeated. Gustaf followed up his success, and at once began a victorious march up the Rhine. Erfurt, Würzburg, Mentz, Frankfort, and Nuremberg, one after another, fell into his hands. In April, 1632, Tilly once more dared to face his opponent in the field. His army was again defeated, and himself mortally wounded. Gustaf continued his victorious march through Bavaria. At Nuremberg he was received with enthusiasm.

But the tide of events began to turn when Wallenstein once more received the command. Not inferior to Tilly in military science, he far surpassed him in cunning and personal influence. Crowds of adventurers, from Italy, Scotland, Ireland, and other countries, flocked to his standard. Prague was retaken, the Saxons driven out of Bohemia, while Pappenheim was sent to cope with the French, who had now taken up arms, and were under the command of Richelieu. At Nuremberg the armies of Gustaf and Wallenstein came into close quarters, but both generals were too cunning to begin the attack. At last Gustaf found a favourable opportunity. Hearing while in Bavaria that Wallenstein was plundering Saxony, he turned suddenly back, and came upon his enemy before he had time to entrench himself. A desperate battle was fought at Lützen, on November 6th, 1632. The Swedes in the end won the day; but Gustaf himself was shot through the back, having lost his way in the mist, and galloped into a body of the enemy's horse.

So died Gustaf Adolf, a worthy descendant of Gustaf Vasa. The latter had, in the midst of the greatest difficulties, laid the foundation of the kingdom : the former had so extended it abroad as to make it one of the greatest powers of Europe. It is difficult of course to decide how far he was actuated by political, and how far by religious motives. His ambition seems to have been the creation of a great Protestant Papacy, in which Sweden should have a paramount influence. At home he did much to promote the interests of his country by furthering the cause of education and political reform. To him was due the system by which the four estates voted as distinct bodies in the *riksdag*. While Kristina, Gustaf's infant daughter, was in her infancy, the Marshal Oxenstjerna had the management of affairs abroad. This man had all the caution and much of the skill, but lacked the personal power and energy, of Gustaf; and the cause of Sweden in Germany became the cause of a number of petty princes, each striving to secure what he could for himself. The war continued, with wavering success till the peace of Westphalia was signed, on October 24th, 1648. Two of Gustaf's objects were at least gained. Liberty of conscience was allowed in Europe to all Protestants, whether Lutherans or Calvinists ; and Sweden had guaranteed to her the permanent possession of the mouths of the Oder and the Vistula, as well as the west of Pomerania.

In 1644, Kristina reigned in her own person. Though her great intellectual abilities and her zeal in encouraging arts and sciences have rendered her famous, not only in her own country, but in Europe generally, she was far from fitted for the task of government. By her reckless extravagance in spending public funds in objects of art, and in rewarding her own favourites, on whom she was continually lavishing new titles of nobility, she drew upon her the ill-will of her subjects, and in 1654 she abdicated in favour of her cousin, Karl Gustaf of the Palatinate, who had long in vain sought her hand.

Karl's short reign was distinguished by wars with Poland and Denmark, in which he displayed that warlike spirit for which his family were so renowned. By the peace of Röskilde, in 1658, the southern provinces of Halland, Skåne, and Bleking became at last the permanent possession of Sweden. Further hostilities however soon broke out, and owing to the great abilities of the Swedish admiral, Wrangel, the power of Denmark would have been completely crushed, had it not been for the interference of England and Holland.

In 1660 Karl died suddenly, and for fourteen years the country was under a regency, whose members only quarrelled among themselves. Meanwhile the exchequer was rapidly emptied, the army and navy diminished, and the defences of the kingdom were allowed to fall into decay. When Karl XI. came of age, in 1672, Holland and Denmark took advantage of the defenceless state of the country to declare war. This war, after the Swedes, notwithstanding the valour of Karl and his general, Otto Königsmark, had suffered several disasters, was finally concluded by the general peace of St. Germains, in 1679, which was confirmed by the marriage of Karl with the Danish princess, Ulrika Eleanora. Karl now turned his attention to home politics. Seeing that the only chance of reform lay in quashing the power of the nobles, to whose quarrels the late disasters were due, he threw himself on the people, and by their help passed two measures which, though perhaps otherwise indefensible, were rendered necessary by the circumstances of the time. The first of these, passed in 1680, was a "Statute of Reduction," by which lands squandered by Kristina and other sovereigns were restored to the crown. The second was a still more arbitrary measure. By it absolute power (*suveränetet*) was given to the king, while the *råd* was reduced once more to a consultative body. These measures proved satisfactory in their results. The exchequer was filled, the army and navy placed on a safe footing, and the land restored to order. To Karl is also mainly due the *indelta* system, by which the army is quartered on the lands, and supported by the peasant farmers.[14]

All the good which Karl XI. did was undone by his son Karl XII., who succeeded on his father's death, in 1697. This most heroic warrior has, by his military skill, his daring exploits, and his no less daring escapes, gained as great a name as any Swedish king. But his enterprising spirit proved to Sweden worse than a mere waste of strength. It expended the exchequer, deprived the country of its best soldiers, and only provoked the long continued hostility of Russia. While Karl was carrying on a war in Poland and in the very heart of Russia—which, however desperate and valiantly fought, ended in the disastrous defeat of Pultava, in 1709—Peter the Great was building on Swedish territory the future capital of Russia. While Karl afterwards remained in Turkey, egging on the Sultan to assist him in avenging his losses, the Russians and Danes were making havoc in Sweden. The last years of his life were spent in wars at home, carried on in the same desperate manner as his attacks in distant countries. Peter recognized his great abilities, and now sought to use him as a tool against his rivals in Europe. A secret treaty had already been formed with his favourite Gortz, when Karl was shot at the age of thirty-six, while engaged in storming the Norwegian town of Frederikshald in 1718. The Russians, however, continued their hostilities, and July and August of the next year were marked by the destruction of one town after another on the west coast of the Baltic.

[14] See pp. 199—202.

Karl XII.'s death marks an epoch in Swedish history. Ever since the time of Gustaf Vasa the greatness of Sweden had been bound up with the greatness of her kings, who, by their genius, courage, and, above all, personal influence, had raised Sweden to its high position. We now come to a period which marks the perpetual struggle of different powers within the state for pre-eminence, while, without, the hardly won provinces beyond the Baltic were, one by one, swallowed up by neighbouring countries.

The nobles took advantage of the disputes which followed about the succession to enforce on Ulrika, and afterwards her husband Fredrik I., a new constitution, finally completed in 1720. The king's power was now reduced almost entirely to the appointment of inferior offices, and a triple vote in the *råd* over which he presided. The sixteen members of this body were chosen by the king, but only out of triple the number first elected by a special court belonging to the three first estates.[15] All administrative functions were put into the hands of the *råd*; while legislative functions, as well as the appointment and control of taxes, were left to the *riksdag*, which was to consist, as formerly, of the four estates, viz. nobles, clergy, burghers, and peasants. Practically the power of both *råd* and *riksdag* were limited, and the influence of the lower estate much curtailed by the appointment of a sort of select committee (called *sekreta utskottet*) consisting of 100 members, chosen out of the three first estates. To this committee were left a large number of important questions.

From this time we find the beginning of party poli-

[15] I.e., nobles, clergy, and burghers.

tics. The two chief factions which appear during the greater part of the eighteenth century were known as the *Mössor* "caps" and *Hattar* "hats." The first were so named by King Fredrik, who said that they deserved the name of *nattmössor* "nightcaps" in consequence of their effeminate character They retorted by giving the name of "hats" to their political opponents. What divided these parties was not any question of political or social reform, but a difference of foreign policy. The *Mössor* at first, led by the great statesman Arvid Horn, protested against reliance on any foreign power, but were always suspected of sympathy with Russia, and at last made a formal treaty with that power and England.

The *Hattar* on the other hand were consistent in their adherence to France, and when they came into power they succeeded, through the influence of Gyllenborg and Tessin, in making an alliance with that country. The *Mössor* have the honour of giving effect, in 1734, to a new code of laws (the work of a thirty-eight years' revision of the old codes), and of passing many liberal laws in the direction of the liberty of the press and freedom of industries and trade. The later policy of the *Mössor* was prevented by their antagonists from having full play; while that of the *Hattar* brought about two disastrous wars with Russia and Prussia respectively. The first, in 1741—1743, ended in the loss of part of Finland; the second, in 1756—1762, caused financial difficulties from which the country was long in recovering itself. Both parties are alike liable to a charge of avarice, which made them not shrink from accepting the bribes freely offered them by France, England, and Russia.

The sovereigns who reigned during this period —Ulrika, Fredrik I., and Adolph Fredrik—were essentially foreigners, and exercised little or no influence on public affairs. The accession of the native king Gustaf III.in 1771 marked an important change in this respect. Attached by birth to his country, he was an enthusiastic patriot. His education, and especially his study of history, fostered these feelings. He compared the glories of Sweden under the powerful personal kings, to the miserable wreck which it had become by the divisions of rival parties and dependence on foreign powers, and, ignoring all differences of circumstance, he believed that the recovery of Swedish independence and power could only be attained by a powerful and influential monarchy. At the same time his vanity gave him pleasure in reflecting that the powerful and influential monarch was, in this case, to be himself, the worthy descendant of his great and noble ancestors. Being defeated by the *Mössor* in an attempt to reconcile the conflicting parties, he determined to carry out his plans by a great *coup d'état*. Nothing shows more clearly the feebleness of the Swedish statesmen than the easy way in which they allowed Gustaf to win over the army, imprison the *råd* in the palace at Stockholm, and compel them to sign his new constitution. Administrative functions were now restored to the king. He was to consult with the *råd*, but they were allowed no vote. The *riksdag* was to confine itself to the legislature, but might pass no laws without the royal consent. At the same time the king might not create new laws, or impose new taxes without a vote of the *riksdag*. These measures brought on Sweden, and on Gustaf especially, the wrath of Denmark and Russia. The former had reason to fear that Sweden would, if it recovered power, seek to possess itself of Norway; while Catherine saw in them a determination to check her encroachments in the east. Hostilities were averted for a time by skilful diplomacy, and by the balance of the allied powers, but broke out in 1788.

Meanwhile, Gustaf had made himself unpopular with the lower orders by laws checking the free distillation of spirits and the freedom of the press, and the nobles were glad to take advantage of any popular ill-feeling to avenge their loss of political privileges. A plot to disunite Finland, and make it a power nominally only independent of Russia, caused the first outbreak of the war. While Gustaf was away in Finland, with generals whom he dared not wholly trust, the Danes seized the opportunity to make an attack on Sweden from the Norwegian frontier. Gustaf was only too glad of an excuse for returning to Sweden. He now determined to imitate the exploits of his ancestor and namesake. He went to Dalarne, and there announced himself as the people's king : he was soon surrounded by bands of enthusiastic volunteers. Meanwhile, England and Prussia had interfered in the war with Denmark, and danger from that quarter was at an end. Gustaf had now only the nobles to fear : the three lower orders were loud in his praises. He seized the opportunity. In the three lower estates of the *riksdag*, in 1789, he carried a motion known as *Säkerhetsakten*, " The Security Act," which, while it reserved several privileges to the *ofrälse*,[16] gave the king almost an absolute power. In 1790 the war

[16] See above, p. 75.

with Russia, after losses on both sides, was brought
to an end. But the nobles were not too ready to
bear with meekness the unconstitutional violence by
which their privileges were now still further checked.
They were besides irritated by Gustaf's persistence
in taking up the cause of the French king against
the Revolutionists, and so threatening the enfeebled
country with another war. Things were at last
brought to a climax by an act of revenge, which
reminds us once more of the horrors of the Folkungar reigns. The king was shot by a pistol,
doubly loaded, at a masquerade in the king's
theatre at Stockholm, by a desperate young noble
named Ankarström, and died, after thirteen days'
agony, on the 29th of March, 1792. The fortitude
with which Gustaf bore his suffering, taking measures
to provide for the regency of his kingdom, reconciled
many among the nobles, and roused the people to
a pitch of enthusiasm. No Swedish king ever possessed such a strange mixture of almost effeminate
weakness and real courage. By his friendship with
Louis XVI. were introduced into the Swedish court
the manners and customs of Paris. In this way he
directly did more even than Bernadotte himself
to give that French character which has so stamped
itself on modern Sweden.

After Gustaf's death the fluctuation of foreign
policy depended much on the whim of those in
power, but also on the constant changes in European politics produced by the disturbed state of
France. Gustaf's brother, Duke Karl, who was now
left as regent, made an alliance with the republican
party against the Bourbons, and so increased the
ill-feeling of Russia. Gustaf Adolf, the son of
Gustaf III., who arrived at his majority in 1796,

out of personal dislike to Napoleon took the part
of his enemies, and in 1804-5 joined the triple
alliance of Austria, Russia, and England against
him.   This resulted in the loss of Pomerania.
When the alliance between England and Russia
was broken, Sweden wavered.   In the April of the
year 1807 she concluded an armistice with Napoleon ; but after the treaty of Tilsit reverted to her
former policy.[17]   By opening her ports to English
traders, she brought upon herself, in 1808, a fresh
Russian invasion, which ended in her being forced
to cede all that remained in Finland.

Sweden had thus lost all her lands beyond the
Baltic.   Plots now first began to be formed for
joining Norway with Sweden, under the Danish
prince Kristian August of Augustenburg.   A con-
spiracy, supported by the army, proved successful.
Gustaf was forced to abdicate, and his uncle, Duke
Karl (the former regent) was declared king ; while
Kristian, under the title of Karl August, was appointed heir to the throne.   On his death, the nobles,
who had all along disapproved of the anti-Napoleon
policy of Gustaf, appointed as Karl's successor Bernadotte, the most illustrious of Napoleon's generals.
This measure had not the intended result of strength-
ening an alliance with France.   The coldness already existing between Bernadotte and Napoleon
was changed to an attitude of direct hostility, when
Bernadotte saw the shameful way in which Napoleon, after having used Sweden as a tool against
England, consented to her dismemberment.   Bernadotte joined with spirit in an alliance with England
against Napoleon, whose power was just weakened
by the disastrous retreat from Moscow ; in return

[17] See Alison's " History of Europe," ch. xlvi.

for which conduct, Sweden was rewarded by England at the Congress of Vienna, in 1814, by the acquisition of Norway.

The Norwegians were not so willing to accept this new condition of things. They were ready enough to be free of their allegiance to Denmark, but sought to avail themselves of this opportunity to return to their former state of independence. Knowing beforehand the turn which things were likely to take, they had already, before the congress, drawn up a new constitution, at Eidsvold, at the south of the Mjösen Lake, and had elected a Danish prince, Kristian Frederik, as king. An invasion of Bernadotte, supported by an English fleet on their coasts, compelled them to accept Karl XIII. as their king and Bernadotte as his successor, while the latter agreed to accept their new constitution.

Thus Sweden and Norway were once more united as two kingdoms under one king. From this time the northern kingdoms have exercised no important influence on European politics. Not without reason they have continued to regard Russia as their natural foe, and England as their natural ally. In the Crimean war, in 1855, the Swedes actually allied themselves with England and France against their old enemy. The relations between Sweden and Norway have not been always too friendly, and once or twice there has been the danger of a permanent breach between the two countries. These feelings were prompted in a measure by the difference in the political constitutions of the two countries, that of Norway being much more democratic in its character than that of the sister kingdom. The efforts made by Bernadotte—who came to the two thrones in 1818, under the title of Karl XIV.—to bring the Norwegian government under the control of Sweden, were obviously connected with his policy to increase the power and influence of the aristocracy in Sweden itself. The measure of the Norwegian *storthing* to abolish hereditary nobility, in 1821, was carried in the teeth of the king's veto.[18] Mutual goodwill was again restored when Karl was succeeded by his more liberal-minded son, Oscar I., in 1844. Freedom of the press was now allowed in Sweden. The modes of electing the members of he *riksdag* and *storthing* were improved, so as to make these bodies more representative. As great progress was now made in industries and commerce as had been made in science and literature under the more aristocratic reign of Karl XIV. During the reign of Karl XV., who succeeded Oscar in 1859, radical changes were made in the Swedish constitution. By these, which became law in 1866, the distinct political status of the four old estates was done away with, and two chambers, both elective, were established.[19] Thus the constitution of Sweden has been brought more into harmony with that of Norway, and the way has been prepared by which the countries may possibly be more completely united at some future day.

[18] See p. 188.   [19] See pp. 182—184.

CHAPTER V. .

LANGUAGE, LITERATURE, AND ART.

THE early language of Scandinavia is usually called Old Norse. By its speakers it was known as " Our Northern tongue," or " the Danish tongue." From it are derived three distinct literary languages, having much in common, but yet sufficiently distinct to be justly regarded as different languages, viz. Icelandic, Swedish, and Danish. Of these the first has altered but little in form from the original Norse, still retaining the case-endings of the nouns, as well as much of the declension of the verb, but its pronunciation has greatly changed. The conservative character of the language is due, partly, to the influence of the Saga literature, which helped to preserve that language (much in the same way that English has been preserved to the eye, though changed to the ear, during the last three centuries by the authorized version of the Bible) ; partly to the isolated position of the island, which shut it off from the corrupting influences produced by intercourse with foreign countries. In Sweden and Norway, on the other hand, we find almost as great a difference between the modern and ancient languages, as between our modern English and Anglo-Saxon. In both languages the old case-endings and verbal terminations have been dropped, except where the former have been retained in isolated phrases, in which their original force is no longer felt. Both, but Danish especially, have received a large admixture of foreign words, borrowed chiefly from Low German. In common with Icelandic, they have both retained two characteristics which the old language developed during the 9th century, and which distinguish the Scandinavian languages from the rest of the Teutonic family, viz. the post-positive article and the passive termination. By the former is meant the definite pronoun placed after the noun as a suffix, which quite accidentally has precisely the same form as the indefinite article, or first numeral. Thus we get in Swedish, in the masc. *en förening*, "a club," *föreningen*, "the club;" in Danish, *en forening, foreningen;* in the neuter, in both languages, *et land*, "a land," *landet*, "the land." In the plural the form of the post-positive article is in Swedish usually *ne* or *na*, as *föreningar*, "clubs," *föreningarne*, "the clubs," *länder*, "lands," *länderna*, "the lands:" in Danish *ne*, as *foreningerne, landene.* This peculiarity is said to have originated from the position of the pronoun between the noun and the adjective which followed it, a position retained even when the adjective was dropped. The passive termination which in Danish and Swedish is now *s*, in Icelandic *st* (pronounced *ts*) and earlier *z*, arose out of *sik*, the accusative of the pronoun, which became *sk*, and was afterwards softened into *z st* or *s;* so that the form was originally reflexive or middle, as it still frequently is in Icelandic. Thus we have in Swedish, *Jag kallas, de kallas*, "I am called," "they are called;" in Danish, *Jeg kaldes, de kaldes.*

The retention of the *a* in such verbs as *kalla* and in the plural of such nouns as *föreningar*, is peculiar to Swedish: the Danes prefer the *e* sound. That of these two languages Swedish has most preserved its original character, is to be seen in its retention of the ancient forms of many words, such as *fors* "waterfall," *husfru* "housewife;" cf. Danish *fos, hustrue;* and of many words, such as *dimma* "fog," now completely lost in Danish; as well as the longer pronunciation of the vowels, which in Denmark is much chopped. In other respects the pronunciation is clearer and more accurate. Final consonants are seldom dropped, as in Danish very commonly. Thus *jeg*, in Danish, is pronounced *yé—land, lan.* This pronunciation has in some cases led to the insertion of a *d* in the orthography, where not required on philological grounds, as in *fjäld;* cf. Swedish *fjäll*, English *fell.*

The greatest contrast between Swedish and Danish lies in the pronunciation of the consonantal sounds, represented by *g, k* or *kj,* and *sk.* In Danish the *g* and *k* remain hard before all vowels. In Swedish in almost all parts of the country these sounds remain hard before the vowels *a, o, u,* and *å;* but are softened before *e, i, y, ä* and *ö; g* in such cases takes the sound of consonantal *y.* Thus the word *gästgifvaregård* is pronounced *yestyivare-gord,* which easily passes into *yeshiverigord.* The same change takes place after *l* and *r,* as in *elg, borg;* otherwise a final *g* remains hard. In English the final *g* has in almost all words passed into a *y* or *w,* as *day, bow*—cf. Swedish *dag, båge;* but otherwise the change seems governed by no general rule. Curiously enough, in all the three component parts of *gästgifvaregård,* viz., *guest,*

giver, and *yard*, the English pronunciation is dia-
metrically opposite to the Swedish.   This soften-
ing of the *g* seems to have been once common in
the vernacular before other vowels.   Thus we know
that Gustaf was popularly called " *Justa.*"   *J* is
in both languages the common symbol for the *y*
sound ; *k* or *kj* (as it is usually spelt in Danish)
when softened becomes *ch*, as in *kyrka*, "a church,"
and *köpa*, "to buy."   These are pronounced *chyrka*
and *chöpa*.   In the first word we have gone further
in English, and softened both *k*'s ; while the
Scotch, like the Danes, have retained both.   From
the word *köpa* comes *köping*, " a market-town,"
which occurs very frequently in names of places,
as Jönköping, Norrköping, &c.   It is pronounced
in   quick   speaking   almost   exactly   like   our
equivalent Chipping, as in Chipping-Norton, Chip-
ping-Camden.   Similarly the first half of what the
Swedes spell Köpenhamn,[1] is pronounced Chippen,
as in Chippenham.   Other variations of this sound,
as in our *shop, swop* (for old *chop*), do not occur.
Sk before the lighter vowels softens into *sh ;* thus
skilling becomes, as with us, *shilling*.   At the end
of words it remains hard, as in *Engelsk, Dansk ;*
whereas with us it is always softened at the end of
words, as in *English, Danish ;* and usually at the
beginning, as in *shell, shame, sharp, sheen*—corresponding to Swedish *skal, skam, skarp*, and *sken.*
The last of these words only is softened in Swedish.
On the other hand, we have *scale, scab, scathe*, corresponding to Swedish *skål, skabb*, and *skada.*

The vowels of Swedish and of Danish (as pronounced in Norway) are very similar.   *A e* and *i*
have the usual continental pronunciation ; *o*, besides

---

[1] Ovr Copenhagen.

having the short *o* sound, as in *of*, is often pronounced *oo*. Thus *dom, prof, rost*, are pronounced
as their English equivalents, *doom, proof, roost*.
Y has much the sound of a long French *i*,
while *u* is pronounced either as a long *u* or *yu*. Of
the longer vowels *å* is pronounced as *o*, either as in
long (Swedish *lång*) or as in *loan* (Swedish *lån*) ; in
some parts, *au*, from which no doubt it has arisen,
appears as its vernacular sound: *ä* and *ö* are pronounced nearly as in German. In Danish a long
vowel is frequently expressed by doubling it, thus
aa is used for *å, ee ii uu* for the long *e i* and *u*. In
the corresponding Swedish forms these are usually
simple.

One of the most striking features of Swedish is
its accent, which is more marked than in perhaps
any modern European language. Even in ordinary
conversation the language has quite a musical
ring. By some it is supposed that this is due to
the musical character of the people.

Though the written language of Norway has
since the Union been identical with that of Denmark, as spoken it varies considerably from it,
and approaches more nearly the pronunciation of
Swedish. It varies very considerably in different
parts. In the more northerly *amts* the letters *k g*, and
sk are generally softened before the light vowels ; in
the south, and especially in Kristiania, they are frequently retained hard. The pronunciation is usually
slower than in Denmark, and final letters are less
frequently dropped. In many of the more secluded
parts the old dialects partly remain, but usually in
very corrupt forms. Attempts have lately been
made to collect them, and out of these reconstruct
the old Norse.

There is an essential difference of character between the ancient literature of Scandinavia, and
that of mediæval and modern times.   The spirit of
the latter is essentially foreign, and only comparatively few writers have done more than
stamp something of their own character, on ideas
and style, both borrowed from the great literary
countries of Europe.   With the ancient writings
it was far otherwise.   We here meet with a great
body of literature essentially national, unique in its
matter and treatment, and occupying an honoured
and independent place in European literature.
The art of writing, as distinguished from the use of
runes, of which we have already spoken in Chapter
II., was introduced with Christianity ; but it was
not till the early part of the twelfth century that, as
far as our knowledge goes, we get any written
literary production.   The twelfth and thirteenth
centuries comprise the golden age of Scandinavian literature.   The literary activity of this
period found its central point in Iceland, whose
people seems to have received a special impulse
in this direction, from their early contact with the
ancient culture of Ireland.   This they were able to
develope, in comparative peace from those political
and religious commotions which disturbed the
Scandinavian peninsula.   The chief feature of this ·
early literature is the saga.   A *saga*[2] is strictly
speaking a story or history, generally that of a
favourite hero—a sort of *prose epic* in fact, describing
his genealogy, birth, *wiking* exploits, and quarrels,
&c., until his death.   The two greatest heroes of
the sagas are the two Olafs.   The telling of

---

[2] Strictly speaking a "saying," but always in the sense of a
"history" or "story," never a "legend."

these sagas was one of the great sources of entertainment at the *things* and religious festivals of the
Northmen. They were handed down for centuries
before they began to write them ; and as soon as they
began to write them, they seem at once to have lost
the power of telling them. Very few of these sagas
have been preserved to us in their original form.
They were soon put together, and out of them
more continuous histories were compiled. Thus
Snorri Sturluson composed his history of the early
kings of Norway out of the sagas of the several
kings. The sagas are one of the most valuable
sources we possess of the early history of Scandinavia. The simple, almost childlike style, entirely
free from bombast, the touches of human nature, the
pictures of domestic life, as well as the rhythmical
character of the language, give them a charm which
it is difficult to describe. In the sagas were often
incorporated small poems, the songs which the
poets sang to commemorate some special heroic
deed or tragical act ; but those we now find so
interwoven, are frequently of a later date.

Most of the early poems are very different from
the sagas. They are believed by Dr. Vigfusson [3]
to belong most of them to quite a different school,
which arose among the settlers in the Scottish
isles, who came in even closer contact than the
Icelanders with the Kelts. Of this class are the
Helgi lays, which form part of an epic trilogy ; and
several ballads, of which *Vegtamskviða* is said to be
the most beautiful ; and others which are of a
dramatic, and even comic, character. Another class,
to which belong the great Wolsung lays, are ascribed to a still earlier time, probably before the

[3] See Prolegomena to Sturlunga Saga, clxxxiii—cxciii.

wiking raids began.   The Wolsung lays form the
locus classicus for the older forms of Scandinavian
mythology.   Of the later poems contemporary with
the sagas, we have some preserved by Snorri in
what is called the *Edda,* a sort of Ars Poetica of
the time.   This work is specially valuable, as giving
a very full account of the later Scandinavian
mythology.

As the saga declined there grew up in Scandinavia a totally different class of literature.   Ecclesiastical writings of all kinds, homilies, legends,
service-books, &c. &c., now took the place of the
genuine sagas.   Parallel with these are found
ballads (*folkvisor*), chiefly of a popular character,
based partly on the heathen superstitions, partly
on the legends of saints.   These were gradually
eclipsed by the court romances and the ballads of
chivalry, which belong mainly to the thirteenth
century.   These, with collections of laws,[4] which in
Sweden are very numerous, and translations of
foreign works, form the great mass of mediæval
literature.   More interesting than these just described, are two works, one by an unknown Swedish
writer of the thirteenth century, called *Um Styrilse
Kununga ok Höfdinga,*" " Of the Government of
Kings and Princes;" and a Norwegian work of
about the same date, generally known as *Speculum
Regale (Konungs Skuggsiá),* or "The King's Mirror,"
a discourse on court manners, physical geography,
&c., in the form of a dialogue between father and
son.   In this century began to be written the
famous Rime Chronicles, by anonymous authors,
which give in riming couplets the events of Swe-

---

[4] The whole corpus of early Swedish laws has been published by
Dr. Schlyter.

dish history, from the disputes of the Folkungar kings down to the reign of the Stures. They are chiefly valuable as being the earliest sources of anything like a contemporary and uninterrupted history of Sweden.

To the fourteenth century belongs the first translation of parts of the Bible into Swedish, for the favourite saint Birgitta, by her confessor Matthias, and others.

With the art of printing and the Reformation a new literary era began. The writings of this period are chiefly of a religious kind. Of the greatest importance are the new and complete translations of the Bible under the patronage of Gustaf Vasa, by Laurentius Andreæ and Laurentius Petri, 1526 —1541. The latter, together with his brother, Olaus Petri, published a large number of hymns, psalms, postils, and other theological treatises, all tending to give permanence to the New Learning.

The sixteenth century is marked as being the first age of anything that can be called dramatic poetry. The mediæval mysteries and moralities had never found their way into Scandinavia. The early dramas were entirely of a didactic character, designed especially as a means of instruction in the schools and universities. They consisted chiefly of Bible stories, arranged in the form of dialogues, followed by an epilogue giving the moral of the play. No attempt was made to bring out into prominence the characters of the persons represented. The best examples are the *Tobie Comedia*, by Olaus Petri, and *Holofernis och Judiths Comedia*, by an unknown writer.

With the beginning of the seventeenth century the character of the drama changed. The subjects were now borrowed mostly either from the Greek classics or from Swedish history. To the former class belongs the *Comedia Tisbe* (Thisbe), of Magnus Olai Asteropherus, and the tragedy "*Troijenborgh*" (giving a dramatic account of the siege of Troy), by Nicolaus Holgeri Catonius; of the latter class are the historical dramas of Messenius, who also wrote a complete history of Sweden in fifteen volumes, partly in prose and partly in verse. Most of his works were written while in prison at Umeå, where he had been imprisoned by Gustaf on the charge of Jesuitical plots.

A great impulse was given by Queen Kristina to literature of all kinds. It was for the benefit of the young nobles of her court that Georg Stjernhjelm, the "father of Swedish poetry," composed his master-piece *Hercules,* an allegorical didactic poem in hexameters. Its chief interest lies in the description it gives of the manners and customs of the seventeenth century. He also composed small dramatic pieces called *balletter*, which were played at court festivals, among which *Den Fångne Cupido*—"The Imprisoned Cupid," and *Parnassus Triumphans* are the best known. He also wrote several lyric poems, and was the first to introduce the sonnet into Sweden. But his poems were formed for the most part after the patterns of the Greek and Roman classics. Stjernhjelm was followed by a large school of imitators, who were far inferior to their master. It was against the effeminate productions of this school that the first Swedish satirist, Samuel von Triewald, directed his famous poem *Satir mot våra Dumma Poeter*—"Satire against our Dummy Poets"—about 1720. Triewald was one of a new school of poets, whose leaders, Dahlstjerna and Frese, deserted the classical models, and turned to the modern schools of Italy, France, and Germany.

The last half of the seventeenth century was marked by an enormous advance in science of all kinds. One of the most noted men of his day was Olof Rudbeck. In botany, medicine, and more especially archæology he gained a great name. In his archæological views he was guided certainly more by patriotic feelings than by scientific research. He maintained that Sweden was at once the garden of Eden and the Atlantis of the Greeks, and that from her all civilization had sprung. His famous work *Atlantica*, in which these opinions were expressed, was for a long time very popular both at home and abroad, and did much to foster that archæological spirit for which the Swedes have long been so distinguished. Rudbeck was followed in archæology by Peringskiöld—father and son ; and in chemistry by Hjärne. Celsius became illustrious by his researches in astronomy and physics. At the same time Rydelius (died 1738) gained distinction as the first Swedish philosopher; he was an adherent of the school of Descartes, and reckoned among his many pupils Dalin and Linnæus.

The political events of the eighteenth century had an important influence on literature. By the marriage of Adolf Fredrik with Louisa Ulrika the French taste became more and more prominent ; Corneille, Racine, Lafontaine, and Voltaire were now the models which were chiefly imitated. A little before this Dalin, the earliest Swedish historian, had made the English school of Dryden, Addison, Pope, and Swift his chief models, and caused something like a revolution in the language.

The Swedish *Argus*, which he edited (1732—1734), was simply an imitation of the *Spectator*. Dalin composed several poems, but his greatest work was undoubtedly *Svea rikes Historia*, which long continued to be the classical history of the country.

In the year 1707, (i.e. one year before the birth of Dalin), was born by far the greatest intellect that Sweden has produced. Karl von Linné is called by Swedes "the king of flowers." A man of mean birth, so stupid at Latin and Greek that his parents and schoolmaster alike condemned him to a shoemaker's trade, he by degrees made himself one of the greatest men in Europe. In natural philosophy and every branch of natural history he proved a master. In botany and zoology especially he will always be remembered as having been the first to perfect in anything like a systematic and scientific manner the classification of plants and animals. His botanical system has now, it is true, been discarded; but even the natural system, which has superseded it, is formed on lines which Linnæus himself sketched out, but did not live to complete. A very large number of even the names of the natural orders now commonly employed are already found in his lectures contained in a MS. first published soon after his death.[5] Linnæus died in 1778, and was buried in Upsala cathedral. A plain stone with an inscription marks his grave, and a monument in the taste of the time was afterwards raised in one of the chapels which surround the building; but a far more beautiful monument of his work is the pretty little country farm at Hammarby (near Upsala) where he lived—its garden of wild flowers

It was published at Hamburg, under the title *Prælectiones in rdines naturales plantarum*, in 1792.

HAMMARBY FARM.

Page 124.

which he planted, growing together in a luxurious
and tangled profusion ; and the queer little audi-
torium, with its desks and forms, where he used
to lecture to those who thronged to hear him from
all parts of Europe.

Almost contemporary with Linnæus lived Svedenborg, or Swedenborg, a name probably better
known in England than even that of Linnæus himself. With us it is associated with the religious system which he originated, and which has continued
to find a home in England, though almost forgotten
in Sweden itself. It is not generally known that
Swedenborg was one of the greatest scientists
which Sweden has ever produced. He distinguished
himself in almost every branch of scientific knowledge, and to him is said to have been at first
entrusted the original plan for the great Trollhätta
Canal.[6] But his scientific knowledge and skill
were in later life rendered useless for practical
purposes by his devotion to his new religious ideas.
A man of more practical service, though perhaps
not really so highly gifted, was Polhem, who is
regarded as having been the greatest engineer
Sweden has ever produced.

Gustaf III. gave little encouragement to the
study of science and philosophy, but poets were
welcomed at his court. For dramatic representations he had an absolute passion. His tastes were
derived from his early connexion with the French
court, and the poets of this day were most of the
orthodox French type. • Of these Kellgren and
Leopold are by far the most conspicuous. The
former was a sort of court poet to Gustaf, and gave
the poetical dress to historical dramas which the

[6] See pp. 169, 170.

king himself composed.   He was also distinguished as a writer of lyric poems and satires.   Of the latter *Ljusets Fiender*—" Enemies of the Light "— is one of the best. Leopold, who lived to a blind old age, wrote also chiefly in lyrics ; but he was rather a philosopher writing in verse than a true poet.

But at this time a new school was already rising, which entirely refused to be bound by the fetters of a foreign taste.   Bellman was one of the greatest favourites, and certainly the most original, of all Swedish poets ; but his poems were almost entirely of a popular and generally humorous character, and attracted in his own day little notice among the higher classes.   It was otherwise when the graver but more ambitious Thorild, whose one object in life—according to his own account—was " to interpret all nature and reform all the world," openly attacked the French school.   A violent controversy arose between himself and Kellgren, supported each by his colleagues on either side. Thorild's views at last prevailed, and the bitter enmity between him and Kellgren ceased.   One of the latter's best poems—*Nya Skapelsen*, " The New Creation "—shows clearly the marks of Thorild's influence.

The love of freedom which was awakened by the writings of Rousseau in France, and was fostered in Germany by the poems of Schiller and Göthe, gave a new impulse to the thought and literature of Sweden.   The French school now began rapidly to decline.   During this transition period Wallin, whom Tegnér has called "the David's harp of the north," wrote his hymns and religious songs, most of which have been incorporated into the Church Psalm-book.

The early part of the nineteenth century was marked in Sweden by the rise of two new schools of literature, commonly known as the *Romantic* and the *Götic* school. The former, which derived its spirit from the writings of the German philosopher Schegel, was a reaction from the cold materialism of the eighteenth century. Its writers loved to dwell on the imaginative and ideal, rather than the outer world ; they drew the subjects of their works chiefly from the middle ages, or still earlier *wiking* days. From *The Fosforos,* a literary paper published under their patronage, they got in Sweden the name of *Fosforists.* Their leader was Atterbom (died 1855), who chiefly distinguished himself for the celebrated review of Swedish literature called *Svenska Siare och Skalder,*—" Swedish Seers and Poets," but was also their best poet. Much of their literary activity was wasted by their continued and useless attacks on the Swedish Academy, which still tried to keep alive the dying spirit of the French school. A writer who had much sympathy with the *Fosforists,* but rose above the narrowness which often characterized the school, and kept aloof from its literary disputes, was Almqvist. He was by far the most voluminous writer of his day, and has left poetical works of all kinds—fiction, philosophy, history, and even mathematics. He even composed tunes to some of his poems. His fortunes in life were as various as his works. Having been in turn a politician, a peasant farmer, the tutor of a school, parish priest, and an army chaplain, he next became a publisher. Accused of murder, he afterwards took refuge in the United States, and there became the secretary of Abraham

Lincoln. On the death of the latter he returned
to Europe, and remained till his death at Bremen
under the title of Professor Westermann.

The *Gotic* school resembled the *Fosforist* in
going back to early history for its ideas, but
differed from it in appealing for its ideal, not to the
fanciful and imaginative, but rather to the natural
and simple social life. It was in fact a reaction
from the courtly affectations which had long
become the aim of social culture. The historical
side of this school was represented by Geijer (died
1847), who is distinguished as being one of the
first historians who attempted anything like a
philosophical treatment of history. If his views on
some points have now been generally given up, it
is because so much fresh light has been thrown on
the subject by more recent researches, made in
the critical spirit to which Geijer gave the first
impulse. The greatest writer on the poetical side
of the school is Tegnér, who is universally acknowledged to be the greatest Swedish poet. His
poems are almost entirely lyrical in character.
By far the most popular is *Fritiofs Saga*, a
romantic poem, consisting of twenty-four loosely
connected pieces. The subjects are derived from
a post-classical saga. A poem almost better known
to English readers through the translation of
Longfellow is *Nattvards Barnen*—" The Children
of the Lord's Supper." A celebrated contemporary
of Tegnér was Per Henrik Ling, who attempted to
restore the manly character of the early Scandinavian races, at once by poetical writings in the
spirit of the ancient poems, and by the more
practical system of gymnastics. He is said to have
exercised a great influence on Tegnér. As a poet

he is now almost forgotten; but he will always be remembered as "the father of Swedish gymnastics."[7] Standing apart from either school, was the short-lived poet Stagnelius (died 1823). Though he lived only thirty years, he produced several lyric, epic, and dramatic poems; of these the most beautiful is *Martyrerna*—"The Martyrs." His writings are marked by a somewhat morbid, and almost Manichean, view of the transitoriness of all that is earthly, which puts him in striking contrast to the light-hearted, nature-loving poets of his time.

While Geijer was engaged in his philosophical history, another writer, Fryxell, began in 1823 to bring out a history of a more popular character, designed chiefly for schools. This work was contained in forty-six volumes, and takes the history down to the beginning of Gustaf III.'s reign).[8] Both Geijer and Fryxell have also written several poems.

Fredrik Cederborgh (died 1835) was the first to lead the way in works of fiction. His romances, which were chiefly of a comical character, give a lively description of the manners and customs of his day. He was followed by a large number of inferior imitators. The only Swedish novelist who has gained much reputation beyond the limits of the country is Fredrika Bremer (died 1865). Her early works give beautiful descriptions of country life, in which she took a keen interest, and were published under the title of *Teckningar ur hvardagslifvet*—"Descriptions out of Every-day Life." Her later works are more abstruse and

[7] See p. 198.
[8] Fryxell died in the spring of the current year, 1881.

K

didactic in character, and consequently not so generally popular. At the same time Sophia Margareta von Knorring wrote novels describing scenes from high life; and a little later Emilie Carlén published novels which give very pleasing pictures of the coast life of the Bohuslän peasant. The works of Crusenstolpe are confined chiefly to historical romance, but are more valuable for their elegant style than their historical matter.

The greatest scientist of this century in Sweden was Berzelius, one of the greatest chemists the world has ever known. To him is due the discovery of what is known as the law of combining proportions, and of the fact that animal bodies are subject to the same chemical laws as organic matter.

Ever since the Kalmar Union, Norwegian culture was closely connected with, and for a large part directly derived from, Denmark. The founding of the University at Copenhagen, in 1479, tended to centralize culture in the Danish capital. Thither were sent those who had been already taught in the schools of the larger Norwegian towns, and so were brought in contact with the foreign culture of Europe. This dependence on Danish culture became, however, gradually weaker with the growing up of a large and influential commercial class, which brought the Norwegians into more immediate connexion with other countries, especially with England and France. Thus there grew up a feeling of patriotism known by the Norwegians as *norskehed*, which began to show itself more distinctly towards the close of the century; and the democratic ideas of Rousseau and others

NORTH SEA

SKAGER RAK

Liakenäs (the Naze)

Schleswig

Jutland

Kristiania Fjord

Kattegat

Bornholm

Vener L.

Vener L.

W

BALTIC SEA

Öland

Gotland Fog.

Gulf of Riga

R

U

S

London: Sampson Low, Marston, Searle, & Rivington.

so
ua
ng

a-
ed
u-
al

e
rt
g
d

found a ready home in a country where something like social equality had existed for centuries in all the rural districts. With the new constitution of 1814, and the founding of a home university at Kristiania, this national character was further developed; and this century—in spite of some opposition on the part of such a man as Velhaven, who still clung to Danish culture—has seen the outgrowth of a true national literature in the works of Ibsen and Björnson.

It remains to mention the most important writers connected with Norway. All other poets are thrown into the shade by Holberg (died 1754), at once the greatest and one of the earliest poets of Norway. He was born in Bergen; took his degree at Copenhagen; studied in the universities of Oxford and Paris, and afterwards in Rome. He thus gained that knowledge of history which enabled him to produce valuable historical works. Most of his later life was spent at Copenhagen. But it is not to his early studies, but to the knowledge of human nature which he gained by his travels in foreign countries, that his real success must be attributed, viz., the production of comedies, which place him among the first of dramatic poets. Unlike Holberg, Tullin (died 1765), a lyric poet, best known for his celebrated May-Day Song, spent all his life in Kristiania, his native town. Like Dalin, he made the English and French writers his models, and was the first to introduce the ornate polished taste of those schools into Danish literature. Of what may be called the pure Norwegian school, the best-known writers are Brun, Storm, Zetlitz, and Klaus Frimann. These, under the leadership of Vessel, were some of the most pro-

minent members of " The Norsk Society," who
made it their chief object to cast ridicule on the
Danish Ewald, the imitator of the sentimentalities
of the German Klopstock.

The Norwegian patriotic school reached its
height in the poems of the favourite Vergeland,
whose view of life as a battle, in which man can
only hope to regain Paradise by social freedom
and brotherly love, is brought out in such poems
as *Shabelsen, Mennesket og Messias*—" The Creation, Mankind, and Messiah." Vergeland found a
violent and bitter enemy in Velhaven, whose satire
Norges Dæmring—"Norway's Twilight," produced
a literary war, which lasted till Vergeland's death in
1845. To Velhaven, with his Danish and aristocratic
sympathies, which ran counter to the prevailing
spirit, is due the praise of having saved his country
from being so engrossed in its own ideas of social
liberty as to shut itself out from the culture which
other lands had to offer.[9] His style was calm,
dignified, and chaste, but, notwithstanding, wanting
in originality and imagination. It is rather as a
critic and a satirist than as a true poet, that he has
left a name behind him.

Meanwhile Asbjörnsen, the great Norwegian
naturalist, and Jorgen Moe, were rousing in Norway
a less narrow and bigoted national spirit, by
publishing to the world the ancient folk-lore, in
which Scandinavia is so rich. The spirit thus
awakened has produced two of the greatest writers
of which the North can boast. The popular romances of Björnstjerne Björnson, and his saga
dramas and beautiful little lyric poems, will be read

[9] For the contrast between these two poets, see Gosse's " Studies
in North. Lit.," pp. 9—16.

with pleasure long after his violent Republican speeches and political personalities have been forgotten. No less a genius, though utterly different in character, is the unpatriotic Ibsen,[1] whose historical plays, and satires on social life, have already gained him a popularity, even among foreign nations, such as no Scandinavian has enjoyed since the days of Holberg.[2]

The architecture of Scandinavia, like its literature, was mainly borrowed from other countries. Building, as an art, was introduced with Christianity. It was brought to the country by the early missionaries. Many of these, especially in the eleventh century, came from England; but as the first churches were built of wood, traces of English influence in Sweden, except perhaps in Bohuslän, are now lost. It is chiefly from the north of France, a great centre of mediæval architecture, that traces of a more permanent influence are manifest. From the twelfth to the fifteenth century, not only the art, but in many cases the actual architects, came from that country. On the other hand, in the southern provinces, which, in the middle ages, were a part of Denmark, the prevalent types of architecture show that the art was introduced from Germany, especially from the tracts bordering on the Rhine. This is particularly true of the cathedral at Lund, which was begun probably in the twelfth century. In parts of the east coast, and particularly, in the island of Gotland, the Swedes have to thank, in the first instance, the wealthy Hanse towns;

---

[1] For a full account of this poet, see Gosse's "Studies," pp. 35—97.
[2] One of his most popular plays, *Samfundets Stötter* has lately been adapted, and put on an English stage.

but in this interesting island the art received a development which is acknowledged to be unique.

The history of architectural development in Sweden runs in parallel lines to that in England and on the Continent, but in detail there are considerable differences. The most striking difference is the absence of a style corresponding in character to Early English. The Romanesque style continued with little alteration as late as the year 1220, when a few of the features which with us are characteristic of Early English (such as the pointed arch, trefoil-headed arcades, more graceful foliage) began by degrees to be introduced. This mixed style continued till about the year 1300, by which time the Romanesque features had died out, and a completely new style, corresponding to our Decorated, was rather suddenly introduced. Thus, roughly speaking, the time of our Early English was covered by a style which must be regarded as a transition between Romanesque and Decorated (or *Gothic*, as Swedish archæologists prefer to style it). Again, the later development of Gothic, which began at the end of the fourteenth century and continued to a certain extent through the fifteenth, hardly deserves (like the Perpendicular in England, or the Flamboyant in France) to be considered a separate style. It is rather a debased form of Decorated.

The architectural interest of the country is absorbed almost entirely by the Romanesque and Transition styles. Of the first there are numerous examples, chiefly of country churches, very well preserved. These are of several forms. One of the most usual is a nave, with a rectangular

chancel, and apse, and a western tower. A good
example of this type is the church at Våmb,
near Skofde in Vestergotland.
Round churches, imitated by
the crusaders from the Church
of the Holy Sepulchre, are
of rare occurrence. Such are
those of Voxtorp and Hagby
near Kalmar, and Solna in
Stockholm. A still more remarkable form is that of St.
Lars,[3] at Visby, in Gotland,
which is built in the shape of
a Greek cross, with four massive pillars supporting the
central roof. But, perhaps,
the most striking example of
this date is the crypt of the
cathedral at Lund. It lies
under the whole of the choir
and transepts, and is as much
as 120 feet by 84. It is supported by eighteen pillars.
Each pillar is differently decorated. Embracing one is
the figure of a giant—no less
a personage than the celebrated Jätte Finn, who was
then and there turned into
stone by St. Laurence, while
attempting to destroy the
church which the Saint had

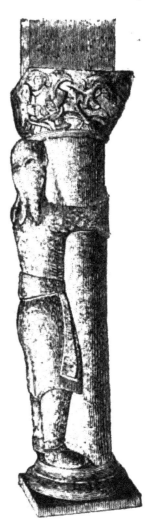

A PILLAR IN THE
CRYPT OF LUND
CATHEDRAL.

[3] This, like all the Visby churches excepting the cathedral—
St. Mary's, is now a ruin.

employed him to build. Sitting about another
pillar, in the most uncomfortable attitude, are
the figures of his wife and child. At the east
end is the original stone altar dedicated to St.
John the Baptist, and in a corner the beautifully
decorated holy well, whose waters, they say, never

CAPITAL OF A PILLAR IN LUND CATHEDRAL.

dry up. At Dalby, only a few miles from
Lund, is the only other crypt in Sweden or Norway.

As a rule, the examples of the pure Romanesque
style are very free of ornamentation. The pillars
are usually quite plain, with cushion capitals ; the
windows small, with one light, sometimes, but
generally only in the tower, with two.

To the Transition style many of the finest

churches in Sweden belong. Lund, which had been nearly destroyed by fire, was rebuilt with greater magnificence. To this period belongs the nave, with its massive pillars and richly carved doorways. The greater part of Linköping Cathedral was built about the same time, as also part of that of Upsala. It is quite impossible to give an adequate idea of the rich variety which marks the carving of this period. The quaint animals, for example, which adorn the capitals of the pillars at Lund, surpass everything in grotesqueness, and point to a powerful imagination, as well as great manual skill, on the part of the carvers. But it was in Gotland that the architecture of this period received the most unique development. There is hardly a church in the whole island—and there are over ninety of them—which has not something beautiful or interesting about it. These churches usually consist of a nave, a short chancel with an apse, a western tower nearly the breadth of the nave, abruptly narrowed off above into an awkwardly-shaped octagonal spire. The walls, which are usually very thick, without buttresses, rest on a narrow plinth. They are sometimes, as at Stånga, decorated with groups of figures nearly life-size, carved in stone. The most beautiful feature on the outside of these churches are the southern doorways, or " portals," as they call them, consisting of shallow porches, with elaborately-carved figures on the tympanum and capitals of the pilasters. The most frequent arrangement of the inside of the churches is peculiar, or nearly so, to the island. In the centre of the nave (which, if we exclude the tower, is nearly square) is a beautiful pillar, connected by pointed arches with brackets in the same style, resting on the tops of the chancel and western arches, and on the north and south walls.[4]   The fonts are quaintly adorned with grotesque creatures, looking like enormous frogs, occasionally figured in the act of devouring men.   They have happily been more frequently allowed to remain than in the churches of the mainland.   Over the churchyard gates are often lofty, sometimes two-storied, porches.   These were intended to protect the churchyards, when made places of refuge in war.   Some churches, as at Gothem and Lärbro, were once defended by castles near the churchyard; but the latter have now been mostly destroyed as useless.   On Öland some churches, as at Alböke, had, for a similar purpose it is believed, a second western tower. From the appearance thus given, they are commonly known as "saddle churches."   These are probably of an earlier date.   One church at Visby called Helge Ands, or the church of the "Holy Spirit," deserves special mention, from its unique construction.   The nave is octagonal in form, and consists of two distinct stories divided by a vaulted roof.   Both the lower and upper roof rest on four pillars.   Those of the lower story are octagonal with round arches; those of the upper, round with pointed arches.   In the centre of the lower roof is an octagonal hole, intended probably to admit light and sound from one story to the other. The two stories have a chancel in common, which ends in an apse enclosed in a rectangular wall. The church originally belonged to a hospital guild; and it is supposed by Hildebrand, that the rich

---

[4] It is most probable that these pillars as well as the "portals" are of later date, probably fourteenth century.

INTERIOR OF HAMRA CHURCH, GOTLAND.

Page 138.

members of the guild occupied one story, the
poorer inmates of the institution the other ;[5] a distinction which would seem to show that the pew
and gallery spirit of the eighteenth century was not
altogether unknown in the thirteenth.

Some of the Swedish churches, especially those
of Skåne, have arcades, with round or trefoil
arches, running under the roof, between the shallow
buttresses. The gables of the nave, choir, and
saddle-backed tower are often decorated with
corbie-steps.[6] The western wall is frequently
marked by depressions, forming shallow niches,
blind windows, crosses, and other decorations, now
for the most part whitewashed, and contrasting
curiously with the brick walls. Occasionally, as
at Torsång near Falun, the niches still retain
remnants of quaint figures.

The most remarkable specimen of Decorated
architecture is the cathedral of Upsala, completed in the fifteenth century. It was built by
French architects. The outside walls are entirely
of brick. Though certainly once a fine building,
before the outside was mutilated by fire, it cannot
be compared for a moment with the best cathedrals
of England, France, or Germany. The beautiful
church of St. Katarina in Visby, belongs also to
this period.

The fifteenth century was in Sweden a great
era of church restoration. The old flat timber
roofs of the early periods were now replaced by
brick vaults, chiefly remarkable for their plainness.
The latter are now to be seen in very many village
churches. The best examples of this date next

[5] Den kyrkligá konsten under Sver. Medelt., pp. 43, 44.
[6] The Swedes call them *trappgaflar*, or " step-gables."

to Upsala Cathedral are the nunnery church at Vadstena, and St. Peter's at Malmö.

One of the most picturesque features in the Church of Sweden, especially frequent in country districts, are the so-called *klockstaplar*, or " bell turrets." These are built separate from the church, either in the churchyard or outside, sometimes at several hundred yards' distance ; as for example, that of Danmark, near Upsala. They are built in many different forms, but always of wood. The most ancient form, as at the church of St. Lars in Söderköping, is a cross-gabled wooden box, open underneath, and surmounted by a spire : it is supported by slanting beams reaching to the ground. Others are entirely enclosed, and resemble to some extent an old-fashioned windmill. The earliest *klockstaplar* must be of the fourteenth or fifteenth century ;[7] but many are as late as the seventeenth, or even later.

The architecture of Norway was borrowed mainly from England and France ; but the churches having been built almost entirely of wood, comparatively few have survived. The only remaining stone churches of much importance are the cathedrals of Trondhjem and Stavanger. The former, even as it now stands, injured by constant conflagrations, partly fallen in ruins, patched up from time to time, is still perhaps the finest cathedral in the north. The main parts of the building fall under four groups : the little chapel at the northeast, built in plain Romanesque, about 1093 ;[8]

---

[7] One of them is found attached to the ruined monastery of Nydala, in Småland, and so must be earlier than the Reformation.

[8] This building is by tradition identified with St. Clement's, a chapel built by Olaf Tryggvason, but the style is clearly later. It may very likely be the original Christ Church, see below, p. 238.

the transept and lower stages of the tower in French Norman style, built in the latter half of the twelfth century : the greater part of the nave, built about 1240-50 ; and lastly, the western front, added about the close of the same century. This last must once have been exceedingly beautiful, but unfortunately only the lower part of the original front has been preserved.[9] A complete restoration has been set on foot, supported by Government and private subscriptions, and the work is rapidly progressing. The cathedral of Stavanger is a much plainer structure, with a massive Norman nave, probably late twelfth century, and a fourteenth century chancel, with richly decorated windows, probably of French architecture. The enormous seventeenth-century pulpit, with its quaint carved and painted scenes from the Old Testament, is not the least striking feature in the church.

But by far the most interesting of Norwegian buildings are the ancient wooden churches (*Stave-kirker*). Many churches, such as that of Urnäs, on the Sogne Fjord, have retained the old Roman-esque wooden arches, carved door-posts, or some other ancient remains ; but only two have at all completely preserved their ancient exterior. These are Hiterdal in Telemark, and Borgund in Lärdal. Hiterdal, the most ancient, probably of the twelfth century, looks from the outside like a group of buildings piled on the top of each other so as to form a gradual ascent of four stages, rising from the east, north, and south sides, and culminating in the west. Each stage, except the lowest, has a small spired turret, and the two lowest have at

---

[9] For a further notice of the history of the cathedral, see p. 238.

the east end an apse. The roofs are relieved throughout by projecting gables. Round the lowest stage there is an open arcade with round arches, originally used for depositing arms, &c.,

BORGUND CHURCH.

before entering the church. The roofs are mainly covered with scale-like wooden shingles. This church has been excellently restored, in 1850, by Nebelong, a Norwegian architect. Hardly less curious, and still more picturesque, is the Church of Borgund, chiefly distinguished from that of Hiterdal by the absence of the central turret and the substitution of neat little dormer windows in the roof for the somewhat clumsy gables. The curious projections, at the corners of the gables of the tower and higher roof of the nave are intended to represent serpent heads, a favourite Norwegian ornament, especially on the ancient ships. The cusped arch of the southern doorway makes it probable that this church was not built before at least the end of the thirteenth century. It is extremely interesting to notice, in this and the other timber churches, with what ingenuity the prevalent styles of stone architecture were adapted to a different material.

The churches in Scandinavia—in Sweden especially—have suffered less from Puritanical zeal than from the restorations of the seventeenth and eighteenth centuries. Externally, broad church-warden windows with round heads have taken the place of the original Romanesque or Gothic. Frequently copper-roofed towers or spires have been added. Internally, the whole, including the ancient frescoes, has been whitewashed. Huge pulpits and altar-pieces of white and gold, with chubby cherubs holding up folds of tasselled drapery in one hand and golden trumpets in the other, hovering among clouds of solid wood ; hour-glasses, now—perhaps unfortunately—no longer used ; massive brass candlesticks, often very fine—are the most striking features of a modern Swedish church. Ancient crucifixes, altar triptychs, &c., still remain in many churches ; but are frequently stowed away in some lumber hole, or sent off for a consideration to the national museum at Stockholm.

In domestic architecture Scandinavia has little to boast. A few old timber houses, with over-hanging stories and carved beams, have survived in Norway, especially in Telemark. In Sweden the best known, and almost only ancient wooden house, is Ornäs farm, near Falun, said to have been built at the close of the fourteenth century. Its historical interest as the scene of one of Gustaf Vasa's narrowest escapes, has fortunately preserved it.[1] The most striking features are the two galleries and winding staircase, in front. Even the modern wooden villas in Sweden, such as those on the islands and shores of the Mälar Lake, are very light and pretty.

Painting in Scandinavia was, during the middle ages, confined to the decoration of churches. Not many of these ancient frescoes have now survived. The most beautiful specimens are those of Risinge church (in Östergötland), and Råda (in Vermland). The latter is one of the very few ancient churches still remaining in Sweden. Outside it is singularly plain, being without tower or turret of any kind. Inside, the whole chancel, walls and roof (which is so cusped as to form a trefoil arch), is completely covered with paintings, containing, in elaborate canopies and divided by beautiful lines of orna-mental work, rows of prophets, evangelists, and saints, and under them a row of flowing drapery To the fourteenth and fifteenth centuries chiefly belong the elaborate triptychs already alluded to. To a large extent they came either directly from the Hanse towns, or were executed by workmen who came from them. A very fair example re-mains at Vadstena. As works of art, however, they

[1] See p. 92, illustration.

INTERIOR OF RÅDA CHURCH, IN SWEDEN.

cannot, especially the later specimens, be compared to the paintings at Råda.

Even in the eighteenth century Sweden still depended much on foreign artists. Ehrenstrahl, a well-known painter at the beginning of that century, came from Hamburg. The taste of the age of Gustaf III. may be judged from the ceiling of the chapel in Stockholm *slott*, by Taravel, on which are represented a number of little cherubs trying to cling to an invisibly-suspended cross. The only really great artist which Scandinavia has produced is the Norwegian Tidemand, who died in 1876. His pictures comprise the most beautiful illustrations of peasant life. One of the most charming is that called *Fanatikerne*—" The Fanatics "—describing a ranter preaching in a cottage. The variety of expression which he has managed to produce on the hearers' faces is very remarkable. There is in the Göteborg museum a group of four beautiful pictures by him, describing peasant courtship, the dressing of the bride, the wedding ceremony in church, and, finally, the first christening feast.

Scandinavia has not in sculpture produced any artist to be compared with Thorvaldsen, of Denmark ; but the names of Sergel and Fogelberg are remembered with gratitude by the Swedes, as being the men who have done most to decorate their towns with the statues of their historical celebrities.

It is rather a strange thing that a country, which has produced such celebrated performers as the violinist Ole Bull, and such exquisite vocalists as Jenny Lind and Christine Nilsson, and whose people are so enthusiastically musical, has turned out no musical composers of any great celebrity.

CHAPTER VI.

OCCUPATION, INDUSTRIES, ETC.

ONE whose acquaintance with Scandinavia is confined to its appearance on the map, will be sur-
prised to find that so large a country contains
a population not much exceeding six millions.
Relatively to the size of the two countries, the
population of Scandinavia to Great Britain bears
the proportion of about eight per cent. Of this population less than a third belongs to Norway.[1] The
paucity of population is mainly due to the physical
character of the country. By far the larger part of
its surface consists of barren rock. It is only where
alluvial deposits have been left that cultivation is
possible. This is chiefly the case by the banks of
the larger lakes, in parts of the valleys, and
especially near the mouths of the rivers. In some
parts, especially on the Sogne Fjord, considerable
tracts of fertile land have been formed along the
sides of the fjord by the abrasion of the rocks
above. In Sweden the alluvial soil is more extensive. But even here great difficulties have to be
met in cutting down forests and clearing the land,
before it is fit for cultivation. This work is now

---

[1] The total population was, in 1879, 6,385,801. Of these,
4,578,901 belonged to Sweden, 1,806,900 to Norway.

being carried out with some vigour, great facilities being afforded by Government ; and the population is, in spite of emigration, on the whole steadily increasing. The proportion of country under cultivation in Sweden is now about ten per cent. of the whole ; in Norway it is scarcely three per cent.

In Sweden rather more than half of the farm lands are devoted to agriculture. Farming operations have very much improved of late years by the introduction of better machinery, improved systems of manuring, and superior breeds of cattle. The same object has been much facilitated by the formation of agricultural societies in each *län*, and the institution of farming schools (*landtbruks skolor*), the latter being under the direct control of Government. One great drawback is the cost of coal, which makes the introduction of steam too expensive to be remunerative. Horse-power has therefore still to be used in grinding, ploughing, &c.; while it is only in some favoured districts that this can be supplemented by the use of water-mills. Windmills are also employed in some parts. Compared with Norway, the farm buildings are substantial, being built chiefly of plaster-covered timber on massive stone foundations, reaching frequently up to the first story. For the roofs, thatch is most frequently used. This is commonly kept in its place by frames of pine made of series of parallel beams like rafters, only crossing each other diagonally at the top, giving it something of the appearance of a *cheval-de-frise*. In the southern provinces the buildings are occasionally in the half-timbered style so common in the southern and western counties of England.

The prevailing crops of the country are rye, barley, and oats. Wheat is also grown, but chiefly in the south. Less important crops are potatoes, hops, flax, and hemp. Owing to the dampness of the climate, and, in some places, the swampiness of the soil, various methods of drying the crops are adopted, especially in the more northerly districts. Hay is very frequently hung up on long rails, to dry in the wind and sun. Here it has sometimes in rainy weather to hang for weeks before it is fit to carry. The hay-carts—used also for other farm purposes—are very oddly shaped. They are very long and narrow, and taper sometimes to a single plank at the bottom. In the south hay is often tossed by machinery, and made into cocks—English fashion. A similar method to that described is frequently employed also for drying the corn, but another is often substituted. Birch poles, about the size of our English hop-poles, are fixed at intervals in the field ; round these the sheaves of corn are hung so as to form small cylindrical stacks, giving the field a picturesque bristling appearance. Oats are also frequently made up into pretty conical cocks, tied together at the top so as to throw off the rain, and looking not unlike old-fashioned pointed beehives. A still more peculiar method is employed for drying peas. A large number of poles are fixed in the ground, in a circle about ten feet in diameter ; their tops are tied together in a point, so that the whole forms a sort of hut, outside which the peas are fastened. The hollow inside insures due ventilation, and enables the peas to dry without danger of heating. Flax is, where possible, laid out to dry on the bare rocks which protrude here and there through the soil, or is made up into minute little cocks, or laid against low rails. Hops are usually cultivated close by the farmhouses, in little patches so small as to require not more than twenty or thirty poles, put very close together. The crops are exceedingly poor, and only sufficient for home brewing. For ploughing, and almost all farm purposes, oxen are very largely employed in all parts of the country. The ploughs are oddly shaped—invariably with one handle—and have much the look of the pictures we sometimes see of Virgil's plough as described in the " Georgics." The process of ploughing has a very awkward and comical appearance. The ploughman, in order to get a firm grasp of the handle, has to walk half sideways with an uncomfortable waddling gait. The women take a very large part in field labour of all kinds. Fields are occasionally divided by walls made of loose unmortared stone ; but by far the commonest contrivance is a wooden fence, made usually of long thin pine boards run up diagonally from the ground, and supported at intervals by upright birch poles. This system of fencing is common throughout Norway and Sweden as well as Gotland (where such a fence is still called a *tun*), and must be extremely ancient. It forms quite a characteristic feature of Scandinavian landscape. In other respects farming in Sweden is much like that in most parts of England.

The methods of farming employed in Norway are in the main similar to those used in Sweden. Hay and corn are almost always dried in the ways above described. The main differences are necessitated by the different character of the country. By far the larger part of the cultivated land is

devoted to the hay crop. The paucity of land
available for this purpose makes the farmer use his
utmost endeavours to utilize every inch of it.
Every little patch of ground between the rocks
and bushes is mown with the greatest care. Even
though the crop, as sometimes happens on the
banks of wet or shady places, consists only of a
medley of ferns and flowers, these are ruthlessly
cut, and stowed away for the winter consumption.
The instrument usually employed is a minute
scythe, used with one hand. Only in the broader
fields of some of the larger valleys is an ordinary
large scythe of any use. Ponies and sledges are
generally employed in loading. The advantage of
sledges is that they can be used without danger of
upsetting on uneven and hilly ground. The building in which the hay is stowed is called a *storhus*
"large house." [2] It is built of two stories, the lower
being used as a stable, while the upper forms the
hayloft. This is approached by a gangway of
stones and planks, arranged on an inclined plane,
so that the pony can carry the load at once into
the loft without the necessity of any appliances
for lifting. In some cases the hay is grown on the
top of the fjeld. In such cases the stowing presents the greatest difficulties. To carry the hay
down the zigzag paths would be the work of endless labour, if feasible at all. Various means are
adopted to meet this difficulty. Sometimes the
hay is let down on sledges swung over the precipice to the valley or fjord below, whence it is con-
veyed in carts or boats to its destination. Another
method is still more singular. A tight rope is

[2] So called because it is the largest building on the farm : the
word, oddly enough, has no connexion with our "store house."

fixed from the hayfield above to the valley below, so inclined as to form with the ground an angle of about forty-five degrees. Along this rope large bundles of hay are let down by means of a sliding pulley attached to the rope by which they are bound. It is impossible to describe the extraordinary effect both of sight and sound produced by this contrivance, when seen or heard at a distance. The bundle looks like some great bird of prey, shrieking as it rushes down at a tremendous pace through the air, till at last it comes down with a thud upon the ground below. The hay season begins about the middle of July, and continues in some parts of the country till the end of August. The same field is cut sometimes twice, or even three times. Even the early crops are usually very poor and thin.

In the valley of Gudbrandsdal, parts of which are very dry, an ingenious system of irrigation has been devised. Water is carried from the streams, which intersect the valley, often for many miles in long wooden troughs, formed out of the trunks of young pines cut lengthwise and hollowed out in the middle. Similar troughs carry the water down on to the farms where it is wanted, and furnish also the supply required for various domestic uses. Of cereals, by far the most important is barley, from which the *fladbröd*, " flat bread," the staple food of the country is chiefly made.[3] Both threshing and grinding are done by water-power, a water-mill being an almost invariable accompaniment of a Norwegian farm.

The farm buildings are usually placed so as to form the four, or more frequently only three, dis-

[3] Vide p. 218.

connected sides of a quadrangle. This arrangement is also frequent in Sweden. Besides the
storhus already mentioned, the buildings mainly
consist of three, that in which the farmer and his
family reside, in which also the large guest-chamber
is usually to be found; that reserved for the kitchen
and domestic servants ; the third containing the
dairy and store-room—a very necessary part, where
the farms are far separated from water and railway
communication. These form the nucleus round
which a large number of sheds and outbuildings
of various kinds are clustered, giving quite the
appearance of a small village. Great skill is shown
in the construction of these houses. A flat foundation is first secured by building out a pile of large
loose stones from the side of the slope. When
stones are not at hand, the same result is obtained
by resting a. framework of wood on wooden pillars,
cut to the size required by the exigencies of the
ground. In this latter case the space underneath
the house is left open. The walls are built of
square trunks, crossing each other, and neatly
fitted together at the corners. The crevices between the trunks are filled up with moss, and the
walls lined inside with smooth upright boards.
In the better houses, overlapping horizontal boards
are fixed on the outside of the building. The roof
is made of timber covered with tiles, or rough
coarse slates, arranged diagonally. When neither
of these can be got, earth is employed, the wood
being first covered with a coating of birch bark
to keep out the wet. The earth is soon covered,
and kept in its place, by a medley of moss, ferns,
and flowers. These, with the rich brown colour
the walls get with age, and the rough corners of

the buildings, give a very picturesque appearance. In all the more civilized places the houses are painted white, and have red tile roofs, which quite destroy the artistic effect. Not uncommonly the walls are stained a pretty dull red. In other parts, as often in Sweden, green is a more favourite colour.

Besides the fertile patches in the valleys, a large part of the fjeld bears coarse kinds of grass, on which the animals are sent to graze in the summer. This gives rise to a second class of farms scattered among the mountains, much larger in extent, but each held by the same proprietor as some farm in the valley below. Such farms are called *säters*. On the spurs of the high mountain land which stretch out into the fjords, these mountain farms occupy a more or less isolated position, lying between the region of scrub below and the barren rocks above, being shut off on either side by precipices, only approached by steep zigzag paths. On this account they are usually kept by dependants of the farm below. The stock kept is often very large, consisting mainly of cows, of which there are sometimes as many as 400; and the main business of the farm is the production of butter and cheese. Besides these a considerable number of sheep and goats are usually kept. These climb up among the rocks, and feed upon the grass which the cows cannot reach. The goats feed to a large extent on the young branches of the dwarf birch. Each *säter* consists of a group of hovels, varying usually, from two or three to a dozen in number, but sometimes reaching as many as thirty or forty. Each hovel is about twelve feet by six, and six to eight feet high. They are built of loose stone walls and turf roofs. The

entrance is always at one of the gable ends. The
building sometimes is divided by a cross partition
into two rooms, the antechamber being used as
a bedroom, the inner as a dairy.   Not unfrequently, especially when built on sloping ground,
it has two stories, the lower being used as a
stable.   Sometimes, when the *säter* is large, one
building is reserved for the common purpose of
bedroom and kitchen.   In such cases, the fire-
place is distinguished from the rest of the floor
by a boundary of stones, while a hole in the roof
above serves as a chimney.   When the *säter* is
near the home farm, or the proprietor is poor
and cannot afford to keep a resident upon it, the
business has to be done by the farm servant below,
who is responsible for the arduous task of ascend-
ing and descending daily with the milk.   For
calling the cattle for milking a rude horn is sometimes used, and the herdsman is not unfrequently
the musician of the district.   The farmer cannot
afford to lose even the scrub.   The branches of
the dwarf birch are in many places cut and dried
like hay, and made into tall conical stacks, being
largely used to feed the sheep and goats in the
winter.   The twigs of the white birch are occasionally cut in the same way in the poorer parts
of Sweden for the use of sheep.

Next to farming, the most important industry
in the country is foresting.   The enormous extent
of forest in Sweden has already been noticed.   Only
a small part of this is sufficiently accessible to be
of any practical value.   The whole available area
of forest is now estimated at about 63,000 square
miles.   By far the larger part of this lies in the
north and middle of the country.   By the banks

of the great rivers in the north, and in all parts of
Dalarne and Gestrikland, the timber trade is driven
with great briskness. Formerly the forests were
cut down in the most reckless manner, no care
being taken to plant young trees to replace the
old. Since 1869, the management of the forests
has been placed under the control of government.
A special committee was afterwards formed to
direct the carrying out of improvements, and these
were still further advanced by building foresting
schools (*skogsskolor*) throughout the country. The
industry is now carried on with greater care and
economy. The timber, which consists mainly of
red and white deal, is used principally for building
and other farm purposes, for fuel in steamboats
and railway engines, for charcoal in the preparation
of steel. It is also largely used in the building of
boats, making of oars, &c., &c. Birch is used
almost entirely for firewood. The trees are usually
felled in the autumn and spring. When cut they
are allowed to soak for some time in the water of
the lakes and larger rivers, and then sawn in the
mills which abound in the great forest districts,
and are carried by rail or water to their destination. In the latter case an ingenious contrivance
is sometimes used. A large number of trunks are
joined together by iron loops so as to form a continuous chain. Two such chains are joined to the
angles at the base of a triangle of wood—usually
a large snow-plough—which answers the double
purpose of cutting the water with its point like
the bow of a ship, and keeping the chains apart. At
the further end is a cross piece of timber. In
this loose frame the trunks are put, and towed down
by small steamers by a rope attached to the apex

of the triangle. It is a very curious sight to see
these little steamboats, puffing and toiling with
their train, which is sometimes as much as a
quarter of a mile long, behind them. It is obvious
that such an arrangement is only possible on lakes
or on smooth and fairly straight canals. In tortuous or rapid rivers, the trunks must constantly
catch in the rocks or banks of the stream.

In Norway foresting plays a comparatively un-
important part in the industries of the country.
It is only by the banks of the larger rivers, and in
the less mountainous regions about Kristiania that
it is carried on to a very large extent. The usual
plan adopted for the carriage of the timber is to
float it down the rivers in the early spring, when
they are very full and the current strong. In many
parts of the country the timber is used only for
home purposes. Each farmer has usually certain
rights, protected by Government, of cutting down
trees in the neighbouring forests, and this work is
generally given to the charge of a special work-
man. In cutting the timber, water-mills with small
circular saws are usually employed. Sometimes
these mills occur together in picturesque groups,
the water being divided by wooden troughs, from
which are thrown up white jets of foam.

One great danger to which both countries are
liable is the breaking out of fire. It is not an uncommon thing to see large tracts of country
covered with a wilderness of bare rocks and
blackened stumps, showing where the forest once
was. Not far from Kristiania several miles of
forest were thus completely devastated a few years
ago, the fire being caused in this case by the
spark from a railway engine.

One of the most productive industries, especially in Sweden, is that of mining. The most important minerals by far are iron and copper. The kinds of iron ore most abundant are those usually known as metallic oxides, which lie in the primitive rocks. They are always black, and never red. It is quite possible therefore for a visitor to go down a Swedish mine without the least danger of staining his clothes. Ore is found in a great many parts of Sweden, but the most important mines are those in Vermland in the west, in Vestmanland at the west of the Mälar lake, and at Dannemora in Upland, north of Stockholm. The iron-mines of Norway lie quite in the south, principally in Telemark and about the small seaport of Arendal. The most celebrated mine in Sweden, though not so extensive as some of those in Vermland and Vestmanland, is that of Dannemora. The ore of this mine is some of the purest in the world. The mine itself is very striking, a large open quarry some 500 feet deep, its bottom more or less covered with the snow and ice, which has fallen and frozen during the winter, and remains gradually melting till the next winter. This gulf is descended by a series of ladders suspended to the sides. From the bottom a lower shaft descends for about 100 feet, among dripping rocks, from which a number of passages branch in various directions. The ore is dislodged by blasting, and lifted to the surface in iron buckets, worked by windlasses. The machinery is moved partly by steam, but chiefly by water-power, aqueducts being carried from the lake Grufsjön close by. Some of the richest hills in iron ore are Taberg,[4] near the south corner of the Vetter, and Gellivara, in Lap-

[4] See above, p. 28.

land, but, chiefly owing to their inconvenient situations, neither are at present worked.

Iron works are numerous in all parts of the mining districts, especially along the railways, lakes, and rivers. Some of the largest of these are the great Domnarfvet works, some few miles south of Falun. Charcoal burnt on the spot is invariably used for fuel in the blasting furnaces. The method employed for converting the crude iron into malleable iron and steel is that known as the Bessemer process. The men employed are the Dalkarlar of the district, who are strong, able-bodied, and very hard-working men, unlike the ordinary Swedish workmen. It is a curious sight to see them bustling about with nothing on but their wooden shoes, long white shirts, and face-defenders.

The chief copper-mines in Sweden are those in Falun, in Dalarne, and Åtvidaberg, in Östergötland; but another is also worked in Åreskutan, a mountain to the west of Östersund, near Rörås, in Norway. The mines of Falun are extremely ancient, having been worked at least as early as the thirteenth century, under the superintendence of the Hansers, who then practically monopolized the trade and industries of the country. An old tradition goes so far as to say, that copper from this mine was sent for the vessels of Solomon's temple. It is from this mine that the town received its ancient name of *Kopparberget*, "The Copper-Mine." It is probably this industry which did much to foster that independence of character which has always so marked the people of Dalarne. The shafts of this mine descend, the deepest of them, to 1200 feet. The most striking features about them are the water-wheels, some of them forty feet in diameter, which are driven by aqueducts running from the Runn lake. The water falls with enormous violence over the edge of a cutting. Great danger has been incurred, once or twice, by the falling in of the ground. The greatest disaster of this kind happened in 1687, when the mine was so filled with water, that for several years it could not be worked. Near Falun the country is the most dreary and desolate wilderness, all signs of vegetation having been completely destroyed by the poisonous copper-smoke.

The most important copper-mines in Norway are those near Kåfjord, a branch of the Alten Fjord, in the extreme north, and Rörås, a town on the fjeld, south-east of Trondhjem. The former is entirely worked by an English company, and the miners are almost exclusively Finns.

Next to copper, the most valuable of the Norwegian resources in minerals is silver. The celebrated mines of Kongsberg, a town not very far west of Kristiania, show a steadily increasing yield. The annual produce is now worth about 22,000*l.* The Norwegian silver has the reputation of being extremely pure and excellent. On the other hand, the mines of Sala, in Sweden, have very much fallen off, and would hardly be worth working, except for the lead ore which they contain. The silver work of Norway has long been celebrated. Beautiful silver tankards, apostle spoons, brooches, &c., many of them some centuries old, were once possessed by the peasants in many parts of the country. Unfortunately for the people, either poverty or a mercenary spirit has allowed them to part with these too readily, and most have found their way into museums and private collections of antiquities. They are now comparatively very rare. The modern work is also very pretty. It consists mainly of spoons, brooches, bracelets, and dress ornaments in filigree work, distinguished by its spiral twists and its round pendants ; but the latter give it rather a flimsy appearance.

Gold is found only in small quantities, both in Sweden and Norway. Of other metals the most important is nickel. In Norway this metal was once very plentiful, and formed one of the country's most valuable resources. But it has lately very much decreased, and is now comparatively insignificant.

Of other minerals, coal, cobalt, sulphur, vitriol, and allum deserve mention. If we except Bear Island,[1] coal is found at present only in Skåne. Hitherto the collieries have not been very successful, and hardly repay the cost of working ; but the yield is steadily increasing, and now amounts to about 5,000,000 cubic feet per annum. The coal is very similar in character to the smokeless Welsh coal.

Besides the above-mentioned industries, there are scattered throughout the country several factories of different kinds, but mainly in the south. The most productive of these are the iron-foundries, spinning-mills, and cloth-factories. The most important foundries are those of Motala, where railway engines and machinery of all kinds are made. The chief centre of stuff factories of all kinds is the town of Norrköping, in Östergötland. This busy town owes its existence to the Motala river, which supplies the power for driving a large number of watermills. Next in productive-

[1] See p. 13.

ness are the sugar factories. This is chiefly confined to the manufacture of beet-root sugar.
The largest beet farms and factories are those
at Landskrona on the Swedish coast, near the
Sound, and Arlöf, near Malmö. The manufacture of tobacco is by no means insignificant.
Large fields of tobacco are grown near Stockholm
and elsewhere. The leaves are hung up and dried
in colossal airy sheds erected on the spot. Of the
rest, the breweries and match factories most deserve
mention. The largest of these is Carnegie's great
porter brewery near Göteborg. Attached to it is
also a cane-sugar factory, the largest by far of any
in Sweden. Norwegian ale, made in Bavarian
style, is very much prized, and largely exported
to Sweden and Denmark, as well as more distant
countries. The chief match factories are those of
Sogndal, on a branch of the Sogne fjord, in Norway, and Jönköping, at the south of the Vetter
lake, in Sweden. At the latter more than a thousand workmen are employed. The best matches
are those made out of the aspen poplar. There is
an ingenious machine by which a whole trunk is
cut spirally into one long thin plank, out of which
the matches are cut. Besides the regular factories,
a very great deal of industrial labour, such as weaving, spinning, and the like, is done by the peasants
themselves, in their own houses. Homespun cloth,
a rough material known as *vadmal*, is worn in
very many parts of both Sweden and Norway, and
home-made linen fetches a high price in foreign
countries.

Second, perhaps, only to agriculture in importance, both from the number of men employed and
the wealth produced, are the fisheries of Norway.

M

Something has already been said of the kinds of fish found along the Scandinavian coasts.[6]   It remains to give some short account of the principal features of this branch of industry.   In the north the land is so poor and the farms so small, that, besides those who make fishing their only business, almost every farmer combines with his agricultural work the occupation of fishing.   It is in these districts that the greatest abundance of fish is taken.   By far the most important are the cod and herring fisheries.   Of the cod fisheries there are chiefly two.   The first is the great Lofoten fishery, which lasts from February till the beginning of May.   It is impossible to give an adequate idea of the marvellous change in the whole appearance of the country during this season.   What in summer time is a desolate region, with no signs of life except the occasional homestead among the patches of green beneath the great masses of rocky mountains, is now covered with the temporary wooden huts of the fishermen, and is full of life and bustle.   The water swarms with boats belonging to the fishermen and traders, who come in crowds in their boats to carry off their purchases. The fish caught are divided into two kinds, called *stockfisk*, " stickfish," and *klipfisk*, "rockfish."   The former are at once stuck up on poles and allowed to dry till the summer, when they are taken away.   The *klipfisk* are split open, salted, and sold on the spot to the traders in so-called *jägts*, a sloop with a single mast, and one large square sail. On deck the fish are piled in the form of a stack, and taken to their various destinations, where they are dried on the rocks, whence their name.   In

---

[6] See above, pp. 36, 37.

the summer time the *jägts* may be often seen carrying freights of timber stacked in a similar manner. The best oil is that which is allowed to drop from the liver as it decays. This is afterwards packed in barrels, and shipped for home and foreign consumption ; but only a very small proportion of the article sold as cod-liver oil is really extracted from the cod. The second cod fishery is that of Finland, which takes place in the early autumn, · but it is not so productive as the Lofoten fishery. The value of the cod fisheries may be best appreciated from the fact that, out of the sum of 1,635,611*l.* produced by the whole of the fishing industries in Norway in the year 1877, 1,078,333*l.* were derived from the cod fisheries alone. In these fisheries it is estimated that as many as 66,386 men and 15,676 boats were employed.

Of the herring fisheries, by far the most important is that of Nordland and Tromsö, which takes place in the late autumn. Summer herrings are also caught in large quantities in several parts, but more especially in Romsdal and the northern coasts. Less important fisheries are those in which mackerel, lobsters, &c., are taken.

The fisheries in Sweden are insignificant when compared with those of Norway. Besides cod, mackerel, and herrings, which are caught, but not in very large quantities, almost entirely on the south-west coasts, there is a species of fish which abounds in the Gulf of Bothnia. This is the *strömming*, a fish much like a herring, only far smaller. They are caught with a seine net, cured like herrings, and exported largely to Finmark and Russia.

It remains to say a few words about the commerce

of the two kingdoms. Sweden appears to have inherited, to a large extent, the trade which gave the Hanse towns so important a position in the middle ages, and has become one of the most important trading-people in the world. By far the greater part of her trade is carried on with England. The Statistical Tables show that in 1877, out of the total value of imports amounting to about sixteen millions and three quarters sterling, four millions and three quarters came from Great Britain. While of the exports amounting in value to about twelve millions sterling, six millions and a half are sent to that country. These consist mainly of timber (including also wooden fibre for paper, matches, &c.), iron, and steel, especially steel rails. The chief imports by far are coal, and gold and silver bullion. Of the commerce carried on with other countries, the most important is that with north Germany (including the Hanseatic towns), Prussia, and Denmark. Oats are exported largely to the continent, in exchange for wheat, hops, &c.; while farming implements and machinery are imported from the United States, and sugar, coffee, tobacco, &c., from different parts of the world.

The chief seaports of Sweden are Stockholm, Göteborg, Gefle, and Malmö. There are besides a large number of smaller ports along the coast.

The trade of Norway is on an average rather more than half that of Sweden. Its imports are much the same in kind as those of Sweden, except that it imports larger quantities of meat, corn (principally barley), and stuffs, mainly from Denmark and the German towns, and iron rails from England. The trade with Hamburg is enormous, its imports from that single town being nearly equivalent in value to the whole of those from Great Britain. In its exports it differs from Sweden mainly in the enormous exportation of fish. This alone, if we include the cod-liver oil, amounts on an average to the value of nearly two millions sterling. On the other hand, the exportation of metal is inconsiderable. The chief emporiums of Norway are Kristiania, Bergen, and Trondhjem : next to these Frederikstad, Drammen, Kristiansand, and Stavanger, are most important. There is a very considerable trade carried on between Norway and Sweden, each country having a separate tariff, and exacting customs from the other. The exports from Norway to Sweden are much larger than the imports she receives from that country. This is mainly because Norway is herself already far better supplied with those metals which Sweden exports than Sweden is with fish, which she therefore imports very largely from the sister country.

The south of Sweden is being more and more opened up by new railroads, which are continually increasing. The larger main lines are most of them the property of the State, and under the Home Department of the government, who appoint directors in various districts. On none of the lines is the passenger traffic large ; but on some of them, especially those which lie in the great forest and mining districts—as that, for example, between Falun and Gefle—there is a considerable traffic in timber and minerals. From most of the larger termini there are usually two trains a day, one of which, the day-train, starts early in the morning ; the second, the night-train, late in the

evening. Travelling, as a rule, is very slow, most
of the trains stopping at all the stations, and that
for a considerable time. There are besides much
longer stoppages, of twenty minutes to half-an-
hour, arranged for breakfast and dinner. Expresses are very few, stop rather frequently, and
are not very fast. Except expresses, all trains
have three classes. A large number, especially on
local lines, are what are called *blandade*, or "mixed"
trains, i. e. are partly passenger and partly goods
trains. Even the regular goods trains have a few
passenger carriages attached. The lines are
usually very lightly constructed. The chief difficulty in making them lies in the cuttings which
have occasionally to be made in the gneiss rock,
and the solid foundation of gravel required when
the line has to run, as often happens, over miles of
marsh. Rivers and lakes are frequently crossed by
what are called "swing-bridges" (*svång broar*),
which are drawn on one side to allow steamers
to pass. They are made of iron and look very light,
and form quite a pretty feature in the landscape.

In Norway the enormous difficulties of the
country make the construction of railways an extremely costly and difficult task. The only railways of any size are those which connect Kristiania with Stockholm and Trondhjem. The rest
are merely local lines between Kristiania and the
busy little trading-towns of the south, such as
Drammen and Kongsberg. A more important line
is being constructed between Bergen and Vossevangen. The enormous labour and engineering
skill required for such an undertaking will be easily
understood, when we mention the fact that there
are to be fifty tunnels blasted out of the solid

gneiss rock within the distance of as many English miles. The railways in Norway are entirely under government, and the trains are not generally any faster than in the sister country.

A far more important means of communication in both countries is that afforded by steamboats. It is only by visiting the country, or at least carefully studying a large map, that we can realize to what a very large extent the population of the country lies near navigable water in one form or another. It would probably be an understatement to say that at least nine-tenths of the aggregate population of the two countries live within two or three miles of some steamer station. All along the coast, in and out of the creeks and fjords, round the shores and islands of the larger lakes, on all the larger rivers, steamers are constantly plying, carrying passengers and goods at rates considerably lower than the third-class passenger fares of an English train. Some of the coasting steamers (as those which ply only between the larger towns, and those which carry the fortnightly mails to the North Cape) are very large, and beautifully fitted out, some of them 1000 tons burden and more. The more local steamers, especially those on the Swedish lakes and Norwegian fjords, are often small, some not larger than a common English tug. They all carry goods, and frequently cattle, as well as passengers. They are usually well filled, especially in the summer months. They are essentially to Sweden and Norway what railways are to ourselves—a continual bond of connexion between different parts of the country. In Sweden steamers depart and arrive with extraordinary regularity; in Norway it is very different. The times of arrival

are published, it is true, in the weekly *kom-
munikationer* (official time-tables), and that with
the same preciseness as in Sweden, but they
bear only an approximate relation to the actual
times.   This is partly due to the many interruptions from storm, and more especially fog,
which among the closely-packed islands of the
coast makes it necessary to stop sometimes for
several hours together ; but it is chiefly owing to
the general disregard of seasons, which arises out
of the uncertainty of the weather.   The captain
who knows he may be stopped before very long, is
glad to leave a station as soon as he can.   Thus a
steamer is as often before its time by half an hour
or more, as it is behind it.   A traveller whose
steamer is advertised at two a.m., may be roused at
one only to wait till five ; or, on the other hand,
he may wake up with a start on hearing the
steamer's whistle at twelve.   Very great skill is
required in the navigation of the coasts of Sweden
and Norway, on account of the number of islands
and sunken rocks, and many of the captains are
retired naval officers.

The internal communications of Sweden are
much facilitated by the construction of canals between the large lakes and rivers.   Thus steamers
are, for example, able, by means of the Trollhätta
and Göta canals (which unite the Vener and Vetter
lakes with the Gota river), and the Södertelge and
other canals, to ply the whole way across country
between Göteborg and Stockholm.   The Trollhätta
canal is one of the most remarkable products of
engineering skill.   The difficulty met with by the
Trollhätta falls [7] is overcome by a series of locks.

[7] See p. 27.

It is a very remarkable sight to see a full-sized steamer climbing up the side of a hill, step by step, as it moves from one lock to another. This great work has taken centuries to complete. Schemes for uniting the larger lakes with the Baltic were contemplated in the times of Sten Sture the younger, and Gustaf Vasa ; but the first effort to realize them was the construction of Karl's dike (*Karlsgraf*), near Venersborg. The work was commenced by Karl IX., but nothing important was effected till the beginning of the eighteenth century, when Karl XII. commissioned Svedenborg and Polhem to draw up schemes for the erection of sluices at Trollhätta. The former does not appear to have taken a very active part, but Polhelm actually commenced an enormous sluice, sixty feet deep, remains of which are still visible. This and two other sluices were nearly completed by his successor Viman, when, in 1755, the whole work was destroyed, it is believed maliciously, by the sudden discharge over the falls of an enormous quantity of timber. It was not till 1800 that the old canal was at last completed, under the directions of Erik Nordevall. The western half of the Göta canal was opened in 1822, in spite of enormous opposition and difficulties of all kinds ; and was followed ten years later by the eastern half, so that the communication across the country was completed. In 1832 the new Trollhätta canal, with its eleven locks, was begun, and opened in 1844. This is that now in common use; but the older canal, with its three large locks, is still used for smaller craft. Hardly less wonderful than the locks themselves is the narrow cutting above. For about a mile long it is blasted out of the solid gneiss rock. As it is

only twenty-three feet broad, and much curved,
steamers can only crawl at the rate of some two
miles an hour, and have to stop at intervals in
sidings to let other vessels pass.   The whole length
of the course, between Göteborg and Söderköping
on the Baltic, is about 240 English miles.   There
are in all seventy-four locks or sluices; the latter are
always used where a large ascent has to be made
at once, in which case they occur in groups of two,
three, or four, ranged like so many steps in a staircase.   The breadth of the canal is 48 feet at the surface, the depth 10 feet.   The locks are 120 feet long,
by 23 feet broad.   The highest point which the canal
reaches is 296 English feet above the level of the
sea ; it lies about midway between the Vener and
Vetter.

In the south of Sweden, since the opening
of so many railways, roads have become of little
use, except for purposes of local traffic ; but in the
north of Sweden, and throughout the whole of
Norway, they are of very great importance, and
long journeys are taken entirely, or at least mainly,
by road.   In both countries facilities for travelling
are given by special laws, which regulate the system
of posting and entertainment.   These laws date
originally from at least the thirteenth century.   In
Sweden they were made or confirmed by Earl
Birger,[8] not so much for the benefit of the traveller,
as the protection of the peasant from the growing
power of the nobles.   They differ in detail in the
two countries, but are the same in principle.   The
roads are divided into stages, varying from five to
twelve miles in length.   At the end of each stage
is a station or a farm, where horses and vehicle are

[8] See p. 74.

changed, being hired in an ordinary way for one stage only. The peasants who live round a station are obliged in a regular order to provide horses for the traveller, at a tariff fixed by law ; and the keeper of the station to provide food and lodging, if required, at a reasonable charge. The country stations, called in Sweden *gästgifvaregårdar*, and in Norway *skydsstationer*, are often of the most meagre description, especially on the less frequented roads of Norway ; but the system is of the greatest advantage to the traveller, who would otherwise be at the mercy of the honesty or caprice of the peasantry. To the latter it is in some respects a doubtful advantage. They sometimes have to send out their horses when they are most required for field work, or are already jaded ; and some years ago the prices paid could hardly be regarded as a fair compensation. But these have now been raised very considerably, especially in all the stages where the road is very steep : in such cases far more than the actual distance is paid for. In Norway there are two kinds of stations, called respectively *faste* and *tilsigelse*. At the first a certain number of reserve horses belonging to the station-master are always kept, so that, unless the road is exceptionally crowded, the traveller has only to wait while the fresh horse is being put in. At the *tilsigelse* stations he has to wait till a message has been sent to the peasant whose turn it is to provide a horse, and the horse has been brought. As this peasant may happen to live several miles away, there is often a long delay, sometimes for hours. This may be obviated by sending beforehand, either by the regular post or a special messenger, a written order called a *forbud*, mentioning the time at which the horse and vehicle are required. The *tilsigelse* stations are now rapidly giving way to *faste* on all the main roads. In Sweden a certain number of horses, taken in turn from the surrounding farms, are kept in readiness at every station—a system which is convenient to the traveller, but a great burden to the farmer, who may have to send his horses to the station without any remuneration.

The average cost of posting in Norway for a single person is about threepence an English mile ; for two together, fivepence. A book is published every year, called the *lommereisetourbok*, "pocket-travelling-book," giving the distances between each station in Norway, and the exact price to be paid. The usual vehicle for a single traveller is what is called a *carjol*. It has a small seat much resembling that of a tricycle, supported on a frame of ash. This projects behind, so as to carry as much of the luggage as can be strapped on ; and in front is so long as to allow the traveller to stretch his legs at full length. There are no springs, but their absence is partly made up for by the enormous length of the shafts. The harness is of the simplest character ; there are no blinkers, and a curious contrivance in lieu of a saddle. It consists of two flat pieces of wood, about circular, which rest on the animal's back, and are joined by a curved piece of wood or iron over the top. A soft piece of sheepskin is often placed underneath to prevent galling. The great object of the harness arrangements is to save leather, which, owing to the scarcity of oak-trees, is a very expensive article. Ropes are very often made to supply the place of reins. A whip is seldom used, not because the animals are so spirited as not to require it, but simply because the peasants, who are really very fond of their horses, will not allow them—hard-worked as they already are—to be overdriven. A Norwegian pony is a sprightly animal enough, when well fed and in good condition, and will tear on with a light *carjol* at the rate of ten miles an hour or more ; but, as a

NORWEGIAN CARJOL AND PONY.

rule, very frequently, even on level ground, they can hardly be induced to go more than four. There is also another vehicle very commonly, in some parts universally, used ; it is called a *stolkjär*, "seat-cart"—a rough, small cart, with one broad seat resting on a spring : but as there is no spring under the framework of the cart, a very uncomfortable, jarring sensation in the feet is the inevitable result.

One of the most important roads of Norway is that which follows the valley of the Lågen (Gudbrandsdal) and the Romsdal, and forms the greater part of the route from Kristiania to Molde. Branching off from this, at Dombås, is the road to Trondhjem, which, after leading over the Dovre Fjeld, follows the Gula valley. There is a second road between Kristiania and Trondhjem by Rörås, which follows the Glommen and Gula valleys. There are two chief roads connecting Kristiania with the Sogne Fjord and the west—one through Valders district, the other through Hallingdal. They meet at the head of the Lärdal valley. Another road leads out of Trondhjem in a northerly direction, as far as Kongsmoen, at the head of Folden Fjord. North of this point there are no roads, and all communication is by water. Many of the routes in Norway, especially in the west, combine water and land stages. This is the case especially with the great western route from Molde to Bergen, which crosses lakes and fjords, and is nearly as much by water as by land; and with that again between Lärdalsören and Bergen. The water stages are arranged on the same principles as those on the hard road. For boatmen and boats there is a definite tariff fixed by law; and they are provided for in regular order by the peasants in each district. It will thus be seen that even the roads in Norway are remarkably few. It is only in the south that the nature of the country admits of anything like a network of them. They are generally very well made, being composed mostly of a fine gravel, except where they cross the sandhills so frequent in the larger valleys, which makes it impossible in some parts to construct a hard road. Some of the roads show great engineering skill, being blasted out of the solid gneiss rock. A very remarkable specimen is the famous zigzag in the rock at Stalheim, by which descent is made into the Nårödal valley.

In Norway the roads were originally made by government, but are kept in good order by the *bönder* through whose farms the land passes, posts and stones being put up at intervals to mark the distance for which each proprietor is responsible. In Sweden regular grants are made by government for the maintenance of the roads, which have to be kept in good repair, as in Norway, by the land proprietors. Some roads have been made at the expense of public benefactors. Thus at Jonsered, near Göteborg, there is a stone by the roadside stating that the road was made at the expense of Baron Clas Alströmer, in 1749. The improvement and management of the high roads, bridges, and canals is under the direct control of a body of engineers, which is regularly organized after the manner of a military corps. In the case of war these may be called out for any engineering work in the army.

CHAPTER VII.

RELIGION, GOVERNMENT, INSTITUTIONS, ETC.

ALTHOUGH the *riksdag* at Vesterås, in 1527,[1] gave the first blow to Roman Catholicism in Sweden, Lutheranism was not definitely established as the state religion till the meeting at Upsala, in 1593, when the people feared that the Roman Catholic King Sigismund would attempt to force the old religion upon them.[2] There can be little doubt that the succession of bishops remained unbroken. In Norway the Reformation was carried out by Kristian III., who ascended the Danish throne in 1533. It was forced upon the people with great rigour, and even violence, and in many cases the *overseers* of the Lutheran Church of Denmark were put in the place of ejected bishops. In both Sweden and Norway the church was established on extremely Erastian principles. The bishops and clergy are in fact little or nothing more than state officials, responsible to government for the religion, and to some extent the education of the people. The ritual and services differ in detail in the two countries, but in general character are very similar. In Sweden the ritual is exceedingly simple. The

[1] See p. 95.
[2] I.e., as defined in the Augsburg Confession, see p. 98,

priest wears throughout the service a black gown without sleeves, much like a commoner's gown at Oxford, only longer. He holds in his hand a long white handkerchief, intended apparently for ornament and not for use. In Norway he usually wears a large full gown, and a ruff, which gives him a singularly old-fashioned appearance, like a gentleman in a picture of the seventeenth century. This garment is generally, but not always, afterwards exchanged for a chasuble, which is laid on the altar and put on by the clerk shortly before the collect, and taken off again before the sermon. The services are very few. The most important is the ante-Communion service—which still goes by the name of High Mass (Sw. *Högmessa;* Dan. *Höimesse*)—on Sunday morning. There are a large number of hymns from an authorized Psalm-book interspersed. The sermon, preceded by a long exordium, is almost always a discourse on the Gospel for the day, which has in most cases been retained from the mediæval office. This is repeated in Sweden, in Norway usually read for the first time, from the pulpit. The Collect, Epistle, and most of the prayers are said or sung by the priest in front of the altar facing the people. Celebrations of the Holy Communion (*Nattsvarden*) are very few. Even in cathedrals they are seldom oftener than once a month.[3] Sometimes in the Swedish towns they are held alternately on Saturday afternoons and Sunday mornings. In towns it is not an uncommon thing for men to attend this service in black evening dress. The altar rails usually form a half-oval or semicircle round the front of the altar, which has behind it a huge picture or reredos and

---

[3] At Trondhjem and Lund they are weekly.

N

two large candlesticks.   In Sweden the chasuble is
generally not used except on great feast-days or in
cathedral celebrations.   The chief parts of the
ancient office are in the order here given as
follows :—The *Gloria in excelsis,* with its two parts
inverted, and divided by the *Kyrie Eleison,* forming
a sort of introit ; the *Collect, Epistle, Gradual,* and
Gospel; the *Creed* (always the Apostles') ; the
Sursum Corda (much mutilated) ; the *Institution*
(without any prayer of consecration); the *Ter-*
sanctus ; the *Lord's Prayer ;* the *Agnus Dei ;* after
which follows the Communion of the Elements ;
which is followed by the *post-Communion.*   Of the
parts inserted the most important are a long ex-
hortation, much resembling our " Dearly beloved in
the Lord," a prayer for worthy reception, and a
thanksgiving prayer after the Communion.   In
the villages of Sweden and Norway this is
almost the only service which is held ; and as there
are frequently in the more out-of-the-way parts
two or more churches in one *pastorat,* it constantly
happens that there is only one regular service in a
fortnight or three weeks.   In the towns there are
also morning and evening services, consisting now
usually of a long discourse upon some part of the
catechism, or a fixed passage of Holy Scripture,
and a few prayers not unlike our ordinary type of
family prayer.   Not even in cathedrals, with few
exceptions, as at Lunds, is there any regular daily
service.   The character of church music varies of
course . very much, far more than its amount.
Almost every part of the service is sung.   Even the
Epistle and Gospel are in Norway frequently
monotoned or inflected.   Organs, where they exist
(as in all towns and large village churches), are

placed usually in a western gallery called *läktare*,[4] where the choir also sit. In Norway the psalms are precented by the village clerk, dressed in a frock coat—an official who looks quite as important as the priest himself. In Sweden the pastor usually performs this office. The singing is commonly, to an English taste, extremely slow and drawled ; but in country villages especially it is very congregational and hearty.

It is an extremely difficult and delicate task for a foreigner to describe the religious character or condition of a people. At best he can do little more than state the results of his own observations, leaving the reader to judge for himself. What is, perhaps, most striking is the great difference with regard to religious observances between different classes, especially as it is in some respects unlike our common experience in England. The poor in both Sweden and Norway are very much attached to their church and pastor. On a fine Sunday the churches, which even for the population are very scanty, are often crammed, though the people have sometimes to drive or row the distance of ten miles or more. When in church they join heartily and look attentive. Among the middle and higher classes, with the men especially, it is different. All, it is true, belong nominally to the established church, and nearly all are confirmed, and communicate at least once a year. But the services, except by women, are badly attended. There is often a painful deadness about them. The churches do not look cared for. The sacred asso-

---

[4] From *Lectorium*, originally used of the rood-screen from which the epistles and gospels were read, and afterwards applied to a gallery of any kind.

ciations of the buildings do not prevent their
being used for other, even secular, purposes. Thus
churches are often used even for profane concerts.
The Storkyrka in Stockholm was used last year
(1880) as the place of meeting for the great
Educational Congress of the three kingdoms,
Sweden, Norway, and Denmark; and was the
scene of a stormy discussion on the desirability of a
purely secular education. Little reverence is paid
to church furniture, even though it has been employed for the most sacred purposes. The lower
room of the museum at Stockholm presents a
melancholy spectacle of ancient fonts, triptychs,
crucifixes, and much more, which have been taken
from the churches to which they properly belong.

The absence of anything like strong church
feeling is probably mainly due to the constitution
of the church. The clergy are a number of state
officials, paid to perform certain duties. The laity
have therefore none of the interest and enthusiasm
inspired by the feeling that they are themselves
members of the church, and consequently there is
the skeleton of a political hierarchy without any
religious life and vigour. It may be due in part
also to the social position of the clergy. Men of
the highest ability and most independent spirit will
not as a rule undertake an office where freedom of
action is hindered by petty and vexatious government regulations. As state officials the clergy are
poorly paid, consequently they are drawn chiefly
from the peasant-farmer (*bonde*) class. In the
country villages this has its advantages. The
pastor is a sort of *maximus inter pares*, with much
the same interests and sympathies in secular
matters as his flock. He wins their friendship

without losing their respect. On Sunday he is their teacher and adviser, in the weekday he is their personal friend. But in the towns the pastor, though far more learned in the technical part of his duties, is often inferior in social standing to the greater part of his congregation. Nor is there, as in England, any system of parish visiting, by which the pastor may gain respect as a hard-working and self-denying parish priest. The pastor is essentially a preacher, and, if he fails to extract an interesting or attractive sermon out of the few texts allowed him by government, he must expect to be a nobody.

The church organization of the middle ages is in a large measure still retained. Sweden is divided into twelve dioceses (*stifts*), viz. Upsala, Linköping, Skara, Strengnäs, Vesterås, Vexiö, Lund, Göteborg, Kalmar, Karlstad, Hernösand, and Visby. The see of the one archbishopric is at Upsala. Besides the bishops of these sees, the chief pastor (*pastor primarius*) of Stockholm, which is extra-diocesan, holds a position practically equivalent to that of a bishop. Every *stift* is divided into *Prosteries*, each *Prosteri* being under the jurisdiction of a *Prost*, an officer much like a rural dean with us. The *Prosteries* are divided again into *Pastorats*, a *Pastorat* being all that is under one rector (*kyrko-herde*), and containing in turn one, two, or more *socknar*, or districts with churches. In Norway there are six *stifts*, Kristiania, Hamar, Kristiansand, Bergen, Trondhjem, and Tromsö. In Sweden each *stift*, as well as the church of Stockholm, is governed by a consistory, which decides local questions, subject to the right of appeal to the king and minister of ecclesiastical affairs. More general questions are discussed by the *kyrkomöte*, a convocation of bishops and representatives of both clergy and laity, which meets every five years.

Church patronage in this country is somewhat complicated. In the case of bishops all the clergy in the diocese vote in the first instance. The king elects, out of those who have received most votes, the candidate he pleases. Incumbents (*kyrko-herdar*) for ordinary livings are appointed by the consistory and parish—the parish being obliged to elect one of three chosen by the consistory.[5] Clergy, in addition to their university and ordination examinations, are required to pass another in pastoral and dogmatic theology before they can enter upon a living.

In Norway all ecclesiastical offices are filled up by a special committee of the council (*råd*), who elect, as in Sweden, one of the three who have received most votes in the first election by the diocese or parish. In both countries the clergy are very fair scholars in the classics, ecclesiastical history, and dogmatic theology, and sometimes in Hebrew and Philosophy.

For government purposes Sweden is divided into *läns* and *härads*. The *län* corresponds in size to an English county, the *härad* or *lagsting* is equivalent to our old English division of "hundred."

According to the Constitution of 1866, the Swedish Diet (*riksdag*) consists of two Chambers.[6] The Upper Chamber is composed of members who must be at least thirty-five years of age, and pay

---

[5] In livings in the king's gift the parish has the right of choosing a fourth candidate, who frequently gets the appointment.
[6] See Stat. Handbook, pp. 117—120.

taxes on real property of a value not less than
80,000 *kronor* (4444*l.*), or on an income not less
than 4000 *kronor* (222*l.*) per annum. They are
elected by the *landsting* of the *län* and the free
burghers of the towns, in as near as possible
the proportion of 1 in 30,000 of the population. Each member is elected for nine years,
and receives no emolument. This chamber is intended to represent the wealth and, to a large
extent, the land interest of the nation. Members
of the chamber are elected as vacancies occur, and
there is no general election. The members of the
Lower Chamber are only required to be twenty-
five years of age, and to be paying taxes or rates
on real property of the value of 6000 *kronor*
(333*l.*), or an annual income of 800 *kronor* (44*l.*)
They are elected by a complicated system of compound voting, in such a way as to secure the
proportion of 1 in every 10,000 of the town,
and 1 in every 30,000 of the country population. The whole chamber is re-elected every three
years, vacancies in the meanwhile being filled
up by interim elections. Its members receive,
in addition to their travelling expenses, a sum
not exceeding 1200 *kronor* (66*l.*). This limitation has some beneficial results : it makes the
members anxious to avoid a lengthened session,
and " obstruction " is said to be a thing unknown.

The *riksdag* meets regularly every year, beginning with the 15th of January. The *riksdag*
at once selects from its members several select
committees, such as the *Constitution Committee,*
State Committee, Taxation Committee, &c., whose
business it is to prepare bills belonging to their
special departments. The members of these com-

mittees must be taken equally from both chambers.
Voting is made by ballot—a system which leads
to a large amount of small speaking, as the only
means a member has of making known his opinions
in the house. The *riksdag* has the power of making,
annulling, or altering laws, and levying or re-
mitting taxes ; but every measure, excepting those
affecting taxes, must, besides being passed by a
majority of both houses, receive the royal assent
before it can become law.

The functions of government are vested in the
king and the ministry (*statsråd*) of ten, seven of
whom have portfolios, and are each at the head of
some department ; the remaining three have only
a consultative voice. The seven departments are
Justice, Foreign Affairs, Land Defence, Sea Defence, Home, Finance, and Ecclesiastical Affairs
(including Education). Under some of these are
also colleges and other administrative bodies, who
superintend some special business connected with
the several departments, *e. g.* the College of Commerce, Army Administration, and others.

The king has a larger share of independence
and power than in many constitutional governments. In the legislature he has the right of himself bringing forward measures, as well as vetoing
what the *riksdag* may have passed. He appoints
the ministers—the only restriction being that they
must be native Swedes, of pure evangelical learning—and out of their number selects the prime-
minister (*statsminister*). He may not, however,
declare peace or war, or exercise any important
functions of government, without laying the matter
before the *råd*. In all cases the reasons for the
advice given have to be entered in a protocol, and

the minister is responsible for his advice before a a special court, selected out of the members of the *riksdag.* The king himself is not responsible for his actions.

The local government of every *län*, including the collecting of taxes, distribution of public funds, maintenance of order and discipline, &c., is under the general superintendence of a magistrate called *landshöfding.* In each *län* is held a *landsting* —an assembly which, in addition to the part it takes in the election of the members of the upper house, decides many questions of local interest, such as those connected with agricultural improvements, means of communication, education, &c., within the *län.* The regular session of the *landsting* lasts for about a week in the month of September.

For executive purposes the *län* is divided into *fögderies,* each *fögderi* being under the surveillance of a *kronofogde* and a *häradsskrifvare.* The former has to provide for the maintenance of public order and discipline, and to see that the decisions of the local courts are carried out; the latter is a sort of secretary, whose duty it is to draw up and revise terriers and other public documents connected with the *fögderi.* Under every *kronofogde* there are several less important officials, called *länsmän,* whose business it is to assist him in his duties, or take his place in their several sub-districts, and act as local bailiffs or constables. Stockholm has a special municipal government of its own, under the superintendence of an officer called *ståthållare,* who provides for the collection of taxes and all monetary matters; and a *polismästare,* who acts as judge in a police-court, in which breaches of order and decency and other small offences are tried.

The court of first instance in the country (both for civil and criminal cases) is called the *härads-rätt*. It is a sort of local assize, held in each *härad*, under the jurisdiction of a judge called *häradshöfding*, who moves in circuit in districts called *domsagor*, and containing one, two, or several *härads*. The sessions of these courts take place usually three times a year, but in some cases only twice.

The jury (*häradsnämd*) consists of twelve peasants (*bönder*), elected in rotation, whose verdict holds good only in cases where they unanimously disagree with the decision of the *härads-höfding*, otherwise the decision of the latter must be followed. The corresponding court in the towns is the *rådsturätt* or *rådstugurätt*, which is under the jurisdiction of the mayor (*borg-mästare*) and town councillors (*rådmän*). This court meets at least every Monday (excepting holidays, when it meets on the next ordinary day). In the larger towns it is divided into at least two departments, for civil and criminal cases respectively. In Stockholm there are as many as seven.

The courts of second instance (*hofrätter*) are three—belonging one to each of the three ancient kingdoms of which Sweden is composed, viz. Svea, Göta, and the old Danish provinces in the south, Skåne and Blekinge. These courts meet at Stockholm, Jönköping, and Kristianstad respectively. Besides the president, assessors, secretaries, &c., the two former consist of twenty-five, but the *Skånska hofratt* of only ten members, who are in each case elected permanently. The regular sessions are from the 14th of January to the 31st of May, and from the 1st of October to the 20th of December. But a division of the court sits also through the summer.

The highest court of appeal, or *konungens högsta domstol*, consists normally of twelve members, appointed by, and acting in the name of, the king, who, when present, has the right of two votes. The office is permanent, unless any of the members be found either incapable or guilty of flagrant injustice or corrupt practices. Such cases are examined by a special court of forty persons, elected every third year by the *riksdag*.

Besides these regular courts, there are special courts for military offenders—the three grades being the *krigsrätt, krigshofrätt*, and the ordinary court of final appeal, assisted by two officers of high rank.

The diet of Norway is called the *storthing*, or "Great Parliament." Its members are elected every three years by means of a compound system of voting, closely resembling that employed for electing the members of the lower house in Sweden, so arranged that, as near as may be, the town members shall represent the proportion of one-third of the whole. The voters in the first instance must be at least twenty-five years of age, and possess real property to at least the value of 300 *kronor* (16*l.*) No person may be returned as member who has not resided in the country at least ten years, and is not at the time of election as much as thirty years old. The members are paid for their services.

The *storthing* assembles as a rule annually, beginning on the first business day of February.

Its first duty is to elect one fourth of its body. This forms the *lagthing*, or upper house, the remaining three-quarters constituting the *odels-thing* or lower house. The functions of the *storthing* are nearly the same as those of the Swedish *riksdag*, but its method of procedure is very different. Every important measure must be first introduced in the *odelsthing*, either by the government or a private member. If passed, the *lagthing* may at once reject or pass it, in which latter case it has only to receive the royal assent to become law ; or it may send the bill down with amendments to the *odelsthing*, who, in their turn, may reject, pass, or amend it. If the *lagthing* then refuses to accept the amended bill, the two houses meet together, and the measure can only be carried by a majority of two-thirds of the combined houses. The power of the king to throw out a bill passed by the two chambers has this important limitation—that if a bill passes both chambers of three successive parliaments at three distinct ordinary sessions of each parliament (provided no counter-resolution shall have been passed in the interim), it becomes law without requiring the king's assent. It was in this way that the country carried, in the face of the royal opposition and almost at the cost of a civil war, the bill for abolishing the rights of the hereditary nobility in 1821. This power of the *storthing* is now disputed by the king, who refuses to accept a resolution for appointing an army committee which has been repeatedly passed by the *stor-thing ;* and the question is being decided before a special court of arbitration.

The government consists of the king and nine

ministers, seven of whom are at the head of departments corresponding to those of the Swedish
government, except that Post is joined with the
Navy, instead of being under the Home department.

There are two *ministers of state.* One of them,
with two other special ministers, has to attend the
king when absent in Sweden ; the other acts as
prime-minister at the head of the government in
Norway. All the ministers are appointed by the
king, but must be Norwegians by birth. At
present there exists much ill-feeling between the
government and the *storthing,* and some of the
leading Norwegian Radicals are anxious to exclude the government from the meetings of the
latter—a measure which would tend greatly to
diminish the power of the king in the country.

Norway is divided for political purposes into
amts and *fogderies.* The chief magistrate in the
amt is the *amtmand,* who corresponds very nearly
to the *landshöfding* in Sweden. Beneath him is
the *foged,* who superintends the public business
of the *fogderi ;* and beneath the *foged* the *läns-
mänd,* one of whom acts as bailiff or constable in
each parish (*prästgjeld*). The government of the
towns is presided over by an officer called a *byfoged,* who holds special municipal courts.

Courts of justice are, as in Sweden, divided into
three grades. The court of first instance, both
for civil and criminal cases, is held in each parish
by rotation under the presidency of the *sorenskriver,* who combines in his own person the offices
of the Swedish *häradsskrifvare* and *häradshöfding.*
The court of first instance in towns is that of
the *byfoged,* who thus has the chief control both

in the judicature and municipal government. The court of second instance is that of the *stift*. Of these there are two in Kristiania *stift*, one in each of the rest. From these courts there is again an appeal to the supreme court (*höjesteret*), which must, according to the constitution, consist of a judge and not less than six assessors. Ministers, and members of the *storthing* can only be indicted before a special court called *rigsret*, which is elected out of the *lagthing* and supreme court. Besides these there are, as in Sweden, special courts for military and ecclesiastical offenders.

In addition to the regular courts there is in every parish a sort of court of arbitration, under a commissioner and two assessors, chosen monthly. The chief object of this court is to reconcile disputants and prevent unnecessary litigation. If both parties can be brought to terms of agreement, the resolution has simply to be revised and confirmed by the *sorenskriver*, at a trifling cost. The good results of this system may be seen from the fact that in the year 1877, out of 84,369 cases brought before this commissioner, only 13,968 passed for decision to the court of first instance.

Sweden and Norway possess each a national bank. That of Sweden has a capital of 25,000,000 kr., and a reserve fund of 5,000,000 kr., and about 18,000,000 kr. of deposits. The latter has a capital of 12,500,000 kr., a reserve fund of 4,500,000, and about 6,000,000 kr. of deposits. In addition to these, several private banks have the privilege, under certain limitations, of issuing notes having a public currency.

Besides the national banks, there are, in each country, special banks, called *hypotheks*, under

government, which lend money to those purchasing
land. The money is raised on mortgage. The
interest paid being six per cent. on the original
amount, which covers not only the interest, but a
portion of the capital, which is thus paid back in
a fixed term of thirty years.

The annual revenue of Sweden is about
70,000,000 kr. (3,888,000*l.*) ; of Norway, it is
about 45,000,000 kr. (2,500,000*l.*) Both countries
have a small national debt. In Sweden it was, last
year (1880), actually 220,296,129 kr. (12,238,673*l.*)
But this was more than counterbalanced by
rentable state property. In Norway, it was actually 99,632,000 kr., but against this sum there is
rentable state property to the value of 84,200,000
kr., so that the debt was practically only 15,432,000
kr. (857,333*l.*) Both countries therefore may be
justly regarded as being in a flourishing financial
condition.

Education both in Sweden and Norway is com-
pulsory, all children being required to attend
school, who cannot satisfy the authorities that they
are receiving sufficient education at home.

In Sweden, places of instruction may be
divided into three kinds, the *folkskolor* or "people's
schools," answering to our national schools, *allmänna skolor*, "public schools," which are to be
found in all the larger towns, and the universities.
All of these are under the general control of the
ecclesiastical (and educational) department, and
partly under the bishops and clergy of the diocese
to which they belong.

Of the *folkskolor* there is usually one in each
village, in which case they are called *fasta skolor*,
"permanent schools;" but in the larger parishes,

especially in the north, where two or more parishes (*socknar*) are under one pastor, there are often what are called *flyttbara skolor*, "circular schools," which are taught in rotation by the same school-master. This latter system is very common in Norway and the outlying districts of Sweden. The adult schools, where the pupils range from eight to about fifteen years of age (when the scholar is confirmed), are always taught by a certificated teacher, usually a master, who has primarily undergone a course of four years' instruction at one of the seminaries established for the purpose in Stockholm and each of the cathedral towns. The infant schools (*småskolor*) are taught by a mistress who has received instruction at one of the public or private seminaries of a similar kind. All the *folkskolor* are under the management of a board (*råd*), consisting of the pastor as chairman, and members chosen by election from the village, subject to the control of the chapter. The religious instruction is entirely under the management of the pastor. The schools are visited by an inspector, who has to advise the *råd*, and send in two annual reports of the general condition of the school, one to the chapter, and the other to the ecclesiastical department. The minimum of subjects taught, before a pupil can leave school and be confirmed, are reading, writing, arithmetic, church catechism, Bible history, and singing ; but other subjects, such as geometry, geography, history, &c., are also taught. Besides these, popular schools of a more advanced kind, called *folkhögskolor*, designed to give a higher culture to the labouring classes, are being established in different parts of the country.

The public schools, *allmänna läroverk*, or *elementarläroverk*, are of two kinds, the lower (*lägre läroverk*), which correspond to our middle class schools, and the higher (*högre läroverk*), which are more like our public schools, and are intended to a large extent as preparatory to the universities. The course at the latter consists of seven classes, of which the five lowest take a year each to pass through, the two highest two years each. The pupil, therefore, in a regular way takes nine years to pass through the course, and, as he may not be admitted before nine years of age, cannot generally enter the university until he is eighteen. At the end of each year he has to pass an examination. The usual curriculum consists of Latin, Greek, mathematics, natural science, and modern languages ; but some few schools are, in the two upper classes, almost entirely classical, others exclusively modern ; while there is one at Stockholm (*realläroverket*) altogether modern throughout. Sometimes the two sides, or "lines" as they call them, viz. the "Latin line" and the "real line," are combined in one school. In the former line Greek is taught, but only as an alternative for English, which is otherwise a *sine quâ non*. The proportion of those who take up the "real line" exclusively is about twenty-three per cent. In all schools botany is taught in the lower classes. As the scholars are generally then too young to appreciate it, the technicalities of the science often prove very irksome, and only create a distaste for the study in after life. All public schools are in each diocese under the general supervision of the bishop, under the title of *eforus*, who appoints an inspector for each school. Each

O

school is governed by a *rector* as head master, and the masters under him. In the lower schools the rector is appointed by the bishop and consistory ; in the upper, nominally by the king, but practically by the bishop and consistory. To each of the "higher schools" there is a library attached.

In Sweden there are two universities, at Upsala and Lund respectively. The University of Upsala was founded by Sten Sture the elder, in 1477 ; that of Lund, in 1668, by Karl XI. In the autumn term of 1879 there were 1345 students at Upsala, at Lund 581 ; but the latter had increased by the autumn term of 1880 to 709.

The statutes, drawn up in 1876, affect both universities alike. Either university is nominally under a chancellor, who is usually a nobleman or some other distinguished person; and under him a vice-chancellor, who is always the bishop of the diocese. Practically, the university is governed by a *rector*, who is elected out of the ordinary professors and holds office for two years, and two consistories, chosen from the professors, and including also the librarian as an *ex-officio* member. The upper consistory has to deal with the general management and finance of the university, the lower constitutes a sort of board of studies, having under its control the instruction and examination of the students. No student is admitted into the university unless he is provided with a certificate of having passed a previous school examination.

In each university there are four distinct faculties, viz. theology, law, medicine, and philosophy. The last is now subdivided into two sections—the first comprising moral science, history, and language ; the second, mathematics and natural science. In each of these faculties and sections there is a distinct course, divided into different grades. But before the student can study the special subjects belonging to either of the first three faculties, he first must pass a preliminary examination in those branches of the philosophical faculty which are required as a foundation for study in his special faculty. In each faculty there are in theory three degrees—those of "candidate" (*candidat*), "licentiate" (*licentiat*), and *doctor*. In practice these now only form the regular course in the faculties of medicine and philosophy.

In theology the student is usually content with the two necessary examinations in theoretical and practical theology, which enable him to become a *verbi divini magister*, or in popular language a *pastor*. The examination for a *candidat* in theology is perhaps the stiffest of any, and formerly might only be aspired to by one who had already become a *doctor* in philosophy. A *doctor's* degree in this faculty is now only given by the king himself, and the *licentiat* degree has fallen through. A student in laws may similarly, after passing his legal examination, called *rättegångs process*, practice at the bar, and comparatively few can afford the time and expense required to become a *candidat*. In all faculties the *candidat* and *licentiat* degrees are given by examination; the *doctor's* degree may be claimed of right in all faculties but that of theology, by one who writes and defends a treatise.

The philosophical faculty is much the largest, the students who pass out in this faculty being about a third of the whole number.[7] In the

[7] In statistical tables the proportion appears to be much larger, but this is because the number of students put down as belonging to the

autumn term of 1879 the numbers in each faculty were as follows. At Upsala: theology, 327; law, 146; medicine, 179; philosophy, nominally 693. At Lund: theology, 144; law, 61; medicine, 68; philosophy, nominally 308.

For social and disciplinary purposes the students are divided into societies called *nations*, named after the district, usually the diocese, from which their members come. These are under the superveillance of an inspector who is a professor, and one or more curators who are chosen from each *nation* among their own number. In Upsala these clubs are very distinct, and have each their set of rooms in the town. At Lund there is one large general club or union (*förening*), having a building, with library, restaurant, and other public rooms attached. These societies make up to a certain degree the social advantages of the college life in the English universities. At Upsala there is a boating club, but at neither university is there that general development of physical activity by athletic exercises of all kinds which is so characteristic of Oxford and Cambridge university life. Indeed gymnastics and fencing are almost the only hard exercises in which the students engage.

At Upsala there is a special medical institute, called the *Karolinksa Institut*, established in 1667, which, like the university, has the power of examining for the *candidat* and *licentiat* degrees in medicine, and provides special opportunities for medical practice.

Education, both in the universities and the schools, is provided for largely by government

philosophical faculty includes all who have not yet passed the preliminary examination in philosophy.

grants. In the public schools and universities it is paid for partly by fees, in the "folk schools" partly by small fees, but mainly by local rates imposed by the *landsting*. In the universities there are, besides, endowments under supervision of government, which provide small exhibitions, which seldom exceed the sum of 200 kronor (11*l.*), for deserving scholars. The education of women in the middle classes is so far supported by government that grants are made to certain schools, on condition of their receiving a specified number of pupils free of charge.

There are, besides the general schools already spoken of, several also of a more special kind, as, for example, different sorts of military and naval schools at Stockholm, Göteborg, Karlskrona, Karlsborg, &c.; training colleges (called seminaries), especially that for the training of the higher class of schoolmistresses and private governesses at Stockholm; mechanical or "technical" (*tekniska*) and industrial (*slöjd*) schools of various kinds throughout the country. Of the last kinds we may specially notice the *Tekniska högskola* at Stockholm, where students are taught mechanics, applied mathematics, chemistry, the use of machinery, and all branches of knowledge connected with mining, building, engineering, &c.; and the very similar, but somewhat less scientific institution at Göteborg, called *Chalmerska Slöjd-skolan*. There are besides these a large number of popular industrial schools throughout the country, giving instruction in weaving, spinning, and other special industries. The foresting and agricultural schools have already been spoken of.

Great importance is attached in Sweden to gymnastic exercises, both as a means of giving a healthy physique, and also as a specific remedy against certain kinds of bodily ailment. For such purposes the *Gymnastika Centralinstitut* was founded by Per Henrik Ling, the great inventor of Swedish gymnastics.[8] It is divided into three departments ; one to train officers to superintend gymnastics in the army and navy, a second to train teachers of gymnastics for the town and country schools, and a third for the study of gymnastics as a system of medical treatment. This system has been adopted with more or less success in Germany, England, and other foreign countries.

The cause of higher culture in Sweden has been largely promoted by establishing academies in all the chief branches of learning and art. The most important of these are the Swedish Academy, founded by Gustaf III. in 1786, which has been already alluded to in the review of Swedish litera- ture ;[9] the Academy of Natural Science ; the Academy of Literature, History, and Antiquities ; the Academy of Agriculture ; the Academy of Liberal Arts ; the Academy of Music (which examines almost all the teachers of music through- out the country) ; and lastly, the Academy of Military Science.

In Norway the educational machinery is in many respects much like that employed in Sweden. In the "folk schools" the "ambulatory" system is even more common than in the sister country. Public schools are in Norway divided into three instead of only two kinds—upper, middle, and lower. Among the lower, about half are boy- schools or girl-schools ; the other half are mixed.

[8] See pp. 128, 129.   [9] See p. 127.

Otherwise the education of girls is left to private schools. Unlike Sweden, the "real line" is more often adopted in the public schools than the classical. The University of Kristiania was opened in 1813, the year before the separation from Denmark. Like the universities of Sweden, it consists of four faculties—the fourth being divided in a similar way. It is under the general government of a council, one of whom is elected by the professors in each faculty. All lectures are free. As compared with the Swedish universities, the most striking difference is in the small number of students belonging properly to the philosophical faculty. In 1878 the whole number of students was 768. Of these 215 studied law, 199 medicine, 150 theology, while only 81 belonged to the philosophical faculty.[1] Of the latter, 50 studied history and philosophy, 31 natural science; the rest (123) had still to pass in their preliminary philosophical examination. The numbers have been showing a considerable falling off of late years. In 1870 there were as many as 1026 students.

The standing army of Sweden consists of two classes, called respectively *indelta* and *värfvade* troops. The latter, which number about 7000, are always on duty. They consist of life guards, and garrison troops quartered in the chief towns; and three artillery corps, called the Svea, Göta, and Vende regiments, each divided among ten batteries with five guns: they have their headquarters at Stockholm, Göteborg, and Kristianstad, respectively. The *indelta* troops, which form the mass of the

[1] Excluding those engaged in preliminary studies.

regular army, are only on duty at certain times in the year, during which they have to go through regular military discipline and training.   Otherwise they dwell on different small farms, which are allotted to them ; hence the name *indelta*, "apportioned."   This system is exceedingly ancient, dating at least as far back as the time of Karl XI., and probably by him only organized out of the ancient system of land tenure existing from the days of the *wikings*.   The system as at present existing is as follows.   The whole of the land is divided into two kinds, called *frälse*, " free," and *ofrälse*, "unfree." [2]   The first is strictly freehold, being possessed without rent or ordinary taxation ; the second is subject to various kinds of taxes, and in the south especially is often divided into small holdings rented from a larger proprietor.   Every district called a *rote*, which usually contains two farms, carries with it the liability of maintaining a soldier, by providing for him a house, and small farm attached called a *torp* (thorp), and securing its proper cultivation whenever he is absent on service, i. e. for thirty to thirty-six days in each year.   In other cases a horse is provided for, either in addition or instead.   Properly speaking, the latter liability should have fallen upon the *frälse* land, the exemption from taxes having been originally granted in the days of Magnus Ladulås, on condition of providing a horse ready equipped, which was in those days far more costly than all the ordinary taxes.   The whole of this system of land tenure, though it has some economical advantages, is unjust in principle and objectionable in practice ; because it is impossible by it to in-

[2] On the origin of this distinction see p. 75.

crease the army, without injustice to those on whom the increased burden would fall. Some years ago a special committee was appointed to draw up schemes for doing away with the distinction between *frälse* and *ofrälse* land, and supporting the army by direct taxation, without injury to the present holders, or loss to the revenue. The result of its labours was published in 1876,[3] and a change will in all probability before long be effected. The *indelta* troops number altogether about 29,000, consisting of eight regiments of cavalry and eighteen of infantry, named after the districts where they are severally quartered. The whole of the standing army is reckoned at 35,296 men. The reserve forces, *Beväringsmanskap*, "Defence men," are drawn from the mass of male population throughout the country by a general conscription called *allmänna beväring*. Every man is by law liable to serve in the army or navy who is between the ages of twenty and twenty-five; but in times of peace he can only be compelled to attend drill and otherwise receive military training for fifteen days in both his twenty-first and twenty-second years. The whole of the force thus at the disposal of the State amounts to 125,424 men, divided among infantry, cavalry, and artillery. In addition to these there are several volunteer rifle corps, amounting in all to 16.768 men. In time of war even the *frälse* land is liable to provide soldiers or horses, one for every *rote;* this is called the *extra roteringsmanskap.*

Gotland still retains one trace of its ancient independence, in providing an army of its own. This is called *Gotlands nationalbeväring,* which may

[3] Skattejemknings Komiténs Betänkande. Stockholm, 1876.

only be employed for the defence of the island from foreign attack. Every Gotlander from eighteen to sixty years old is liable to serve in it, but after the age of forty-five he belongs to the reserve. This force consists of riflemen (*jägarer*), artillery, and infantry, and numbers in all 7779 men, including officers.

The navy is supported by the land, according to the same general principle as the army. There are, however, two degrees of liability, according to which the taxed land is called *rusthållet* or *rothållet*.[4] The first consists of lands most heavily burdened, and lies on the Bleking coast, near the naval station of Karlskrona; the other of *ofrälse* land, on different parts of the coast. Each man either receives a *torp* or is supported in the house, or at least at the expense of the landholder, and, in addition, receives four-fifths of his clothing expenses. In time of war the *frälse* coast land is subject to an *extra rotering*, for the support of the navy, just as the interior lands for that of the army. The whole of the naval force consists of thirty-one companies, of which twelve have their headquarters at Stockholm, nineteen at Karlskrona, where are also the great naval depôt and training ship. In addition to these is a general conscription of all the sea-coast population, which forms a reserve force amounting to about 28,000, called the *sjöbeväring*, exactly corresponding to the *allmänna beväring*, which forms the army reserve. In addition to this those who belong to the merchant service, and are between the ages of twenty and thirty-five, are liable to be called out in time of war. The regular navy consists of four monitors, each with two guns, and averaging fifteen to six-

---

[4] See Administr. och Statist. Handb. pp. 161, 162.

teen hundred tons; ten smaller ironclads, averaging about 350 tons, with one gun ; one ship of the line with sixty-six guns, one frigate with sixteen guns, four corvettes, and nineteen gunboats, nine with two guns, ten with one gun each; besides a torpedo boat, transports, sailing ships, &c.

In Norway there is nothing corresponding to the *indelta* system, but all the larger farms are liable to provide a horse for the use of the army. Troops are raised partly by enlistment, partly by conscription. Every inhabitant[5] of the country from the age of twenty-three, is bound to serve in the army, nominally for ten years. He is liable to serve for a term of seven years in the line, and three years in the reserve called *landvärn*, which may only be called upon to fight in the defence of the country. He is required to attend drill, &c., about thirty days in each year, for a period of from three to five years. Besides this, all up to the age of forty-five are liable to an extra-ordinary levy, called *landstorm*, in case of great danger. The fighting army is usually limited to 18,000 men, and 750 officers. In 1878 the troops of the line numbered 54,000 men, and the *landvärn* 20,000, besides the guards and train.

The navy is raised partly by voluntary service, partly by conscription. The inhabitants of the towns are liable to serve in the navy from the ages of twenty-two to thirty-five. In 1879 the navy consisted of four ironclad monitors with two guns each, two steam frigates with thirty-nine guns each, two corvettes with sixteen and fourteen guns respectively, and twenty-three small gunboats with one to two guns each, besides transports, &c.

[5] Except the clergy, pilots, and the inhabitants of Finmark.

CHAPTER VIII.

HABITS, CHARACTER, ETC.

THE continual intercourse which both Sweden and Norway have had with other nations, and the constant infusion of strangers, have tended to destroy much that was peculiar both in the habits and character of the people. Stockholm is in many respects an imitation of Paris. Its inhabitants delight in hearing it called "the Paris of the north." The influence of Germany and the Hanse towns has been even larger, not only in some of the larger seaport towns, such as Göteborg and Bergen, but even in the smaller inland towns of Sweden.

If we would get a true idea of the national character, we must turn to the life of the country people. In Norway, and to a large extent in Sweden also, the system of small freeholds has tended to produce a certain independence of character, which, while it makes the peasant landlord contented with poverty, makes him obstinate in refusing to introduce improvements. It is interesting to compare this state of things with the great progress made in farming in those large estates of Sweden which are rented of rich landed proprietors. Socially, the people are perhaps the most democratic in the world. In

Norway this is particularly the case. The relics of aristocracy were stamped out by the resolution of the *storthing* (in 1821), which abolished hereditary titles of nobility. In Sweden, though an aristocracy on feudal principles has existed since the days of Magnus Ladulas, it has never taken a really firm root. The middle class has for the most part consisted of traders, many of them foreigners living in the seaport towns, and not therefore forming a connecting social link between the upper and lower classes. The political power of the aristocracy was taken away by the constitution of 1865, and the people are more and more inclined to look with disfavour on the social privileges of a favoured class. Notwithstanding this, their loyalty is very remarkable. In Norway the king is looked upon with the greatest veneration. Both Norwegians and Swedes have the greatest respect for law and order. Imagine an English crowd meekly submitting to have all the public-houses closed in a populous town like Göteborg, which happened on the occasion of a great local festival some years ago! A Swede will sit patiently in his carriage at a railway station, because it is contrary to the regulations for a passenger to open or shut the door for himself.

The general state of intelligence speaks a great deal for the system of universal education existing both in Sweden and Norway. It would hardly be too much to say that the ordinary peasant knows more than the average small farmer or local dealer in England. The inquisitiveness and outspokenness of the people are very astonishing. This is particularly the case in Norway, where the people are more accustomed to see strangers. The

questions asked are very often of a personal character, e.g.: "How old are you?"—"Are you married?"—" How much money have you got?" Often
they betray a geographical turn of mind, as: "How
many miles is it from here to London?"—"Are
there any fjords in England?" Nothing delights
a peasant more than to be shown the name of his
farm or village on a map. In Sweden especially
the people are extremely fond of books. Every
village nearly has its bookshop. Even the bar-
maid behind the counter of a Swedish *schweitzeri*
spends her leisure moments in reading. One of
the most striking features of character among the
people is their excessive courtesy. This is far
more striking in the lower classes than in the
upper, among whom an off-hand manner is sometimes assumed. It is more marked among Norwegians than among Swedes. The Norwegian
peasant takes off his hat to every one, high or low
—not as a mark of servile respect, but of social
courtesy. The waving of hats, when a fjord
steamer leaves a village station, is almost as striking
a ceremony as the leave-taking of the members of
the House of Commons. Shaking of hands is not
so often a mark of friendly salutation as a token of
gratitude. The *skydsgut,* or postboy, who drives
or sits behind the traveller's *carjol,* will shake hands
on receiving his *drikkepenge,* " drink-money," even
though on counting his fare he grumbles like a
London cabman. In Sweden the custom is much
rarer, except in the more retired districts. There,
bowing and curtseying, especially in the towns,
have quite taken their place. The waitress gives
the prettiest of curtseys as she says her *God natt,
god natt,* "Good night, good night." The waiter

bows almost to his knees as he bids his *adjö* on being paid his little bill.

The courtesy of the Scandinavian character shows itself in many ways in the civilities of every-day life. The peasant housewife herself hands round the dishes. This she does as the owner and giver of the meal. When the meal is over, the party, whether guests or members of the family, one by one shake hands with her, saying, " *Tak for matt* (*mad*)," " Thanks for the meal :" she answers, " *Väl bekommet*, " Good may it do you." Such civilities were once universal in Norway and Sweden, but are rapidly giving way to the commonplace philistinism of modern life.

Kindness and pleasantness of manner are everywhere to be met with. Surliness and ill-humour are extremely rare, and when found are usually the result of drunkenness or some physical defect. Both Swedes and Norwegians are noted for their hospitality. In some of the poorest districts the peasant will give food, which is probably coarse enough, but the best he has, to provide for the casual stranger ; and the kindness received is too often shamefully abused. Tourists, bent only on their own pleasure, are apt to grumble most inconsiderately at fare which, however mean, and even coarse, can only be procured with great cost and labour in districts so separated by mountains from the high roads of communication. They forget, too, that money, in parts of the country where provisions are scarce and almost unattainable, is not always an exact compensation. But this good-nature shows itself not only in the general readiness to provide food and lodging at very moderate charges, but more generally in the considerate courtesy and forbearance in every way shown towards strangers.

The Scandinavians are an essentially pleasure-loving people. We read in the sagas the most graphic accounts of banquets in honour of Woden and Thor, of wedding banquets, funeral banquets, and banquets of all kinds—of the yule ale (*Jul öl*), the funeral ale (*Graf öl*), and the mead. Though the reason or excuse for these banquets has in some cases been changed, and *finkel* and *brännvin* have largely taken the place of ale and mead, the Scandinavians of the nineteenth century do not in this respect come far short of their illustrious ancestors.

By far the greatest of all feasts is that of *Jultid*, "Yule tide," an ancient heathen festival, like many others, adapted to a Christian use. The feast begins with *Jul afton*, or "Christmas Eve."[1] The house is decorated with linen cloths, adorned with Scripture texts. The floor is strewn with straw, symbolizing the straw of the manger. On the hearth a huge fire is lighted, and on the table are placed branch-candlesticks ; both of them are kept burning all the night, partly to symbolize the "Light of the world," partly to drive away malignant spirits. The most characteristic luxuries are the *Jul öl*, "yule ale," and *Jul galt*, "yule boar," a long loaf of bread, which the poverty of the people has long been obliged to substitute for the orthodox Christmas luxury. The domestic animals in the homestead—dogs, cattle, sheep, and horses—are not forgotten ; the latter especially are treated with *Jul öl*, to make them frisky when they bear their

[1] For a full and interesting account of this and other festivals, &c., see Lloyd's "Peasant Life in Sweden," ch. xi.—xix.

riders to church on Christmas morning. A sheaf of corn is even hung up for the birds, on the roof of the house. The Christmas service is performed very early in the morning, when the chancel is lighted up with a splendid display of candles, and the celebrant is attired in a white chasuble with golden orphreys. On the next day the feast is continued. There is a curious confusion between the protomartyr and the Swedish St. Staffan, the celebrated missionary of the north of Sweden. On this day is held the *Staffans Skede*, " Staffan's race." A cavalcade of village youths is accustomed early in the morning to ride helter-skelter from village to village, to commemorate the rides of St. Staffan on his missionary circuits.

The Jul feast is continued up to Epiphany (*Tre Kongers Dag*, lit. " Three Kings' Day "), or sometimes even to St. Knut's Day, January 13th. This period is enlivened with dances, music, games of all kinds, cards, burlesques, and an endless variety of amusement. Candlemas, or *Lilla Jul*, on February 2nd, is also kept as a great day of rejoicing, and is marked by feasting of all kinds.

Easter (*Påsk*) is a far less important feast than *Jul*. It is marked by great bonfires on Easter Eve, and the use of eggs in various forms.

May Day is also celebrated by bonfires. There is also on this day an interesting custom, which reminds us of the processions formerly usual in England, as elsewhere, on Rogation days. A number of children go about singing hymns for the harvest from house to house, carrying branches of birch twigs, which they present to those who put something into the little baskets they take with them. The birch twigs are believed to be productive of a good

P

harvest. The games of the season appear to have symbolical references to the return of spring.

But by far the greatest summer festival is that of Midsummer. On St. Han's Eve (June 23rd), huge bonfires are lighted, round which the peasants dance. Another universal custom is the dance round the *Maj-stång*, "May-pole." These poles, with their withered wreaths and circles, and the rows of faded birches which are planted near the homestead, are long left standing, and form quite a characteristic feature of a Swedish village. The whole ceremony is believed to be a relic of an ancient festival in honour of the sun-god, who is specially symbolized by the circles suspended on the poles. The most striking part of this festival is the abundance of decoration to be seen everywhere, both in town and village. Every house is decorated with wreaths of leaves and flowers. Even the stalls and outhouses of the farms have their bunches of green. In the towns the shops and all public buildings are splendid with verdure. The steamboats, even the little boats which ply from island to island at Stockholm, are loaded with wreaths. One of the favourite flowers used is St. John's wort, which is supposed to have special lovers' charms.

Besides these and other annual feasts, several special occasions are celebrated with great merry-making. Weddings, especially, are marked by many very curious customs, some of which it may be interesting to notice. The betrothal—which may be separated by weeks, months, or years from the wedding—usually takes place on one of the great church feasts ; it is a simple ceremony of exchanging rings, joining hands, &c. After this the exchange of presents begins. The bridegroom must send his psalm-book ; he may also send jewellery and clothes ; but he must not send a pair of shoes, for that would give his bride an opportunity of running away. The bride, in turn, sends scarves, shirts, &c., which must be worn on the wedding-day. This is generally a Sunday. The evening before, the preparatory ceremonies begin. The bride is solemnly attired, usually by the priest's wife in the house of the latter, or of some other friend near the church. In the morning the guests assemble in the house of the bridegroom's father, and after a preliminary banquet proceed in state to the house where the bride is located, whence they proceed in solemn procession to the church. In front is the bridegroom, attended by the bridesmen, or knights, whose original duty was to prevent the bride being carried off by some disappointed lover ; next the trumpeter, fiddlers, and other musicians ; behind them the attendants and friends ; and last the bride, preceded by her maids. The party is usually mounted on horseback. During the ceremony, while the happy couple are kneeling before the altar and receiving the priest's blessing, the bridesmen and bridesmaids hold over them a sort of canopy, called a *pell.* The pew where they sit is decorated with fir and evergreens.

After the service, the procession, now headed by the bridegroom and bride, return to the house of the bride's father, and the great banquet begins. To this feast it is customary for the guests to contribute each their own share. Presents to the bride are now made in money, placed under the great wedding-cake. The banquet

P 2

over, there is a ball, in which the bride and bride-groom are expected to dance with every one present. When this has continued long enough, the bride takes off her crown and gives it to one of her maids, who deems it a mark of great distinction ; or has her shoe taken off—an action originally intended as a gentle hint that it was time to retire. This is a signal for the bridesmaids to hoist the bride upon a chair over their heads, in which exalted position she drinks their health, and makes a little speech intimating a hope that they will be fortunate enough to follow her good example. Then the bridegroom is hoisted similarly by the groomsmen on a chair, or more frequently on their shoulders. After this the happy pair retire to take off their wedding-dresses, and return in their plain clothes to distribute their presents. The guests then depart, but only to continue their feast the next day. Thus it often goes on for several days. When all is over, the bride is expected to entertain separately all who have given her presents.

Funerals are marked by almost as much merry-making as weddings. Two feasts are given by the friends of the deceased ; one on the night before the funeral, much resembling in character an Irish wake ; the second begins on the night after the funeral, and sometimes lasts for several days. The most characteristic part of the service is a panegyric read by the priest in church, giving a short account of the life of the deceased. Baptism is followed by a feast known as *Barns öl,* " child's ale."

As might naturally be supposed, such occasions of mirth and jollity were apt in former times to give rise to much rioting and drunkenness. But great improvements have been effected in this respect, partly by sumptuary laws, and partly, it is hoped, by the better tone of the people themselves, and breaches of order are now of rare occurrence, and when they happen subject the offender to disgrace. Mr. Metcalfe² gives a very amusing account of a wedding in Finmark, in which they seem to have gone to the opposite extreme. The *prest* would allow neither spirits nor dancing, and pronounced them to be "ungodly." Both Swedes and Norwegians have got a bad name for drunkenness, and the bad name clings to them, as it does to the dog in the proverb, in spite of all reforms. Great efforts have been made in both countries to put down the evil. Temperance societies have existed in both countries for more than fifty years, but do not appear to have effected much. In Norway a law was passed some thirty years ago making both the manufacture and sale of spirits in country places illegal.³ Though the law can very easily be evaded in individual cases by obvious means, it has on the whole a very beneficial tendency. The people drink as a rule very mild home-brewed beer, and drunkenness is almost confined to the towns. In Sweden a permissive law has long been in force, by which a majority of householders can prevent the selling of spirits in any place. Private stills have long been illegal in both countries.

In the Swedish towns a system has been devised, generally known as the "Göteborg or Gothenburg system," from its having been first tried as an experiment in that town. It is now adopted in Stockholm and most of the larger towns as well.

---

² Oxonian in Norway, i. pp. 283, 284.   ³ Id. i. p. 172.

In Sweden the public-houses are the monopoly of
the town councils. Formerly they were accustomed
to let them to the highest bidders. According to
the Gothenburg system they are let *en masse* to a
company, who, after paying themselves an interest
of five per cent., hand over the remainder of the
profits to the council for public purposes. The
great advantage of this system is that the keepers
of the houses, who are therefore agents or servants
of the company, have no interest in the amount of
liquor sold, and are not tempted to encourage
drunkenness in their customers. There are also a
number of other regulations, one limiting the
amount of liquor sold, another requiring in certain
cases that the customer shall eat something before
he drinks, and many others. This system is however not as effective as might at first sight be
supposed. It does not in the least affect the
consumption of wine, beer, and porter, which do
not come under the liquor laws, and are sold by
almost all grocers and provision dealers. There is
nothing too to prevent a man buying bottles of
spirits and consuming them *ad libitum* at home.
It is a very common sight to see workmen in the
Swedish towns with suspicious black bottles in their
hands. Besides, the system is said to encourage
tippling. A man having drunk his quota at one
house goes off to another, and arrives at a chronic
muzzy state, without being absolutely and obviously
intoxicated. Still on the whole it has done something to check the evil, and the very existence of
such remedies is also indirectly beneficial as a
public recognition that intemperance is a disgraceful thing, and harmful to the community. Among
women, at any rate, drunkenness is very rare.

The love of gaiety is quite as characteristic of the middle and upper classes as of the lower, and shows itself as much in the more refined pleasures of the ball and opera, as in the more national, if more boisterous, forms of merriment in which the peasants delight. One trait, common to all classes alike, is the love of music. In Norway this shows itself to a large extent, but in Sweden it is universal. We do not refer so much to the great vocalists, such as Jenny Lind and Christine Nilsson, who have made a name in Europe, or even to the exquisite singers who may be heard at the operas and concerts in Stockholm and other large towns ; but to the people as a whole. Every town, however small, has its *trägården*, " the tree-garden," a place something between a park and a square, where a band is constantly playing. In Stockholm such performances continue all the afternoon up to twelve o'clock at night, and attract crowds of listeners, and that even at the " king's tree-garden," which is in the very heart of the city. To hear such music is an occupation at least quite as pleasant as standing in a crush in a dusty park to watch greatness drive sedately by. Very many even of the country villages have their bands, which are very fair ; and there is no opening for the importation of barrel-organs and German bands.

In one respect, however, the Scandinavian of to-day differs very greatly from the Scandinavian of the *wiking* times, viz. his want of energy. This shows itself both in his work and recreation. The peasant will work on steadily all day long, from early morning till late at night. He does not grumble if extra work is given him. He is cheerful and good-natured enough. But there is a want of anything like real energy.　He goes to work with a slow step : he stops to chat with every one he meets : his arms move slowly : he allows himself to be interrupted, and yet he never takes a long rest ; and the result is that in sixteen hours he only gets through as much work as an English labourer would do in twelve.　And yet for all this he is happy, contented, and extremely patient.

In the towns it is much the same.　There is to an Englishman's ideas the most astounding absence of bustle.　Even the dockyards are comparatively quiet. At the bourse there is no excitement.　The men lounge and chat as though the state of the money-market were a matter of the supremest indifference to them.　At Bergen the stillness is only broken in the fish-market, where the clamour and noise would suggest that Billingsgate itself had suddenly been transplanted to Scandinavian soil.　Even in Sweden railways do not appear to have had the disastrous tendency which is sometimes ascribed to them. So far from inspiring energy in others, the trains themselves seem oppressed with the prevailing tor-por ; and move at a pace which reminds the traveller perhaps of one or two very isolated country lines in our own country.

The recreations of the people show the same natural disposition.　The ancient *wikings* were renowned for their athletic exercises, of which they seem to have left their traces in the Scotch games of the present day.　But the Swede and Norwegian now find little or no pleasure in physical exercise.　They prefer croquet to cricket. They care little for sport.　They prefer to sit still and listen to music, sipping their cup of coffee or glass of *snaps*.　They will never walk where they can ride or be driven. Even in skating, with all their opportunities, they show neither the ardour of the English novice nor the skill of the adept. Their notion of a holiday is to be carried in a steamer among the picturesque scenery of a Swedish lake, or the grander glories of the Norwegian fjords. They fail altogether to appreciate the kind of spirit which makes a man risk life and limb for the sake of doing or having done some difficult mountain ascent. Scandinavians are nevertheless by no means wanting in enterprise. They have not, it is true, that love of travelling which makes an Englishman run off to the continent for the sake of change of air and scenery; but they are far more ready than he to leave their country for the sake of some definite object, especially the object of making their way in life. America is the goal of every poor man's ambition. More people emigrate to America from Sweden than from any other country in Europe. Last year (1880) no less than 70,000 emigrated in the first six months of the year. Those who return come back with pockets full of money, and glowing accounts of a land of freedom with high wages, and inspire others with the wish to follow their example. It might be well for them perhaps sometimes if they could ask the advice of those who do not return.

The characteristic want of energy spoken of above, is attributed by some to the poverty of the food. This may partly account for it among the peasant classes. Both in Sweden and Norway the peasants are underfed; a result due mainly to the poverty of the land, and cost of carriage, especially in the north of Sweden and the inland districts of Norway. In such places, the peasant has still to provide to a large extent both his own food and his own clothing. The evil, however, has continued to decrease with the increase of railways and of steam navigation.

The staple food of the Swede is a flat hard rye cake, of a black-brown colour. It is called *knäckebröd*, "brittle bread," and is to be found everywhere, in the very best hotels as much as in the cottage of the meanest peasant. The corresponding *fladbröd* of Norway, though derived from a common ancestor, the bark-bread of ancient days (which even yet is said to be found occasionally in some remote regions), is now thoroughly unlike the *knäckebröd* in taste and character. It is exceedingly thin and crisp, and is made of a mixture of rye, barley, and potatoes. In both countries rye bread and half-rye bread (made of a mixture of rye and barley) are common, and in Norway are gradually supplanting the *fladbröd*, which on the tables of the better-to-do people is now seldom seen. In Sweden there is an abundance of dairy produce of all kinds. In Norway milk is often very scarce, as the cattle are grazing on the fjeld through the summer months ; but this want is made up for by the great abundance of cheese of all kinds. The most peculiar kind of cheese is the *gammel ost*, which is eaten in a very black advanced state of decay, and is often, for olfactory reasons, kept under glass. Eggs are tolerably plentiful in both countries, but are also largely imported from France. Fresh meat, especially in Norway, is both poor and scarce ; but its want is supplied by smoked reindeer, which is brought down by the Lapps during the winter months. It is often so dry and hard, that it has to be chopped with a hatchet. The peasant generally has besides a good supply of bacon. Fish, even in Norway, is far scarcer in the inland districts than might be supposed. Probably this is due in many cases to the want of proper fishing appliances, and to the want of due care in preserving the rivers. Both fish and smoked meat are often eaten raw. In Sweden, raw salmon, *graf lax,*[4] is considered a great delicacy.

The dress of the upper and middle classes is much like that of all Europeans, and varies with the time. A lady of Stockholm is quite as anxious as a lady of London to be dressed in the latest fashions from Paris. One characteristic feature of modern Swedish dress is the white plush peaked cap worn almost universally by boys and young men. It looks particularly curious when combined, as is frequently the case, with the black dress of a waiter, or the coloured livery of a coachman.

Even among the peasantry the old national costumes are rapidly dying out. At the beginning of the century they existed in every Scandinavian village. Now they are only to be found, in Sweden at least, in a few distinct localities, especially in Småland and Dalarne. It is very curious to notice the difference which exists, even in villages bordering on each other. The following description may give some idea at least of the chief peculiarities of some of them. Leksand, Mora, and Rättvik are the three principal villages on the Siljan lake in Dalarne. As these, Leksand especially, represent large parishes, the peasantry may be seen on

---

[4] So called because buried for some time in the ground to give it a high flavour.

a Sunday in large crowds, all wearing their peculiar costumes, a custom about which they are as
particular as about their attendance at church.
The churchyard at Leksand, on a Sunday morning
at ten o'clock—crowded as it is with Sunday-
dressed peasants—is one of the prettiest sights
imaginable. The men wear long thick black
coats, reaching down to the knees, made of coarse
home-spun, called *vadmal* (pronounced *valmar*),
and bordered with bright red. Sometimes they
have a short jacket underneath, made of the same
material. Underneath is an ordinary waistcoat.
On their legs they wear tight sheepskin knee-
breeches of a fustian hue, and very thick woollen
stockings. Their shoes, which are very heavy and
have extremely thick soles, are tied in front with
bows ; and over them hang broad flaps of leather.
Their stiff felt hats are rather high, with narrow
brims, and are slightly rounded off at the top. The
women wear thick *vadmal* dresses, usually blue,
black, or green, with a striped apron of the same
stuff. Both are fastened round the waist with a
belt of silver ornaments. Above is a short-waisted
bodice without sleeves, narrowing into two long
pieces, which go over the shoulders and serve as
braces. In front are suspended a great variety of
neck ornaments, similar to those on the figure of
the Icelandic bride in the South Kensington
Museum. The long white sleeves of the chemise
are very full, and give quite an episcopal appearance.
On the head is worn a tight-fitting cap of white,
red, or party-coloured stuff. The shoes are exactly
like those worn by the men, except that they have
usually narrow, very forward heels, almost coming
⌐ a point, which make their wearers bend for-

ward in walking. At Rättvik, the men commonly wear *vadmal* gaiters; the women black skirts and green bodices, and the most striking high-peaked black caps, trimmed with red. At Mora, the men wear long dirty-white coats, under which is usually visible the leather apron of the week-day; the women, short white jackets with sleeves, coloured kerchiefs over their heads, and boots without heels. The dress of the children is every-where almost exactly like that of their elders, except that very young boys are dressed as girls,

NORWEGIAN WEEKDAY DRESS.

NORWEGIAN HOUSEWIFE'S SUNDAY DRESS.

and the girls usually have red or orange caps,

fitting tight to the back of the head, without a crown.

In Norway, there are almost everywhere traces left of the old national dresses, but these are nowhere so completely preserved as in the parts of Sweden above described. They are to be seen chiefly on Sundays, among the older and less fashionable folk. At Vossevangen, about the Hardanger, and in Telemark, they are perhaps most frequent. The almost universal head-dress of the women is the kerchief, usually printed but sometimes white. Sometimes the kerchief is made to project from the head by means of some stiff material. A still further development is what may be called " the Sunday butterfly bonnet." It is made of white crimped cambric, covering and bent over a butterfly-shaped piece of card, and bound over the forehead with a piece of coloured material. The accompanying illustration gives some idea of a Norwegian matron in her Sunday dress. In Nordfjord, black peaked caps are worn precisely similar to those at Rättvik. The dress of the men in Norway is usually less marked. Short black jackets, and red worsted caps with overhanging peaks, are the rule. Long coats and knee-breeches are now becoming quite exceptional. One article of apparel, found now mostly in Telemark, is very peculiar, viz. trousers with enormously high waists and short braces, which give the wearer much the effect of a boy in his father's trousers.

CHAPTER IX.

TOWNS, ETC.

FEW cities in Europe can boast of a more beautiful situation than the capital of Sweden. The present town lies on a group of islands and on the two sides of the narrow outlet of the beautiful Mälar Lake. It is quite impossible now to decide how early there may have been some settlement on these islands. The first we hear of was after the destruction of the town of Sigtuna by the Esthonians and Carelians in the twelfth century. According to an ancient saga, the inhabitants of Sigtuna, not knowing whither to turn, threw a trunk or *stock*, filled with the treasures of the city, into the water, determining to settle wherever it landed. The trunk came to shore at Agnesnäs, which was hence called *Stockholmen*, "the *stock* island." Doubtless this tradition merely arose as an explanation of the name. The town appears to have been quite insignificant till the time of Birger Jarl, who, about 1251, fortified the three principal islands—Stockholm, which was then called *Helgeandsholmen*, "the Holy Spirit island," from a hospital or "house of the Holy Spirit" erected there ; *Stadsholmen*, "the town island," where the most important buildings still stand ; and *Kedeskär*,

which, since the time of Karl XI., has been called
Riddarholmen, from the *Riddarhus* (House of
Lords), there erected. The town received municipal privileges in 1255-60. Magnus Ladulås completed the fortifications, and erected on the last-
mentioned island a Franciscan nunnery, whence it
was for a time called *Gråmunkeholmen*.

In the fifteenth century the town began to extend
on the mainland on either side, forming the districts
now known as *Norrmalm* and *Södermalm*. We
read that in the year 1484 as many as 15,000 were
cut off by a plague at one time. This was as much
as the whole population of two centuries later.
The cause of this decline was probably the terrible
part which the city played in the political struggles
of the fifteenth and sixteenth centuries. During
this period, it was the scene of some terrible
massacres, such as the *Käpplingemord*, in which the
Swedish burghers were ruthlessly murdered by the
" Hat-brothers," the German supporters of Albrecht;[1] and the terrible " Blood Bath " of the
Danish tyrant Kristian.[2]

Stockholm was celebrated for its almost im-
pregnable strength. . The way in which it was
able to defend itself against Margaret, Kristian,
and Gustaf Vasa, has been already noticed,[3] as
also the famous battle of Brunkeberg, where the
Swedes struggled so manfully for their freedom.[4]
The population increased enormously with the
great political and commercial progress of the
seventeenth century : in 1763 the town is said to
have contained as many as 73,000. After this
the population increased but slowly, until, in 1840,

[1] See above, p. 85.
[2] See above, p. 90.
[3] See pp. 85, 89, 93.
[4] See p. 89.

Q

it reached 84,000.   Since then it has again made
rapid strides, and in 1879 was as much as
173,433.

In Stockholm is the official residence of the king
and court, the seat of government and the highest
court of appeal, and the meeting place of the two
chambers.   The city is, besides, the largest commercial and trading centre of the east coast of
Sweden, especially of the trade with Russia, Finland, and North Germany.   It has no docks, the
tideless lake forming a natural harbour.   The ships
are ranged along the quays in the open water.   A
constant communication is kept up between the
islands and two sides of the lake, by means of
tiny little steamers, which run every few minutes.
There is also a connexion between the chief islands
and the land on either side by bridges.   The beauty
of the city lies in its situation rather than its buildings.   Hardly any of them display good architectural taste.   Most of them are pretentious stuccoed
erections without grace or elegance.   This is remarkably the case with the great palace (*slott*) on
Stadsholm, a perfectly symmetrical, huge, square,
flat-roofed group of buildings, round an open quadrangle, with lower wings in the same style, projecting
on each side of the north and south fronts.   Inside,
the rooms are gorgeous, gilded, magnificent ; they
are filled with the costliest furniture—including
drapery, china, and ornaments of all kinds—which
the art of the eighteenth century could produce.
In one room the whole of the furniture, even the
chairs, are edged with Dresden china.   Such
decorations are due mainly to the taste of
Gustaf III.'s time.

The most interesting building perhaps is the

Riddarholm Church. Outside, the most conspicuous element is the very graceful iron spire (102 feet in height). It was put up in 1835, when a large part of the church had been destroyed by fire. Inside the church are innumerable banners, the trophies of many a hardly-won victory, and the tombs of nearly all the kings and queens from the time of Gustaf Adolf, besides a countless number of heroes and statesmen. The church, being no longer used for service, is cleared of all furniture except the pulpit, and is a perfect picture of gloom and dismalness. It was originally attached to the nunnery erected by Magnus Ladulås, but has, by frequent fires and restorations, entirely lost its ancient character. This is also the case to a great extent with the so-called Storkyrkan, "the Great Church," which has been sadly defaced inside and out. Rarely can be seen such a profusion of gilded cherubs as those which grace the pulpit of this church, or hover among folds of drapery over the royal pew, bearing in their hands a golden crown, ready to drop on the head of the monarch. More pleasing objects are a huge altar-piece of ebony, silver, and ivory, and the seven-branched brazen candlestick, given by Magnus Smek in memory of . his murdered father.[5] Close by Riddarholm Church is the modern House of Parliament, a mean structure enough. The old Riddarhus, just across the bridge on Stadsholm, is a far more pretentious building: here the *Riddar*, or highest estate of the realm, used to meet. A large granite bridge unites Stadsholm with the northern suburb Norrmalm, meeting it in the centre of *Gustaf Adolfs torg*. Two similarly constructed buildings, ornamented

[5] See p. 75.

Q 2

with flattened Grecian columns, fill up the eastern
and western sides of the square. That on the
western side is the official residence of the crown
prince; that on the eastern side is the royal theatre,
made famous by the murder of Gustaf III.[*] One
of the most valuable institutions in Stockholm is
the royal library, which contains some very
precious MSS. and printed editions. Of the former
may be mentioned the *Codex Aureus*, a beautiful
MS. of the Gospels in the old Latin version. It is
beautifully executed on white and purple vellum,
and is said to be of Irish workmanship, belonging
probably to the sixth century. Some plain writing
on the fly-leaf in Anglo-Saxon, states that it was
bought by Earl Ælfric from the *wikings*. It was
deposited in Canterbury Cathedral, whence it found
its way to the Netherlands, and afterwards to
Sweden. Another interesting MS. is the *Practica
Johannis Ardeni de Newark, de arte physicali et de
chirurgiâ*. The writer was a celebrated physician
at the time of the plague. It contains a very large
number of quaint illustrations, describing various
medical remedies. There is also the *Homiliu bok*
(twelfth century), bound in sealskin, the oldest Icelandic MS. known, and a large number of sagas of
the thirteenth and fourteenth centuries, besides the
books of ancient city guilds of the fourteenth and
fifteenth centuries. But the greatest treasure is the
Jättebok, "Giant Book," or "Devil's Bible," the
largest MS. in the world. It is as much as three
feet by two in size, and comprises 150 sheets.
It contains the Vulgate, and some short extracts
from the Fathers. It was brought over from Prague,
when the city was taken in the Thirty Years' War.

[*] See p. 109.

According to tradition it was written by a condemned monk, who was to receive pardon if he
could in one night cover with writing 150 asses'
skins. He is said to have finished his task by the
help of the devil, whose huge ungainly portrait he
has left on the fly-leaf.

There are three interesting museums at Stockholm. The State's Museum has a good collection
of Italian and other masters, besides a large variety
of mediæval armour and clothes. The ecclesio-
logical department has been already noticed.[7] The
Natural History Museum has a large general collection of animals and birds, besides fossils,
minerals, &c. The most interesting to a foreigner
is the Ethnological Museum, which has, in addition
to many other interesting objects, several model
cottages with life-size figures, showing the various
costumes of different parts of the country as they
existed at the beginning of this century.

Göteborg (Gothenburg), in point of population the
second largest town in the country, may be regarded
as the capital of western Sweden. It at present
numbers 76,761. The town lies along the southern
bank of the Göta River, near the mouth. It is
divided throughout by canals, which, together with
the ancient dyke (Vallgraf), have a very striking
effect, and enthusiasts have even called the town
" The Venice of the North." Two interesting old
forts still remain, called respectively Kronan, " the
Crown," and Lejonet, " the Lion," though useless
of course for modern warfare. Old Göteborg was
founded by Karl IX., in 1607, opposite the ancient
town of Elfsborg (a few miles further up the river),
which still gives its name to the *län*. The present

[7] See pp. 143, 180.

town was founded in 1619 by Gustaf Adolf. It
has always been famous for its commerce. In old
days it was the great centre for the herring fishery
in the Skager Rak, but in later times this has
greatly declined. The town has played an important part in the Danish wars. In 1719 especially
it was bravely defended by Lillie against the Danish
admiral " Tordenskjold." There is little of interest
in its public buildings. The German church, with
its copper roof, is rather a fine specimen of the
seventeenth-century architecture. There is a very
fair museum, with a picture gallery containing a
good collection of Swedish pictures. In the
natural history department there is an enormous
whale, caught off the Bohuslän coast.

The town has some fine Horticultural Gardens,
into which the Goteborg folk turn out by
hundreds, to listen to the band, and drink their
snaps or coffee. Here there are some large glass
houses containing one of the finest collections of
orchids in the world. Hardly less pleasing are the
gneiss hillocks which everywhere surround the town,
on which children and others who cannot afford to
visit the Horticultural Gardens love to clamber,
drinking in the bracing air, and gathering the wild
flowers which abound in the richest variety. But
to strangers the greatest interest in the town is its
harbour. Its busy quays with the crowd of
steamers, ranged with their bows shorewards,
present a pleasing picture of life and activity. We
have already made some remarks on the " Gothenburg system."

Gefle, which lies on the Baltic coast, some
100 miles north of Stockholm, is the chief
exporting centre for the timber and iron of

Dalarne and Gestrikland. It has had a very chequered existence. Though frequently laid waste by fire, it has recovered itself with marvellous rapidity. As late as 1869 the greater part was burnt down, and yet it is now as thriving and prosperous as ever. The present town is essentially modern—rows of plastered houses, all the same height, all perfectly straight, with little or nothing to relieve the eye—a picture of dulness and monotony.

Malmö is an ancient town. In the fourteenth century it was, as a fortress and fishing town, one of the most prosperous in the then Danish dominions, but afterwards declined as Copenhagen rose in importance. The harbour was not made till the close of the last century, since which time the town has rapidly gained in size and prosperity, and is now one of the leading export towns of Sweden.

Upsala, the chief university town in Sweden, is situated in Upland, about midway between Stockholm and Gefle. The old town, which lay about three miles to the north-west, is one of the most ancient in the country. In pagan times, it was the seat of the Swedish kings, and the centre of pagan worship. Rising out of the wide plain of Fyrisvall, in front of the quaint little thirteenth-century church, are the barrows known as the " king's hows " (*kungshögar*), supposed to contain the bones of Thor, Woden, and Freya, but, in reality, burying-places of about the fifth century A.D. On one of these the ancient custom of drinking mead out of a silver horn in honour of Thor was lately revived by Karl XIV. A few miles south are the ancient *mora* stones at which the king was elected in the middle ages.

New Upsala rose up in the thirteenth century, on the site of the royal harbour of Östra Åros.[8] The archbishop's seat was changed to the new town by a papal bull in 1276, at which time the foundations of the cathedral had already been laid. The greater part of the building, however, belongs to the fifteenth century.[9] In the chapel beyond the choir is the tomb of Gustaf Vasa. The walls are painted with pictures describing his early adventures and the chief scenes of his life. There are also the tombs of Laurentius Petri and Linnæus,[1] and many other eminent persons. The building is full of interesting relics. Near the altar is preserved the silver shrine of St. Erik, which was laid on the altar when the kings were crowned in the cathedral. There is also a beautiful collection of old church plate, vestments, and crosses. Trinity Church is still more ancient, but has not been used for service for more than 200 years. Among the university institutions the most interesting are the Botanical Gardens and the Library *Carolina Rediviva*. The great treasure of the latter is the *Codex Argenteus*, the well-known fifth-century MS. of Ulphilas' Moeso-Gothic Gospels, bought by Magnus de la Gardie, the Chancellor of the University, and presented to the library in 1669. The MS. is written on purple vellum in gold and silver letters, and bound in massive silver (whence its name).

The most striking feature at Lund (in Skåne), is undoubtedly its Romanesque cathedral. Though the historical interest of the building has been to a large extent destroyed by the late complete restoration to the Romanesque style, it is certainly

---

[8] So called to distinguish it from Vesteråros (Vesterås).
[9] See p. 139.   [1] See p. 124.

one of the finest buildings in Sweden. Its beautiful crypt, with the interesting contents, has already been described.[2] Attached to the library of the university, which contains some very rare and early editions of the classics, is a small museum with a very interesting collection of northern antiquities.

Besides its cathedral,[3] Linköping (in Östergötland) has a very good diocesan library, with several valuable MSS. and an interesting collection of rare rune-calendars, cups, and other curiosities.

Karlskrona, the great naval station of Sweden, was built by Karl XI. on a group of islands on the south coast. The natural harbour formed between them is said to be one of the best in the world.

The limits of this book. prevent anything like a description of the many towns, castles, &c., throughout the country, to which events in Swedish history have given an historical interest. We must content ourselves with mentioning one or two. At the castle (*slott*) at Vadstena, on the Vetter Lake, the window is still shown from which Duke Magnus, the mad son of Gustaf Vasa, threw himself down, at the invitation of a freshwater mermaid, into the moat below ; the staircase up which Karl XII. rode, fully equipped, on a charger as fiery as himself ; and the room where Erik was cruelly confined by his brother Johan.[4] Here also are remains of the monastery founded by the favourite saint, Birgitta (Britta), where queens and princesses sought rest from the anxieties and dangers of political life.

At the castle of Kalmar, opposite Öland, were

[2] See pp. 135, 136.   [3] See p. 137.   [4] See p. 97.

drawn up the articles of the Kalmar Union ;[5] but
the inside has been so much altered from time to
time, that its interest is much lost. Opposite, at
Borgholm, on the island, is a beautiful old castle,
the finest ruin in the country.

But perhaps the most interesting place from an
historical point of view is Visby, on Gotland. Both
the island and town have a history of their own.
Originally a little independent commercial community, but afterwards forced to throw itself
for protection on Sweden ; at one time a leading member of the Hanseatic League, at another
the prey of pirate chieftains such as Ivar Axelsson
Thott, or Danish governors such as Severin Norrby,
who bled the town and country without scruple ;
it did not form part of the Swedish kingdom till
the middle of the seventeenth century. Its ancient
walls, with the thirty-seven towers still standing,
and the twelve churches, all but one in ruins,
point to its former wealth and importance—a
strange contrast to its present shrunken condition.[6]
An infinitely greater number of coins—Roman,
Anglo-Saxon, Cufish, &c.—have been found on the
island than in any other district of Sweden. Some
remarks have already been made on the architectural features of its buildings.[7]

The busy manufacturing town of Norrköping,
"the Swedish Manchester," as it has been sometimes called, and the mining towns of Falun, Sala,
&c., have been already described.[8]

The rest of the Swedish towns are chiefly small

[5] See p. 86.
[6] The total population is now about 7000, whereas in the thirteenth
century the freemen alone numbered 12,000.
[7] Pp. 135, 138, 139.   [8] Pp. 158-160.

ports, having a local trade along the coast or on the margins of the larger lakes.

The capital of Norway lies at the extremity of the eastern bight of the pretty Kristiania Fjord. In front on a projecting point is the ancient fortress of Akershus, dating at least from the beginning of the fourteenth century, which offered a brave and successful resistance to the attacks of Karl XII. in 1716. Behind, on an elevated summit, rises the stuccoed royal palace, the most conspicuous build-ing in the town. Behind it lie its well-kept public gardens, and from it in front runs down the Karl Johans Gade, a street in which the Storthing House and University buildings are situated. Among the latter there are several museums. The archæo-logical department contains an interesting collection of northern antiquities, especially weapons and implements from the *wiking* age. Among other objects there is a very fine *wiking* ship (the largest known), discovered last year (1880), in a barrow near Tönsberg, on the western side of the Kristiania Fjord, where it had been buried with its owner, probably some pirate chieftain, over a thousand years ago. There are also several speci-mens of carved door posts, &c., taken from the ancient wooden churches. The picture gallery contains a valuable collection of pictures of Gude, Tidemand, and other celebrated Norwegian artists.

Far to the north is the picturesque height of St. Hans Haugen, now laid out in walks, from which there is a glorious view of the fjord ; and near by is the Aker River, which runs through the town, forming some very pretty falls. On the way to St. Hans Haugen is the beautiful cemetery, full of white crosses, with graves exquisitely planted with roses and other flowers. The churches are mostly modern and have little interest, if we except the altar-piece in Trinity Church, describing our Lord's baptism, by Tidemand.* Round the town are beautiful patches of rock and pine-woods, which are being rapidly encroached upon by the stately villas of the prosperous inhabitants. Only one or two of the ancient picturesque little wooden cottages still remain in the outskirts.

The foundations of the town were laid in 1624, by Kristian IV. of Denmark, close by the ancient town of Oslo, which had lately been destroyed by fire ; but it was not till the disunion from Denmark (in 1814), that it began to have any importance. At the beginning of the century it only numbered 10,000 inhabitants. The whole population, including that of the suburbs, is now 95,836. It is by far the largest town in Norway, and the chief place of exportation for the timber and iron trades.

Bergen is the great place of export for the fish trade of the country. It is beautifully situated along the sides of a narrow bight (Vågen), and a small lake beyond between two pretty mountain ridges. Thus it is not accessible, except by water, from any considerable distance. The town itself consists mainly of one long, narrow street, intersected by narrow alleys leading down to the quays, and interrupted at intervals by open market-places. Of these the fish-market presents a very busy scene in the early morning of market-days (Wednesdays and Saturdays), when men and women are seen wrangling over the price of the

* See p. 145.

fish with which the boats are often crammed. The long rows of quays, and the red-tiled wooden houses with their pointed gables, are singularly picturesque; the latter are remarkably unlike those of Kristiania or the Swedish towns.

Bergen was for a long time, during the middle ages, the most important town of Norway. It was one of the chief points of conflict in the civil wars of the twelfth century. Here many a bloody battle was fought between the *Birkibeinar* and the *Baglar*.[1] In the days of Håkon IV. it reached its highest prosperity. Part of the hall of this king, and the tower built by him known as Walkendorffs[2] Tårn, are still to be seen on the western side of Vågen, where the ancient city was situated. In those days there were as many as thirty churches and religious houses in or about the town; but these have been almost all destroyed, and the three ancient churches that remain have been so frequently restored as to have lost most of their original character. Afterwards, by a treaty with the Hanse towns, the commerce of Bergen passed into the hands of Germans, who took forcible possession of the ancient part of the town, part of which is still called, after them, "The German quay" (*Den Tyske bryggen*), and exercised a monopoly over the Nordland fish trade. They were not expelled till 1599 by a certain Kristopher Walkendorff, and the monopoly thus passed into the hands of the native Bergen merchants. But the town has never entirely lost its German character, and till lately the service at St. Mary's Church has continued to be held in that language.

Of modern buildings the most interesting is the

---

[1] See pp. 81, 82.   [2] See below.

Museum, which has a splendid collection of northern sea-birds.

Trondhjem, which has a population of 22,544, is built almost entirely on a narrow-necked promontory, formed by a remarkable bend on the river Nid just before it enters Trondhjem Fjord. In ancient times the city was called Nidaros, while the word *Thrándheim* was applied in the sagas to the whole district round the fjord. The town is closely connected with the religious and political history of Norway. Till the liberation (1814) it continued to be the capital of the country. Here most of the early kings were crowned and held their courts. As an archbishopric it exercised spiritual jurisdiction over the whole of Norway and Iceland, as well as the Hebrides, Orkneys, and part of Scotland. Its religious influence first arose from its being the burying-place of Olaf the Saint. His body was, it is said, first moved from its original grave to a little church dedicated by Olaf Tryggvason to St. Clement, in the end of the tenth century, but afterwards placed in a magnificent shrine under the high altar in Christ Church, which was completed about 1093, on the spot, it is said, where St. Olaf was first buried. But it was not till 1151, when Trondhjem was made an archbishopric, that the cathedral rose to grand proportions. From this date additions were constantly made until about the year 1300, the expenses being provided out of the rich offerings made by pilgrims to the shrine.[3] The chapter consisted of twenty-four canons, each of which sang mass at a distant altar within the building. At the time of the Reformation, St. Olaf's shrine itself was sent off to Copenhagen; the relics of the saint, after

[3] For a sketch of the architecture, see pp. 140, 141.

various vicissitudes, were lost. In accordance with the Norwegian Constitution of 1814, the modern kings have always been crowned in the cathedral.

Opposite the town is the little island of Munkholm, where there was once a Benedictine monastery, which was destroyed at the Reformation. The foundations were turned into a fort in the Swedish war of 1658, and this was afterwards used as a prison.

Stavanger is a seaport town on the south-west, near the entrance of the Bukke Fjord. Its chief interest is its fine old cathedral, which has been already described.[4] Its population is 20,288.

In the south, the population of Norway is distributed among several small seaports, of which the largest, Drammen, with a population of 18,851, like Kristiania, exports an enormous quantity of timber. The only other town of any considerable size is Kristiansand, with a population of 12,191, which lies in the prettiest of bays, by the side of a pine-clad hill on the south coast. The more northerly towns subsist mainly upon the local fisheries. The largest of these are Alesund and Kristiansund, which have a population of 5000 and 7000 respectively, and are built on islands on the coast between Trondhjem and Bergen.

North of Trondhjem there are only two towns. The first, Tromsö, with a population of over 5000, lies on a low island not far north of Senjen Island ; the second, Hammerfest, with a population of about 2200, is situated about eighty miles south of the North Cape, on the island of Kval. Both towns are maintained by the Finmark fisheries, and ex-

4 See p. 141.

peditions are made from them periodically to
the Arctic Sea for the purpose of hunting seals,
walruses, &c. They have both grown up almost
entirely during the present century.

The only inland town of Norway is Rörås, on
the mountain south-east of Trondhjem. It owes
its existence to the copper-mines in the neighbourhood.

CHAPTER X.

LAPPS AND FINNS.

WE have in this chapter to speak chiefly of a people very different from the highly civilized Teutonic races, which inhabit the greater part of Scandinavia. In the mountains of the north of Scandinavia and Finland, i.e. in the region usually known as Lapland, have long dwelt a race now called Lapps. This people were in ancient times called Finns, and do not appear to have been clearly distinguished from the Finns proper who inhabited Finland, Carelia, and Esthonia. The so-called Finns of Lapland are spoken of by ancient writers as consisting of two classes, the *Skridfinnar*, " Skate Finns," who inhabited the mountains, and distinguished themselves by their snow skating ; and the *Sjöfinnar*, "Sea Finns," who lived on the seashore and subsisted by fishing. The word *Lapp* is first found in the great Danish historian Saxo Grammaticus, who lived in the twelfth century. The use of *Lappefinner* as by Peter Clausson,[1] to distinguish the *Skridfinnar*, or, as he calls them, *Fjeldfinner*, from the *Sjöfinnar*, shows that it must have been originally used as an appellative. Its origin is exceedingly doubtful. Perhaps the most probable conjecture is that which derives it from a

---

[1] Norrigis Bescrifvelse (Copenhagen, 1632), ch. **xxvii.**

R

Finnish word meaning exile.[2]   There are not sufficient data for deciding the origin of this people.
That they came over from Finland is probable,
both from their early traditions which describe
them as a colony from that country, and the close
philological relationship between the various Lapponic and Finnish dialects.   But this is far from
proving an identity of race.   On the other hand,
the great dissimilarity of their moral and physical
character, of their customs and habits of life, and
of their early religion, almost certainly proves
them to belong to a widely different family of the
human race.   It is very probable that as a conquered people they adopted the language of their
more civilized conquerors the Finns, while still in
Finland, and that the language was prevented
from declining by the constant intercourse between
the two races.   It has been noticed that while the
majority of words are almost exactly alike in the
two dialects as they at present exist, the Lapps
have yet retained several words, and those of the
commonest objects of daily life,[3] which are of a
distinctly different origin.   These are probably
relics of their original language.   The modern
Lapponic language has also, especially in the more
southern dialects, incorporated a large number of
Swedish words.

The time in which the Lapps first came into
Scandinavia is not known; but if the word *Cre-
fennæ*, mentioned by Jornandes in his History of
the Goths,[4] as the name of an early Scandinavian

[2] Vide Scheffer's "History of Lapland," ch. i. p. 3.
[3] E.g. Sun, sky, bear, wolf, fox, &c.   See Dillon's "Winter in
Iceland and Lapland," vol. ii. p. 218.
[4] Ch. iii.

tribe who lived not by agriculture, but by the chase, be a corruption of *Skridfinnar*, they must have come over to the country at least as early as the sixth century A.D.[5] It may be noticed that Jornandes also mentions the "*Finni* mitissimi Scanziæ cultoribus omnibus mitiores," as well as the *Finnaithæ*, as distinct tribes. The Lapps are to the present day called *Finns* by the Norwegians; and the most northerly *amt* is named, after them, Finmark, whereas the Finns themselves are often called by them Kvener.[6]

Of the history of this people we know but little. Some attempts seem to have been made in the fourteenth century to convert the Lapps to Christianity by Magnus Ladulås, in the rough and ready mode of conversion then in vogue; but these appear to have met with little success. Gustaf Vasa set about the work in real earnest, sending missionaries together with the tax-collectors, to instruct the people and baptize them when they assembled to pay their taxes. But it was not till 1600 that the first church was built by order of Karl IX. Gustaf Adolf and Kristina did a great deal towards the culture of the race by building and endowing churches and schools. By the order of the former the Scriptures and other religious books were first translated into Lapponic, and native Lapps were trained as missionary priests. Scheffer, in his " History of Lapland,"[7] published

---

[5] Tacitus, in his Germania, describes the Fenni: but these may have been the Finns of Finland, so that the passage proves nothing as to the date of the immigration of the Lapps.

[6] There is precisely the same distinction between the Finnas and Cwenas in Othere's account of Scandinavia preserved in the beginning of Alfred's History of Orosius.

[7] Ch. viii.

not long after this, gives in full the *testamur* of certain persons asked to be present at a *vivâ voce* examination, at one of these schools. As rendered in the English translation it begins as follows. "We, . . . do certifie, that they altogether sang exactly the Psalms of David translated into Swedish, as they are used in the Swedish churches long ago. Next all and every one in particular did recite the Primer,[8] containing not only the elements of speech, but also the Lord's Prayer, the Apostles' Creed, the Ten Commandments, together with the words of Institution of the Sacraments of Baptism and the Lord's Supper; as also graces before and after meat, with morning and evening prayers, &c, &c." But the Lapps in the more remote districts still continued for a long time many of their old religious beliefs and forms of worship. Their chief gods were two: one—identified by Scheffer with the Scandinavian Thor, and also called *Ajeka*—was represented by an inverted birch stump; the larger end from which the roots grow was supposed to resemble the head of the god. This rude image was usually placed on a table decorated with reindeer horns. The stump had a hammer attached to it, and nails and flint driven into the head, so that the god might strike a light when he pleased. Ajeka was the god of men and the source of life. *Storjunkare,* or *Stora Passa*—the god of animals, especially those of the chase, and of fishes—was worshipped under the symbol of a stone, when possible so shaped·as to resemble a man's head. Round it were placed smaller stones, to represent the god's family. Both

---

[8] This Primer had been translated into Lapponic by Nicolas Andreæ, pastor of Piteå.

gods had their sanctuaries in the open air : these were usually enclosed by a hedge of birch boughs or reindeer horns. The images were sprinkled with the blood of sacrificed reindeer. Besides these gods they offered sacrifices to the sun (*Baive*) and the spirits of the departed, and were accustomed to propitiate the numerous good and evil spirits which were supposed to haunt the mountains and rivers. But perhaps the most curious feature of the religion was their use of magic drums. These were constructed out of hollowed birch trunks, and were generally of an oval shape. One end was covered with parchment, on which were painted, with the juice of alder bark, symbolical figures of their gods, with the sun, moon, and stars, various birds and beasts, and several other more or less unintelligible hieroglyphics. On the top of these the magician placed a bunch of brass rings, and he then struck the drum all round with a forked reindeer-bone hammer. The oracle was determined by the position which the rings, when thus shaken, assumed with reference to the hieroglyphics. Scheffer [9] describes among many others a drum on which Christ and His apostles are represented in lower rank than Ajeka and Stora Passa, showing the gradual transition between the old and new faiths. Other drums represented entirely Christian symbols, showing that the use of magic long survived the introduction of Christianity. Several specimens of magic drums, with the rings and hammers, are preserved in the Ethnological Museum at Stockholm.

Notwithstanding the education they receive, the Lapps of the present day retain to a great extent

[9] "History of Lapland," ch. xi.

the habits of their ancestors. They are still mainly divided into two classes, the Fjeld-Lapps and Sea-Lapps. The latter, which very largely preponderate in numbers,[1] live on the shores of Finmark, and gain their livelihood by fishing. They are not very unlike in habit to the Norwegian fishermen, and frequently intermarry with them. In the year 1875 there were over 1762 of these half-castes. Their children are reckoned as pure Norwegians in the census, so that the Lapps are gradually being absorbed in the Scandinavian population.

The Fjeld-Lapps, on the other hand, live a distinct nomadic life, and rarely marry outside themselves. They wander about with their reindeer on the mountains in the winter months, wherever reindeer-moss is most abundant. In summer they descend to the cooler parts near the coast. They live together in encampments of turf-huts, called *gamme*. Their dress consists chiefly of a reindeer-skin tunic fastened by a belt over a sheep-skin shirt. Their shoes and breeches are also of reindeer-skin. In the coldest weather they often wear in addition tippets of bear-skin over their shoulders. Their food consists chiefly of milk, cheese, and the flesh of the reindeer. The cows are used for milk, the males for drawing their sledges; and when either have grown too old to be serviceable, their ungrateful masters kill them, and either eat them themselves, or salt them down for the winter market. The shape of their ordinary sledge has often been compared to that of a canoe, cut abruptly off behind the back. The reindeer is a stupid animal, and takes long to

[1] See below, p. 248.

train ; but when trained it is both patient and
enduring. An animal in the prime of life will
travel over sixty miles a day ; but this is not ex-
ceeded without risk. The reindeer has wonderful
powers of procuring itself food in winter. By its
acute sense of smell it can scent the moss under
the snow, which it scrapes away with its feet till it
has found the desired delicacy. Sometimes, when
the snow melts and afterwards freezes into a hard
crust, they are unable to get at the moss, and die
in great numbers. The greatest plague which the
animal suffers from is a species of gadfly, called by
Linnæus *oestrus tarandi*,[2] which in the hot summer
months flies over the animal and drops a small
egg : this easily finds its way in the soft skin, and
grows till the following summer, when the larva
is hatched. The insect causes the greatest irritation, which drives the poor creature nearly wild,
until it has made its way out of the skin. The
only relief which the animal can get is by plunging
itself into some lake. The reindeer's greatest enemy
is the wolf, which destroys great numbers of them
in the winter months.

The Lapps are easily distinguished by their small
stature, round heads, and prominent cheek-bones.
They were once much addicted to drunkenness ;
but great good has been lately effected in this
respect by the efforts of the Swedish missionaries.
In point of intelligence the Lapps do not stand
high ; but, like many uncivilized nations, show
great skill in manual labour. What cleverness they
otherwise possess is too often exercised in trying
to outwit their neighbours. Though kind and
hospitable, they are yet mean and treacherous.

[2] Lach. Lapp, vol. i. pp. 280, 293 ; vol. ii. pp. 2, 23.

They are passionately fond of money, which they
will often bury for the sake of security. It is
said that large sums have been lost in this way.
They are the most arrant cowards, and will move
from place to place to avoid the wolves, which they
make no attempt to destroy or drive away. In
their habits they are notorious for want of cleanli-
ness. In Norway the Lapps are treated like other
subjects, and have to provide reindeer and sledges
for posting, at a fixed tariff, just as their southern
neighbours provide horses and carriages.

Only in one instance have the Fjeld-Lapps departed from the traditions of their ancestors. Kau-
tokeino, a small village near the sources of the
Alten River, forms their single fixed settlement. Its
inhabitants depend chiefly on making provisions for
travelling, and the carriage of goods across the
northern fjeld.

The Finns are in every respect superior to the
Lapps. They are considerably taller, and more
strongly built. As workers they are hardy and
industrious. The men employed in working the
Kåfjord copper-mines are almost entirely Finns.[3] A
very large number of them hold farms in Swedish
Lapland and Norrland. They very frequently
marry into Swedish and Norwegian families.

The number of Finns in Sweden in the year 1870
was 14,932 ; of Lapps, 6711. In Norway, in 1875,
the number of Finns was 7594 ; of Lapps, 15,718, of
which only 1073 were nomads. In the same year
the number of tame reindeer in Finmark alone was
estimated at 65,290.

[3] See above, p. 159.

APPENDIX A.

THE italics are used for flowers found only or almost entirely in Lapland. An obelus (†) is placed before the names of flowers which are confined to the southern provinces, including Gotland and Oland. An asterisk (*) signifies that the flower is not indigenous in the British Isles.

Flowering Plants.

Ranunculus *glacialis.
,,   Lingua.
,,   Lenormandi.
,,   lapponicus.
,,   *altaicus*, &c.
Trollius europæus.
Anemone Pulsatilla.
,,   nemorosa.
,,   *Hepatica.
Aquilegia vulgaris.
Aconitum *lycoctonum.
Delphinium Consolida.
Berberis vulgaris.
Nymphæa alba.
Nuphar luteum.
Viola palustris, &c.
Dianthus deltoides.
Silene acaulis, &c.
Lychnis alpina.
,,   *apetala*.
Hypericum montanum, &c.
Geranium sanguineum.
,,   sylvaticum, &c.
Impatiens Noli-me-tangere.
Melilotus alba, &c.

Anthyllis Vulneraria.
Astragalus glycyphyllos.
,,   alpinus, &c.
Vicia †*cassubica (Lund).
Lathyrus macrorhizus.
†*Coronilla Emerus (Gotland).
Spiræa Filipendula.
Rubus Chamæmorus.
,,   saxatilis.
,,   Idæus.
,,   suberectus.
,,   *arcticus*, &c.
Geum rivale.
Potentilla argentea.
,,   fruticosa, &c.
Sibaldia procumbeus.
Alchemilla alpina, &c.
Rosa *alpina*.
Pyrus Malus.
,,   Aucuparia.
Saxifraga stellaris.
,,   rivularis.
,,   aizoides.
,,   *aizoon.
,,   nivalis.

Saxifraga tridactylites, &c.
Parnassia palustris.
Ribes alpinum.
Sedum Telephium.
  ,,   album, &c.
Drossera rotundifolia, &c.
Epilobium angustifolium.
   ,,   alpinum, &c.
Circæa alpina, &c.
Lythrum Salicaria.
Carum *Carui.
Angelica sylvestris.
Cornus suecica.
Viburnum Opulus.
Sambucus nigra.
Lonicera *Xylosteum.
   ,, †Peryclymenum (Lund).
Linnæa borealis.
Galium boreale, &c.
Asperula odorata.
Valeriana officinalis, &c.
Scabiosa succisa.
   ,,   Columbaria.
Centaurea Cyanus, &c.
Serratula tinctoria.
Carduus crispus.
   ,,   acaulis.
   ,,   heterophyllus, &c.
†Onorpordon Acanthium.
Aster Tripolium.
Erigeron acris.
Solidago Virgaurea.
Inula Conyza.
Bidens tripartita.
*Arnica montana.
†*Anthemis tinctoria (Gotland).
Achillea Ptarmica.
Chrysanthemum Leucanthemum.
Tanacetum vulgare.
Artemisia campestris, &c.
Antennaria dioica.
   ,,   var. hyperborea.
Senecio viscosus.
   ,,   sylvaticus, &c.
Cichorium Intybus.
Tragopogon pratensis.
Lactuca muralis.

Mulgedium alpinum.
   ,,   *sibiricum (Ånger-
         manland).
Hieracium umbellatum.
   ,,   Pilosella, &c.
Campanula rotundifolia.
   ,,   patula.
   ,,   *cervicaria(Dalarne).
   ,,   †latifolia, &c.
Jasione montana.
Vaccinium Myrtillus.
   ,,   uliginosum.
   ,,   Vitis-Idæa.
Oxycoccos palustris.
Erica Tetralix.
   ,, cinerea.
Andromeda *hypnoides.
   ,,   polifolia.
   ,,   *tetragona.
Calluna vulgaris.
Phyllodoce (Menziesia) cæru-
lea.
Pyrola uniflora.
   ,, minor.
   ,, secunda, &c.
*Ledum palustre.
Ligustrum vulgare.
Gentiana campestris.
   ,,   tenella.
   ,,   nivalis.
   ,,   *purpurea.
Menyanthes trifoliata.
Echium vulgare.
Anchusa officinalis.
Myosotis palustris, &c.
Hyoscyamus niger.
Solanum Dulcamara.
   ,,   nigrum.
Verbascum Thapsus.
   ,,   Blattaria.
   ,,   subsp. virgatum.
Scrophularia aquatica.
Digitalis purpurea.
Veronica spicata.
   ,,   montana.
   ,,   alpina.
   ,,   saxatilis.

Veronica officinalis.
,, Chamædrys.
,, scutellata, &c.
Dartsia alpina, &c.
Euphrasia officinalis.
Rhinanthus Crista-Galli, &c.
Pedicularis palustris.
,, sylvatica.
,, *SceptrumCarolinum.
Melampyrum pratense.
,, var : montanum.
,, sylvaticum.
,, cristatum.
,, arvense.
Orobanche major, &c.
Lathræa squamaria.
Lycopus europæus.
Calamintha Acinos.
Nepeta Cataria.
†Prunella grandiflora (Gotland).
Galeopsis Tetrahit, &c.
Ajuga pyramidalis.
Pinguicula vulgaris.
Utricularia vulgaris.
Primula veris.
,, farinosa.
,, *sibirica.
Lysimachia vulgaris, &c.
Glaux maritima.
Armeria vulgaris.
,, *sibirica.
Daphne Mezereum.
Salix herbacea, &c.
Myrica Gale.
Orchis militaris.
,, mascula.
,, Morio.

Orchis maculata.
,, pyramidalis.
,, fustulata (Gotland).
,, *sambucina.
,, *hyperborea.
Gymnadenia Conopsea.
Neottia Nidus-avis.
Cypripedium Calceolus.
Habenaria bifolia.
Ophrys muscifera.
†Cephalanthera grandiflora
(Gotland).
,, ensifolia.
,, rubra.
Listera ovata.
,, cordata.
Malaxis paludosa.
Liparis (Malaxis) Loeselii.
Corallorhiza innata.
Iris Pseud-acorus.
Alisma Plantago.
Sagittaria sagittifolia.
Butomus umbellatus.
Paris quadrifolia.
Convallaria majalis.
Polygonatum multiflorum.
,, verticillatum.
Smilicina(Maianthemum)bifolia.
Anthericum †*Liliago (Skåne).
,, †*ramosum (Gotland).
Allium vineale.
,, †Schœnoprasum (Got-
land and Oland).
Acorus Calamus.
*Calla palustris.
Scirpus sylvaticus.

Ferns.

Pteris aquilina.
Cryptogramme crispa.
Asplenium Ruta-muraria.
,, germanicum.
,, septentrionale.
,, Trichomanes.

Asplenium viride.
,, Adiantum-nigrum.
Athyrium Filix-fœmina.
Scolopendrium vulgare.
Woodsia hyperborea.
,, ilvensis.

Cystopteris fragilis (several varieties), &c.
Aspidium Lonchitis.
Nephrodium Filix-mas.
,, spinulosum.
,, cristatum.
,, dilatatum.
,, Thelypteris.
,, Oreopteris.

Polypodium vulgare.
,, Phegopteris.
,, Dryopteris.
†Osmunda regalis.
Ophioglossum vulgatum.
,, var. ambiguum.
Botrychium Lunaria.
,, var. rutaceum.

The above list is a selection of the most interesting plants, and such as seemed best to illustrate the flora of the country. For the fullest information the reader should consult C. T. Hartman's Handbok. The names of all the British plants in this Appendix are according to Hooker's Student's Flora.

APPENDIX B.

TABLE OF THE CHIEF TEUTONIC LANGUAGES AND DIALECTS.[1]

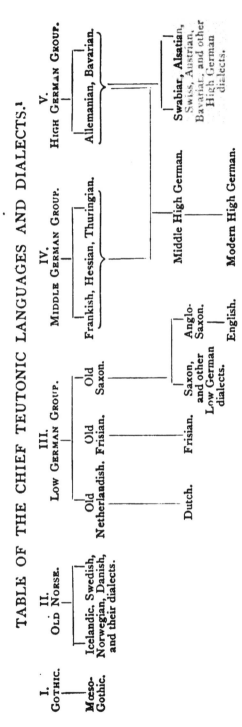

	II. OLD NORSE.	III. LOW GERMAN GROUP.			IV. MIDDLE GERMAN GROUP.	V. HIGH GERMAN GROUP.

I. GOTHIC.

Mœso-Gothic.

Icelandic, Swedish, Norwegian, Danish, and their dialects.

Old Netherlandish. Old Frisian. Old Saxon.

Dutch. Frisian. Saxon, and other Low German dialects. Anglo-Saxon.

English.

Frankish, Hessian, Thuringian.

Middle High German.

Modern High German.

Allemanian, Bavarian.

Swabian, Alsatian, Swiss, Austrian, Bavarian, and other High German dialects.

TABLE OF FINNO-TARTARIC OR URALO-ALTAIC LANGUAGES.[2]

Samoyedic. Finnish. Turkish (Tartaric). Ugric. Mongolian. Tungusian.

Lapponic. Esthonian. Magyaric. West-Finnish.

[1] Taken principally from Siever's articles on German and Gothic languages in the new "Encyclopædia Britannica" (ninth edition).
[2] Taken principally from Hovelacque on the Science of Language.

APPENDIX C.

COINAGE.

1 *krona* = 1s. 1½*d*.
100 *ore* = 1 *krona*.

The chief coins are :—

Of gold, 20 *kronor* ; .10 *kr.*
Of silver, 4 *kr.* ; 2 *kr.* ; 1 *kr.*; *half krona* (50 *öre*) ; *quarter kr.* (25 *öre*) ; 10 *ore.*
Of copper, 5 *öre* ; 2 *öre* ; 1 *öre.*

Other coins, chiefly those belonging to the old Danish and Norwegian currencies, are still used, but are being rapidly called in.

Notes are issued by different banks, of the value of 1000, 500, 100, 50, 10, and 5 *kronor.*

WEIGHTS AND MEASURES ORDINARILY IN USE.

Weights.

1 *skålpund* (scale-pound) = ·937 of 1lb. avoirdupois.
100 *skålp* = 1 *centner.*

In Sweden the *skålpund* is divided into 100 *ort* ; in Norway into 32 *lod.*

Several local systems still exist in Norway, but they are gradually giving way to that here given.

Measures.

In Sweden :—

10 *linier* (lines) = 1 *tum* (thumb).
10 *tum* = 1 *fot* (foot) = ·974 English feet.
10 *fot* = 1 *stång* (pole).
10 *stänger* = 1 *ref.*
360 *ref* = 1 *mil* (mile) = 6·642 English miles.

In Norway :—

10 *tum* = 1 *fot* = 1·029 English feet.
2 *fot* = 1 *alen* (ell).
18,000 *alen* = 1 *mil* = 7·181 English miles.

Small distances are usually calculated, in Sweden especially, by *fjerdingsveg* (quarter-miles).

Square and cubic measurements are based exactly upon long measurements.

DECIMAL SYSTEM OF MEASURES AND WEIGHTS.[1]

Measures.

1 *meter* (m.) = 10 *decimeter* (dm.) = 100 *centimeter* (cm.) = 1000 *millimeter* (mm.)

1 *myriameter* = 10 *kilometer* = 10,000 *meter.*

N.B.—1 *meter* = 3·3681 Swedish feet.

> 1 *myriameter* or *nymil* (new mile) = ·9356 of a Swedish m le.

Weights.

1 *gram* (gr.) = 10 *decigram* (dg.) = 100 *centigram* (cg.) = 1000 *milligram* (mg.)

1 *kilogram* (kg.) = 10 *hektogram* (hg.) = 1000 *gram.*

N.B.—1 *kilogram* = 2·35252 *skålpund.*

---

[1] The decimal system is now exclusively used in all tolls, railways, and in all business which is under the control of the Swedish and Norwegian governments. Efforts are being made to promote its general use throughout the two kingdoms.

APPENDIX D.

BOOKS CHIEFLY CONSULTED IN PREPARING THE WORK.

Forbes : Norway and its Glaciers. Edinburgh, 1853.
Andersson : Svensk Elementar-Flora. Stockholm, 1871.
Palmstroch och Venus : Svensk Flora.
Hooker : School Botany.
Linnæus : Flora Lapponica.
Broch : Royaume de Norvége et de Peuple Norvegien. Kristiania, 1878.
Bergstrand : Lärobok i Geologi.
Torell : Geol. Forskningar i Norge.
Nordenskiold : Om Uppkomsten of s.k. Åsgropar (in Lunds Acta Universitetet).
Montelius, Hildebrand, &c. : Sveriges Historia från äldsta tid till våra dagar.
Geijer : History of Sweden (translation by Turner). London, 1845.
Thompsen : The Relations between Ancient Russia and Scandinavia and the Origin of the Russian State. Oxford, 1877.
Sophus Muller : Dyreornamentiken i Norden (Aarböger for Nordisk Oldkyndighed og Historie, 1880. Parts iii. iv.). Copenhagen.
Fryxell : Berättelser ur Svenska Historien.
Otté : Scandinavian History. London, 1874.
Gardiner : The Thirty Years' War. (Epochs of Modern History.) ·
Ranke : The History of the Popes (translation by Foster).
An Account of Sweden. London, 1694. (Anon.)
Alison : The History of Europe from the Commencement of the French Revolution. Edinburgh.
Hovelacque : On the Science of Language (translation by Keane). London, 1877.
Siever : Articles on German and Gothic Languages, in Encyclopædia Britannica. (9th edition.)
Fornmanna Sögur. Copenhagen, 1825-31.

Snorri Sturluson : Heimskringla. Kristiania, 1868.

Vigfusson: Prolegomena to Sturlunga Saga. Oxford, 1878.

Cleasby and Vigfusson : Icelandic-English Dictionary. Oxford, 1874.

Claëson : Öfversigt af Svenska Språkets och Literaturens Historia. 3rd edition. Stockholm, 1874.

Lassen : Inledning i Norges og Danmarks Literatur. Kristiania, 1878.

Gosse : Studies in the Literature of Northern Europe. 1879.

Hildebrand : Den Kyrkliga Konsten under Sveriges medeltid.

Brunius: Gotlands Konsthistoria.

Bergman : Gotlands Geographi och Historia. Visby, 1879.

Berling : Lund. Korta anteckningar om staden och dess omgifning. Lund, 1879.

Administratif och Statistisk Handbok. Stockholm, 1879.

Annuaire Statistique de la Norvége. Kristiania, 1879.

Almanach de Gotha. 1881.

Skattejemknings Komiténs Betänkande. Stockholm, 1877.

Lloyd : Peasant Life in Sweden. London, 1870.

Metcalfe : Oxonian in Norway. London, 1856.

Laing : Residence in Norway.

„ Tour in Sweden.

Campbell (J. R.) : Articles in Alpine Journal. Vols. iv. v.

Tonsberg : Illustrated Handbook for Travellers (translation). Kristiania, 1875.

Illustreradt Sverige. Stockholm, 1875.

Scheffer : History of Lapland (translation). London, 1704.

Dillon : Winter in Iceland and Lapland. Vol. ii. London, 1840.

Linnæus : Lachesis Lapponica (translation by Smith). London, 1811.

Psalm-books and other Church Service Books, &c.

S

INDEX.

S 2

LONDON :
PRINTED BY GILBERT AND RIVINGTON, LIMITFD,
ST. JOHN'S SQUARE.

A Catalogue of American and Foreign Books Published or Imported by MESSRS. SAMPSON LOW & CO. *can be had on application.*

Crown Buildings, 188, *Fleet Street, London,*
December, 1881.

𝔄 𝔖election from the 𝔏ist of 𝔅ooks

PUBLISHED BY

SAMPSON LOW, MARSTON, SEARLE, & RIVINGTON.

ALPHABETICAL LIST.

A CLASSIFIED *Educational Catalogue of Works* published in Great Britain. Demy 8vo, cloth extra. Second Edition, revised and corrected, 5s.

About Some Fellows. By an ETON BOY, Author of "A Day of my Life." Cloth limp, square 16mo, 2s. 6d.

Adventures of a Young Naturalist. By LUCIEN BIART, with 117 beautiful Illustrations on Wood. Edited and adapted by PARKER GILLMORE. Post 8vo, cloth extra, gilt edges, New Edition, 7s. 6d.

Afghan Knife (The). A Novel. By ROBERT ARMITAGE STERNDALE, Author of " Seonee." Small post 8vo, cloth extra, 6s.

Alcott (Louisa M.) Jimmy's Cruise in the " Pinafore." With 9 Illustrations. Second Edition. Small post 8vo, cloth gilt, 3s. 6d.

—— *Aunt Jo's Scrap-Bag.* Square 16mo, 2s. 6d. (Rose Library, 1s.)

—— *Little Men: Life at Plumfield with Jo's Boys.* Small post 8vo, cloth, gilt edges, 3s. 6d. (Rose Library, Double vol. 2s.)

—— *Little Women.* 1 vol., cloth, gilt edges, 3s. 6d. (Rose Library, 2 vols., 1s. each.)

—— *Old-Fashioned Girl.* Best Edition, small post 8vo, cloth extra, gilt edges, 3s. 6d. (Rose Library, 2s.)

—— *Work and Beginning Again.* A Story of Experience. (Rose Library, 2 vols., 1s. each.)

—— *Shawl Straps.* Small post 8vo, cloth extra, gilt, 3s. 6d.

—— *Eight Cousins; or, the Aunt Hill.* Small post 8vo, with Illustrations, 3s. 6d.

—— *The Rose in Bloom.* Small post 8vo, cloth extra, 3s. 6d.

—— *Under the Lilacs.* Small post 8vo, cloth extra, 5s.

A

Alcott (Louisa M.) Jack and Jill. Small post 8vo, cloth extra, 5s.
"Miss Alcott's stories are thoroughly healthy, full of racy fun and humour . . . exceedingly entertaining . . . . We can recommend the 'Eight Cousins.'"— *Athenæum.*

Aldrich (T. B.) Friar Jerome's Beautiful Book, &c. Selected from "Cloth of Gold," and "Flower and Thorn." 18mo, very choicely printed on hand-made paper, parchment cover, 3s. 6d.

Alpine Ascents and Adventures; or, Rock and Snow Sketches. By H. SCHÜTZ WILSON, of the Alpine Club. With Illustrations by WHYMPER and MARCUS STONE. Crown 8vo, 10s. 6d. 2nd Edition.

Andersen (Hans Christian) Fairy Tales. With Illustrations in Colours by E. V. B. Cheap Edition, in the press.

Angling Literature in England; and Descriptions of Fishing by the Ancients. By O. LAMBERT. With a Notice of some Books on other Piscatorial Subjects. Fcap. 8vo, vellum, top gilt limp, 3s. 6d.

Architecture (The Twenty Styles of). By Dr. W. WOOD, Editor of "The Hundred Greatest Men." Imperial 8vo, with 52 Plates.

Art Education. See "Illustrated Text Books," "Illustrated Dictionary," "Biographies of Great Artists."

Autobiography of Sir G. Gilbert Scott, R.A., F.S.A., &c. Edited by his Son, G. GILBERT SCOTT. With an Introduction by the DEAN OF CHICHESTER, and a Funeral Sermon, preached in Westminster Abbey, by the DEAN OF WESTMINSTER. Also, Portrait on steel from the portrait of the Author by G. RICHMOND, R.A. 1 vol., demy 8vo, cloth extra, 18s.

Autumnal Leaves. By F. G. HEATH. Illustrated by 12 Plates, comprising 252 figures of Autumn Leaves and Leaflets, exquisitely coloured after Nature; 4 Page and 14 Vignette Drawings, by FRED. G. SHORT, of New Forest Scenery, and 12 Initial-letter Leaf Designs by the Author. Cloth, imperial 16mo, gilt edges, with special Cover showing Autumn Leaves printed in colours, price 14s.

THE BAYARD SERIES.

Edited by the late J. HAIN FRISWELL.

Comprising Pleasure Books of Literature produced in the Choicest Style as Companionable Volumes at Home and Abroad.

"We can hardly imagine better books for boys to read or for men to ponder over."— *Times.*

Price 2s. 6d. each Volume, complete in itself, flexible cloth extra, gilt edges, with silk Headbands and Registers.

The Story of the Chevalier Bayard. By M. De Berville.

De Joinville's St. Louis, King of France.

The Essays of Abraham Cowley, including all his Prose Works.

Abdallah; or, The Four Leaves. By Edouard Laboullaye.

The Bayard Series (continued):—

Table-Talk and Opinions of Napoleon Buonaparte.

Vathek : An Oriental Romance. By William Beckford.

The King and the Commons. A Selection of Cavalier and Puritan Songs. Edited by Professor Morley.

Words of Wellington : Maxims and Opinions of the Great Duke.

Dr. Johnson's Rasselas, Prince of Abyssinia. With Notes.

Hazlitt's Round Table. With Biographical Introduction.

The Religio Medici, Hydriotaphia, and the Letter to a Friend. By Sir Thomas Browne, Knt.

Ballad Poetry of the Affections. By Robert Buchanan.

Coleridge's Christabel, and other

Imaginative Poems. With Preface by Algernon C. Swinburne.

Lord Chesterfield's Letters, Sentences, and Maxims. With Introduction by the Editor, and Essay on Chesterfield by M. de Ste.-Beuve, of the French Academy.

Essays in Mosaic. By Thos. Ballantyne.

My Uncle Toby ; his Story and his Friends. Edited by P. Fitzgerald.

Reflections ; or, Moral Sentences and Maxims of the Duke de la Rochefoucald.

Socrates : Memoirs for English Readers from Xenophon's Memorabilia. By Edw. Levien.

Prince Albert's Golden Precepts.

A Case containing 12 Volumes, price 31s. 6d. ; or the Case separately, price 3s. 6d.

Beauty and the Beast. An Old Tale retold, with Pictures by E. V. B. 4to, cloth extra. 10 Illustrations in Colours. 12s. 6d.

Begum's Fortune (The): A New Story. By JULES VERNE. Translated by W. H. G. KINGSTON. Numerous Illustrations. Crown 8vo, cloth, gilt edges, 7s. 6d. ; plainer binding, plain edges, 5s.

Ben Hur: A Tale of the Christ. By L. WALLACE. Crown 8vo, 6s.

Beumers' German Copybooks. In six gradations at 4d. each.

Bickersteth's Hymnal Companion to Book of Common Prayer may be had in various styles and bindings from 1d. to 21s. *Price List and Prospectus will be forwarded on application.*

Bickersteth (Rev. E. H., M.A.) The Reef, and other Parables. 1 vol., square 8vo, with numerous very beautiful Engravings, 2s. 6d.

—— **The Clergyman in his Home.** Small post 8vo, 1s.

—— **The Master's Home-Call; or, Brief Memorials of** Alice Frances Bickersteth. 20th Thousand. 32mo, cloth gilt, 1s.

—— **The Master's Will.** A Funeral Sermon preached on the Death of Mrs. S. Gurney Buxton. Sewn, 6d. ; cloth gilt, 1s.

—— **The Shadow of the Rock.** A Selection of Religious Poetry. 18mo, cloth extra, 2s. 6d.

—— **The Shadowed Home and the Light Beyond.** 7th Edition, crown 8vo, cloth extra, 5s.

Biographies of the Great Artists (*Illustrated*). Each of the
following Volumes is illustrated with from twelve to twenty full-page
Engravings, printed in the best manner, and bound in ornamental
cloth cover, 3s. 6d. Library Edition, bound in a superior style,
and handsomely ornamented, with gilt top; six Volumes, enclosed
in a cloth case, with lid, £1 11s. 6d. each case.

Hogarth.	Giotto.	Figure Painters of
Turner.	Raphael.	Holland.
Rubens.	Van Dyck and Hals.	Michel Angelo.
Holbein.	Titian.	Delaroche and Vernet.
Tintoretto.	Rembrandt.	Landseer.
Little Masters of	Leonardo da Vinci.	Reynolds.
Germany.	Gainsborough and	Velasquez.
Fra Angelico and	Constable.	Mantegna and
Masaccio.	Sir David Wilkie.	Francia.
Fra Bartolommeo.	Van Eyck.	Albert Durer.

Price 2s. 6d. each.

Claude Lorraine.	Sir Thos. Lawrence.	Murillo.
Correggio.	Rousseau & Millet.	Early Italian Sculp-
Watteau, Lannet,	Meissonier.	tors.
and Boucher.	Overbeck.	

" Few things in the way of small books upon great subjects, avowedly cheap and
necessarily brief, have been hitherto so well done as these biographies of the Great
Masters in painting."—*Times.*
" A deserving series."—*Edinburgh Review.*
" Most thoroughly and tastefully edited."—*Spectator.*

Birthday Book. Extracts from the Writings of Theodore
Emerson. Square 16mo, cloth extra, numerous Illustrations, very
choice binding, 3s. 6d.

Birthday Book. Extracts from the Poems of Whittier. Square
16mo, with numerous Illustrations and handsome binding, 3s. 6d.

Black (Wm.) Three Feathers. Small post 8vo, cloth extra, 6s.

—— *Lady Silverdale's Sweetheart, and other Stories.* 1 vol.,
small post 8vo, 6s.

—— *Kilmeny: a Novel.* Small post 8vo, cloth, 6s.

—— *In Silk Attire.* 3rd Edition, small post 8vo, 6s.

—— *A Daughter of Heth.* 11th Edition, small post 8vo, 6s.

—— *Sunrise.* Small post 8vo, 6s.

Blackmore (R. D.) Lorna Doone. 10th Edition, cr. 8vo, 6s.

—— *Alice Lorraine.* 1 vol., small post 8vo, 6th Edition, 6s.

—— *Clara Vaughan.* Revised Edition, 6s.

—— *Cradock Nowell.* New Edition, 6s.

—— *Cripps the Carrier.* 3rd Edition, small post 8vo, 6s.

—— *Mary Anerley.* New Edition, 6s.

—— *Erema; or, My Father's Sin.* With 12 Illustrations,
small post 8vo, 6s.

Blossoms from the King's Garden : Sermons for Children. By the Rev. C. BOSANQUET. 2nd Edition, small post 8vo, cloth extra, 6s.

Blue Banner (The); or, The Adventures of a Mussulman, a Christian, and a Pagan, in the time of the Crusades and Mongol Conquest. Translated from the French of LEON CAHUN. With Seventy-six Wood Engravings. Imperial 16mo, cloth, gilt edges, 7s. 6d.; plainer binding, 5s.

*Bock (Carl). The Head Hunters of Borneo: Up the Mahak-*kam, and Down the Barita; also Journeyings in Sumatra. 1 vol., super-royal 8vo, 32 Coloured Plates, cloth extra, 36s.

Book of the Play. By DUTTON COOK. New and Revised Edition. 1 vol., cloth extra, 7s. 6d.

Boy's Froissart (The). 7s. 6d. *See* "Froissart."

Boy's King Arthur (The). With very fine Illustrations. Square crown 8vo, cloth extra, gilt edges, 7s. 6d. Edited by SIDNEY LANIER, Editor of "The Boy's Froissart."

Boy's Mabinogion (The): being the Original Welsh Legends of King Arthur. Edited for Boys, with an Introduction by SIDNEY LANIER. With numerous very graphic Illustrations. Crown 8vo, cloth, gilt edges, 7s. 6d.

Breton Folk: An Artistic Tour in Brittany. By HENRY BLACKBURN, Author of "Artists and Arabs," "Normandy Pictu-resque," &c. With 171 Illustrations by RANDOLPH CALDECOTT. Imperial 8vo, cloth extra, gilt edges, 21s.

British Goblins: Welsh Folk-Lore, Fairy Mythology, Legends, and Traditions. By WIRT SIKES, United States Consul for Wales, Author of "Rambles and Studies in Old South Wales." Second Edition. 8vo, 18s.

Burnaby (Capt.). See "On Horseback."

Burnham Beeches (Heath, F. G.). With numerous Illustrations and a Map. Crown 8vo, cloth, gilt edges, 3s. 6d Second Edition.
"A pretty description of the Beeches."—*Daily News.*
"A charming little volume."—*Globe.*

Burroughs (John). Pepacton: A Summer Voyage, and other Essays. Small post 8vo, cloth, 7s. 6d.

Butler·(W. F.) The Great Lone Land; an Account of the Red River Expedition, 1869-70. With Illustrations and Map. Fifth and Cheaper Edition, crown 8vo, cloth extra, 7s. 6d.

—— *The Wild North Land; the Story of a Winter Journey* with Dogs across Northern North America. Demy 8vo, cloth, with numerous Woodcuts and a Map, 4th Edition, 18s. Cr. 8vo, 7s. 6d.

—— *Akim-foo: the History of a Failure.* Demy 8vo, cloth, 2nd Edition, 16s. Also, in crown 8vo, 7s. 6d.

—— *Red Cloud.* Crown 8vo, gilt edges, 7s. 6d. [*In the press.*

*C*ADOGAN *(Lady A.) Illustrated Games of Patience.* Twenty-four Diagrams in Colours, with Descriptive Text. Foolscap 4to, cloth extra, gilt edges, 3rd Edition, 12s. 6d.

Cambridge Trifles; or, Splutterings from an Undergraduate Pen. By the Author of "A Day of my Life at Eton," &c. 16mo, cloth extra, 2s. 6d.

Changed Cross (The), and other Religious Poems. 16mo, 2s. 6d.

Child of the Cavern (The) ; or, Strange Doings Underground. By JULES VERNE. Translated by W. H. G. KINGSTON. Numerous Illustrations. Sq. cr. 8vo, gilt edges, 7s. 6d. ; cl., plain edges, 5s.

Child's Play, with 16 Coloured Drawings by E. V. B. Printed on thick paper, with tints, 7s. 6d.

—— *New*. By E. V. B. Similar to the above. *See* New.

—— A New and Cheap Edition of the two above, containing 48 Illustrations by E. V. B., printed in tint, handsomely bound, 3s. 6d.

Choice Editions of Choice Books. 2s. 6d. each, Illustrated by C. W. COPE, R.A., T. CRESWICK, R.A., E. DUNCAN, BIRKET FOSTER, J. C. HORSLEY, A.R.A., G. HICKS, R. REDGRAVE, R.A., C. STONEHOUSE, F. TAYLER, G. THOMAS. H. J. TOWNSHEND, E. H. WEHNERT, HARRISON WEIR, &c.

Bloomfield's Farmer's Boy.	Milton's L'Allegro.
Campbell's Pleasures of Hope.	Poetry of Nature. Harrison Weir.
Coleridge's Ancient Mariner.	Rogers' (Sam.) Pleasures of Memory.
Goldsmith's Deserted Village.	Shakespeare's Songs and Sonnets.
Goldsmith's Vicar of Wakefield.	Tennyson's May Queen.
Gray's Elegy in a Churchyard.	Elizabethan Poets.
Keat's Eve of St. Agnes.	Wordsworth's Pastoral Poems.

"Such works are a glorious beatification for a poet."—*Athenæum.*

Christ in Song. By Dr. PHILIP SCHAFF. A New Edition, Revised, cloth, gilt edges, 6s.

Confessions of a Frivolous Girl (The): A Novel of Fashionable Life. Edited by ROBERT GRANT. Crown 8vo, 6s.

Cornet of Horse (The) : A Story for Boys. By G. A. HENTY. Crown 8vo, cloth extra, gilt edges, numerous graphic Illustrations, 5s.

Cripps the Carrier. 3rd Edition, 6s. *See* BLACKMORE.

Cruise of H.M.S. "Challenger" (The). By W. J. J. SPRY, R.N. With Route Map and many Illustrations. 6th Edition, demy 8vo, cloth, 18s. Cheap Edition, crown 8vo, some of the Illustrations, 7s. 6d.

Cruise of the Walnut Shell (The). An instructive and amusing Story, told in Rhyme, for Children. With 32 Coloured Plates. Square fancy boards, 5s.

Curious Adventures of a Field Cricket. By Dr. ERNEST CANDÈZE. Translated by N. D'ANVERS. With numerous fine Illustrations. Crown 8vo, gilt, 7s. 6d.; plain binding and edges, 5s.

DANA (R. H.) *Two Years before the Mast and Twenty-Four* years After. Revised Edition, with Notes, 12mo, 6s.

Daughter (A) of Heth. By W. BLACK. Crown 8vo, 6s.

Day of My Life (A) ; or, Every Day Experiences at Eton.
By an ETON BOY, Author of "About Some Fellows." 16mo, cloth
extra, 2s. 6d. 6th Thousand.

Diane. By Mrs. MACQUOID. Crown 8vo, 6s.

Dick Cheveley: his Fortunes and Misfortunes. By W. H. G.
KINGSTON. 350 pp., square 16mo, and 22 full-page Illustrations.
Cloth, gilt edges, 7s. 6d.; plainer binding, plain edges, 5s.

Dick Sands, the Boy Captain. By JULES VERNE. With nearly
100 Illustrations, cloth, gilt, 10s. 6d.; plain binding and plain edges, 5s.

EIGHT Cousins. See ALCOTT.

Elementary History (An) of Art. Comprising Architecture,
Sculpture, Painting, and the Applied Arts. By N. D'ANVERS,
Author of "Science Ladders." With a Preface by Professor ROGER
SMITH. New Edition, illustrated with upwards of 200 Wood
Engravings. Crown 8vo, strongly bound in cloth, price 8s. 6d.

Elementary History (An) of Music. Edited by OWEN J.
DULLEA. Including Music among the Ancient Nations ; Music in
the Middle Ages; Music in Italy in the Sixteenth, Seventeenth, and
Eighteenth Centuries; Music in Germany, France, and England.
Illustrated with Portraits of the most eminent Composers, and
Engravings of the Musical Instruments of many Nations. Crown 8vo,
handsomely bound in cloth, price 3s. 6d.

Elinor Dryden. By Mrs. MACQUOID. Crown 8vo, 6s.

Embroidery (Handbook of). By L. HIGGIN. Edited by LADY
MARIAN ALFORD, and published by authority of the Royal School of
Art Needlework. With 16 page Illustrations, Designs for Borders,
&c. Crown 8vo, 5s.

Enchiridion of Epictetus ; and the Golden Verses of Pythagoras.
Translated into English, Prose and Verse; with Notes and Scriptural
References, together with some original Poems. By the Hon. THOS.
TALBOT. Crown 8vo, cloth, 5s.

English Philosophers. Edited by IWAN MULLER, M.A., New
College, Oxon. A Series of Volumes containing short biographies
of the most celebrated English Philosophers, to each of whom is
assigned a separate volume, giving as comprehensive and detailed a
statement of his views and contributions to Philosophy as possible,
explanatory ratherthan critical, opening with a brief biographical sketch,
and concluding with a short general summary, and a bibliographical
appendix. Each Volume contains about 200 pp. Sq. 16mo, 3s. 6d. each.
Bacon. Professor FOWLER, Professor of Logic in Oxford.
Berkeley. Prof. T. H. GREEN, Professor of Moral Philosophy, Oxford.
Hamilton. Professor MONK, Professor of Moral Philosophy, Dublin.
J. S. Mill. HELEN TAYLOR, Editor of "The Works of Buckle," &c.
Mansel. Rev. J. H. HUCKIN, D.D., Head Master of Repton.
Adam Smith. J. A. FARRER, M.A., Author of "Primitive
Manners and Customs."

English Philosophers (continued) :—

Hobbes. A. H. GOSSET, B.A., Fellow of New College, Oxford.

Bentham. G. E. BUCKLE, M.A., Fellow of All Souls', Oxford.

Austin. HARRY JOHNSON, B.A., late Scholar of Queen's College, Oxford.

Hartley. ⎱ E. S. BOWEN, B.A., late Scholar of New College,
James Mill. ⎰   Oxford.

Shaftesbury. ⎱ Professor FOWLER.
Hutcheson. ⎰

Arrangements are in progress for volumes on LOCKE, HUME, PALEY, REID, *&c.*

Episodes of French History. Edited, with Notes, Genealogical, Historical, and other Tables, by GUSTAVE MASSON, B.A.

1. **Charlemagne and the Carlovingians.**
2. **Louis XI. and the Crusades.**
3. Part I. **Francis I. and Charles V.**
   ,, II. **Francis I. and the Renaissance.**
4. **Henry IV. and the End of the Wars of Religion.**

The above Series is based upon M. Guizot's "History of France." Each volume choicely Illustrated, with Maps, 2s. 6d.

Erema ; or, My Father's Sin. See BLACKMORE.

Etcher (The). Containing 36 Examples of the Original Etched-work of Celebrated Artists, amongst others: BIRKET FOSTER, J. E. HODGSON, R.A., COLIN HUNTER, J. P. HESELTINE, ROBERT W. MACBETH, R. S. CHATTOCK, &c. Vol. for 1881, imperial 4to, cloth extra, gilt edges, 2l. 12s. 6d. Monthly, 3s. 6d.

Eton. See "Day of my Life," "Out of School," "About Some Fellows."

*F*ARM *Ballads.* By WILL CARLETON. Boards, 1s. ; cloth, gilt edges, 1s. 6d.

Farm Festivals. By the same Author. Uniform with above.

Farm Legends. By the same Author. See above.

Felkin (R. W.) and Wilson (Rev. C. T.) Uganda and the Egyptian Soudan. An Account of Travel in Eastern and Equatorial Africa ; including a Residence of Two Years at the Court of King Mtesa, and a Description of the Slave Districts of Bahr-el-Ghazel and Darfour. With a New Map of 1200 miles in these Provinces ; numerous Illustrations, and Anthropological, Meteorological, and Geographical Notes. By R. W. FELKIN, F.R.G.S., Member of the Anthropological Institute, &c., &c. ; and the Rev. C. T. WILSON, M.A. Oxon., F.R G.S., Member of the Society of Arts, Hon. Fellow of the Cairo Geographical Society. 2 vols., crown 8vo, cloth, 28s.

Fern Paradise (The) : A Plea for the Culture of Ferns. By F. G. HEATH. New Edition, entirely Rewritten, Illustrated by Eighteen full-page, and numerous other Woodcuts, including 8 Plates of Ferns and Four Photographs, large post 8vo, cloth, gilt edges, 12s. 6d. Sixth Edition.

"All lovers of ferns will be delighted with the illustrated edition of Mr. Heath's "Fern Paradise."—*Saturday Review.*

Fern World (The). By F. G. HEATH. Illustrated by Twelve
Coloured Plates, giving complete Figures (Sixty-four in all) of every
Species of British Fern, printed from Nature; by several full-page
and other Engravings. Cloth, gilt edges, 6th Edition, 12s. 6d.

Few (A) Hints on Proving Wills. Enlarged Edition, 1s.

First Steps in Conversational French Grammar. By F. JULIEN.
Being an Introduction to "Petites Leçons de Conversation et de
Grammaire," by the same Author. Fcap. 8vo, 128 pp., 1s.

Four Lectures on Electric Induction. Delivered at the Royal
Institution, 1878-9. By J. E. H. GORDON, B.A. Cantab. With
numerous Illustrations. Cloth limp, square 16mo, 3s.

Foreign Countries and the British Colonies. Edited by F. S.
PULLING, M.A., Lecturer at Queen's College, Oxford, and formerly
Professor at the Yorkshire College, Leeds. A Series of small Volumes
descriptive of the principal Countries of the World by well-known
Authors, each Country being treated of by a Writer who from
Personal Knowledge is qualified to speak with authority on the Subject.
The Volumes average 180 crown 8vo pages each, contain 2 Maps
and Illustrations, crown 8vo, 3s. 6d.

The following is a List of the Volumes:—

Denmark and Iceland. By E. C. OTTÉ, Author of "Scandinavian
History," &c.

Greece. By L. SERGEANT, B.A., Knight of the Hellenic Order
of the Saviour, Author of "New Greece."

Switzerland. By W. A. P. COOLIDGE, M.A., Fellow of
Magdalen College, Editor of *The Alpine Journal.*

- **Austria.** By D. KAY, F.R.G.S.

Russia. By W. R. MORFILL, M.A., Oriel College, Oxford,
Lecturer on the Ilchester Foundation, &c.

Persia. By Major-Gen. Sir F. J. GOLDSMID, K.C.S.I., Author of
"Telegraph and Travel," &c.

Japan. By S. MOSSMAN, Author of "New Japan," &c.

Peru. By CLEMENTS H. MARKHAM, M.A., C.B.

Canada. By W. FRASER RAE, Author of "Westward by
Rail," "From Newfoundland to Manitoba," &c.

Sweden and Norway. By the Rev. F. H. WOODS, M.A., Fellow
of St. John's College, Oxford.

The West Indies. By C. H. EDEN, F.R.G.S., Author of "Frozen
Asia," &c.

New Zealand.

France. By M. ROBERTS, Author of "The Atelier du Lys,"&c.

Egypt. By S. LANE POOLE, B.A., Author of "Life of E. Lane," &c.

Spain. By the Rev. WENTWORTH WEBSTER, M A.

Turkey-in-Asia. By J. C. McCOAN, M.P.

Australia. By J. F. VESEY FITZGERALD, late Premier of New
South Wales.

Holland. By R. L. POOLE.

Franc (Maude Jeane). The following form one Series, small post 8vo, in uniform cloth bindings, with gilt edges:—

Emily's Choice. 5s.	Silken Cords and Iron Fetters. 4s.
Hall's Vineyard. 4s.	Vermont Vale. 5s.
John's Wife: A Story of Life in South Australia. 4s.	Minnie's Mission. 4s.
Marian; or, The Light of Some One's Home. 5s.	Little Mercy. 5s.
	Beatrice Melton's Discipline. 4s.

Francis (F.) War, Waves, and Wanderings, including a Cruise in the "Lancashire Witch." 2 vols., crown 8vo, cloth extra, 24s.

French Revolution (The Great). Letters written from Paris during the Progress of the Great French Revolution, by Madame J—— to her Husband and Son. Edited by her Great-grandson, M. EDOUARD LOCKROY. From the French. Crown 8vo, cloth, 10s. 6d.

Froissart (The Boy's). Selected from the Chronicles of England, France, Spain, &c. By SIDNEY LANIER. The Volume is fully Illustrated, and uniform with "The Boy's King Arthur." Crown 8vo, cloth, 7s. 6d.

From Newfoundland to Manitoba; a Guide through Canada's Maritime, Mining, and Prairie Provinces. By W. FRASER RAE. Crown 8vo, with several Maps, 6s.

GAMES of Patience. See CADOGAN.

Gentle Life (Queen Edition). 2 vols. in 1, small 4to, 10s. 6d.

THE GENTLE LIFE SERIES.

Price 6s. each; or in calf extra, price 10s. 6d.; Smaller Edition, cloth extra, 2s. 6d.

The Gentle Life. Essays in aid of the Formation of Character of Gentlemen and Gentlewomen. 21st Edition.

About in the World. Essays by Author of "The Gentle Life."

Like unto Christ. A New Translation of Thomas à Kempis "De Imitatione Christi." 2nd Edition.

Familiar Words. An Index Verborum, or Quotation Handbook. Affording an immediate Reference to Phrases and Sentences that have become embedded in the English language. 6s.

Essays by Montaigne. Edited and Annotated by the Author of "The Gentle Life." With Portrait. 2nd Edition.

The Countess of Pembroke's Arcadia. Written by Sir PHILIP SIDNEY. Edited with Notes by Author of "The Gentle Life." 7s. 6d.

The Gentle Life. 2nd Series, 8th Edition.

The Gentle Life Series (continued):—

The Silent Hour: Essays, Original and Selected. By the Author of "The Gentle Life." 3rd Edition.

Half-Length Portraits. Short Studies of Notable Persons. By J. HAIN FRISWELL.

Essays on English Writers, for the Self-improvement of Students in English Literature.

Other People's Windows. By J. HAIN FRISWELL. 3rd Edition.

A Man's Thoughts. By J. HAIN FRISWELL.

German Primer. Being an Introduction to First Steps in German. By M. T. PREU. 2s. 6d.

Getting On in the World; or, Hints on Success in Life. By W. MATHEWS, LL.D. Small post 8vo, cloth, 2s. 6d.; gilt edges, 3s. 6d.

Gilpin's Forest Scenery. Edited by F. G. HEATH. Large post 8vo, with numerous Illustrations. Uniform with "The Fern World," 12s. 6d.

"Deserves to be a favourite in the boudoir as well as in the library."—*Saturday Review.*

"One of the most delightful works ever written."—*Globe.*

Gordon (J. E. H.). See "Four Lectures on Electric Induction," "Physical Treatise on Electricity," &c.

Gouffé. The Royal Cookery Book. By JULES GOUFFÉ; translated and adapted for English use by ALPHONSE GOUFFÉ, Head Pastrycook to her Majesty the Queen. Illustrated with large plates printed in colours. 161 Woodcuts, 8vo, cloth extra, gilt edges, 2l. 2s.

—————— Domestic Edition, half-bound, 10s. 6d.

"By far the ablest and most complete work on cookery that has ever been submitted to the gastronomical world."—*Pall Mall Gazette.*

Great Artists. See "Biographies."

Great Historic Galleries of England (The). Edited by LORD RONALD GOWER, F.S.A., Trustee of the National Portrait Gallery. Illustrated by 24 large and carefully-executed *permanent* Photographs of some of the most celebrated Pictures by the Great Masters. Vol. I., imperial 4to, cloth extra, gilt edges, 36s. Vol. II., with 36 large permanent photographs, £2 12s. 6d.

Great Musicians (The). A Series of Biographies of the Great Musicians. Edited by F. HUEFFER.

1. **Wagner.** By the EDITOR.
2. **Weber.** By Sir JULIUS BENEDICT.
3. **Mendelssohn.** By JOSEPH BENNETT.
4. **Schubert.** By H. F. FROST.
5. **Rossini,** and the Modern Italian School. By H. SUTHERLAND EDWARDS.
6. **Marcello.** By ARRIGO BOITO.
7. **Purcell.** By H. W. CUMMINGS.
8. **English Church Composers.**

*** Dr. Hiller and other distinguished writers, both English and Foreign, have promised contributions. Each Volume is complete in itself. Small post 8vo, cloth extra, 3s.

Guizot's History of France. Translated by ROBERT BLACK.
Super-royal 8vo, very numerous Full-page and other Illustrations. In
8 vols., cloth extra, gilt, each 24s. This work is re-issued in cheaper
Monthly Volumes, at 10s. 6d. each, commencing Nov. 1, 1881. Sub-
scription to the set, £4 4s.
"It supplies a want which has long been felt, and ought to be in the hands of all
students of history."—*Times.*

——————————————————— *Masson's School Edition.* The
History of France from the Earliest Times to the Outbreak of the
Revolution ; abridged from the Translation by Robert Black, M.A.,
with Chronological Index, Historical and Genealogical Tables, &c.
By Professor GUSTAVE MASSON, B.A., Assistant Master at Harrow
School. With 24 full-page Portraits, and many other Illustrations.
1 vol., demy 8vo, 600 pp., cloth extra, 10s. 6d.

Guizot's History of England. In 3 vols. of about 500 pp. each,
containing 60 to 70 Full-page and other Illustrations, cloth extra, gilt,
24s. each.
"For luxury of typography, plainness of print, and beauty of illustration, these
volumes, of which but one has as yet appeared in English, will hold their own
against any production of an age so luxurious as our own in everything, typography
not excepted."—*Times.*

Guyon (Mde.) Life. By UPHAM. 6th Edition, crown 8vo, 6s.

HANDBOOK to the Charities of London. See Low's.

—————— *of Embroidery ; which see.*
Hall (W. W.) How to Live Long ; or, 1408 *Health Maxims,*
. Physical, Mental, and Moral. By W. W. HALL, A.M., M.D.
Small post 8vo, cloth, 2s. 2nd Edition.

Harper's Monthly Magazine. Published Monthly. 160 pages,
fully Illustrated. 1s. With two Serial Novels by celebrated Authors.
    Vol. I. December, 1880, to May, 1881.
      ,, II. May, 1881, to November, 1881.
Each cloth extra, with 400 magnificent illustrations, 8s. 6d.
"'Harper's Magazine' is so thickly sown with excellent illustrations that to count
them would be a work of time ; not that it is a picture magazine, for the engravings
illustrate the text after the manner seen in some of our choicest *editions de luxe.*"—
St. James's Gazette.
"It is so pretty, so big, and so cheap. . . . An extraordinary shillingsworth—
160 large octavo pages, with over a score of articles, and more than three times as
many illustrations."—*Edinburgh Daily Review.*
"An amazing shillingsworth . . . combining choice literature of both nations."—
Nonconformist.

Heart of Africa. Three Years' Travels and Adventures in the
Unexplored Regions of Central Africa, from 1868 to 1871. By Dr
GEORG SCHWEINFURTH. Numerous Illustrations, and large Map.
2 vols., crown 8vo, cloth, 15s.

Heath (Francis George). See "Autumnal Leaves," "Burnham
Beeches," "Fern Paradise," "Fern World," "Gilpin's Forest
Scenery," "Our Woodland Trees," "Peasant Life," "Sylvan Spring,"
"Trees and Ferns," "Where to Find Ferns."

Heber's (Bishop) Illustrated Edition of Hymns. With upwards
of 100 beautiful Engravings. Small 4to, handsomely bound, 7s. 6d.
Morocco, 18s. 6d. and 21s. New and Cheaper Edition, cloth, 3s. 6d.

Heir of Kilfinnan (The). New Story by W. H. G. KINGSTON,
Author of " Snow Shoes and Canoes," &c. With Illustrations. Cloth,
gilt edges, 7s. 6d. ; plainer binding, plain edges, 5s.

History of a Crime (The) ; Deposition of an Eye-witness. The
Story of the Coup d'État. By VICTOR HUGO. Crown 8vo, 6s.

——— *Ancient Art.* Translated from the German of JOHN
WINCKELMANN, by JOHN LODGE, M.D. With very numerous
Plates and Illustrations. 2 vols., 8vo, 36s.

——— *England. See* GUIZOT.

——— *France. See* GUIZOT.

——— *of Russia. See* RAMBAUD.

——— *Merchant Shipping. See* LINDSAY.

——— *United States. See* BRYANT.

History and Principles of Weaving by Hand and by Power. With
several hundred Illustrations. By ALFRED BARLOW. Royal 8vo,
cloth extra, 1l. 5s. Second Edition.

Holmes (O. W.) The Poetical Works of Oliver Wendell Holmes.
In 2 vols., 18mo, exquisitely printed, and chastely bound in limp
cloth, gilt tops, 10s. 6d.

How I Crossed Africa : from the Atlantic to the Indian Ocean,
Through Unknown Countries ; Discovery of the Great Zambesi
Affluents, &c.—Vol. I., The King's Rifle. Vol. II., The Coillard
Family. By Major SERPA PINTO. With 24 full-page and 118 half-
page and smaller Illustrations, 13 small Maps, and 1 large one.
2 vols., demy 8vo, cloth extra, 42s.

How to Live Long. See HALL.

How to get Strong and how to Stay so. By WILLIAM BLAIKIE.
A Manual of Rational, Physical, Gymnastic, and other Exercises.
With Illustrations, small post 8vo, 5s.

Hugo (Victor) "Ninety-Three." Illustrated. Crown 8vo, 6s.

——— *Toilers of the Sea.* Crown 8vo. Illustrated, 6s. ; fancy
boards, 2s. ; cloth, 2s. 6d. ; On large paper with all the original
Illustrations, 10s. 6d.

——— *and his Times.* Translated from the French of A.
BARBOU by ELLEN E. FREWER. 120 Illustrations, many of them
from designs by Victor Hugo himself. Super-royal 8vo, cloth extra,
24s.

———. *See* "History of a Crime," " Victor Hugo and his
Times,"

Hundred Greatest Men (The). 8 portfolios, 21*s.* each, or 4 vols., half morocco, gilt edges, 12 guineas, containing 15 to 20 Portraits each. See below.

"Messrs. SAMPSON Low & Co. are about to issue an important 'International' work, entitled, 'THE HUNDRED GREATEST MEN,' being the Lives and Portraits of the 100 Greatest Men of History, divided into Eight Classes, each Class to form a Monthly Quarto Volume. The Introductions to the volumes are to be written by recognized authorities on the different subjects, the English contributors being DEAN STANLEY, Mr. MATTHEW ARNOLD, Mr. FROUDE, and Professor MAX MÜLLER: in Germany, Professor HELMHOLTZ; in France, MM. TAINE and RENAN; and in America, Mr. EMERSON. The Portraits are to be Reproductions from fine and rare Steel Engravings."—*Academy.*

Hygiene and Public Health (A Treatise on). Edited by A. H. BUCK, M.D. Illustrated by numerous Wood Engravings. In 2 royal 8vo vols., cloth, one guinea each.

Hymnal Companion to Book of Common Prayer. See BICKERSTETH.

ILLUSTRATED Text-Books of Art-Education. Edited by EDWARD J. POYNTER, R.A. Each Volume contains numerous Illustrations, and is strongly bound for the use of Students, price 5*s.* The Volumes now ready are:—

PAINTING.

Classic and Italian. By PERCY R. HEAD. With 50 Illustrations, 5*s.*

German, Flemish, and Dutch. French and Spanish. English and American.

ARCHITECTURE.

Classic and Early Christian.
Gothic and Renaissance. By T. ROGER SMITH. With 50 Illustrations, 5*s.*

SCULPTURE.

Antique: Egyptian and Greek. Italian Sculptors of the 14th and 15th Centuries.

Renaissance and Modern.

ORNAMENT.

Decoration in Colour. | Architectural Ornament.

Illustrations of China and its People. By J. THOMPSON, F.R.G.S. Four Volumes, imperial 4to, each 3*l.* 3*s.*

Illustrated Dictionary (An) of Words used in Art and Archæology. Explaining Terms frequently used in Works on Architecture, Arms, Bronzes, Christian Art, Colour, Costume, Decoration, Devices, Emblems, Heraldry, Lace, Personal Ornaments, Pottery, Painting, Sculpture, &c., with their Derivations. By J. W. MOLLETT, B.A., Officier de l'Instruction Publique (France); Author of "Life of Rembrandt," &c. Illustrated with 600 Wood Engravings. Small 4to, strongly bound in cloth, 12*s.* 6*d.*

In my Indian Garden. By PHIL ROBINSON, Author of "Under the Punkah." With a Preface by EDWIN ARNOLD, M.A., C.S.I., &c. Crown 8vo, limp cloth, 3*s.* 6*d.*

·*Involuntary Voyage (An).* Showing how a Frenchman who abhorred the Sea was most unwillingly and by a series of accidents driven round the World. Numerous Illustrations. Square crown 8vo, cloth extra, 7*s.* 6*d.*; plainer binding, plain edges, 5*s.*

Irving (Washington). Complete Library Edition of his Works in 27 Vols., Copyright, Unabridged, and with the Author's Latest Revisions, called the "Geoffrey Crayon" Edition, handsomely printed in large square 8vo, on superfine laid paper, and each volume, of about 500 pages, will be fully Illustrated. 12*s.* 6*d.* per vol. *See also* "Little Britain."

JACK and Jill. By Miss ALCOTT. Small post 8vo, cloth, gilt edges, 5*s.* With numerous Illustrations.

John Holdsworth, Chief Mate. By W. CLARKE RUSSELL, Author of "Wreck ot the Grosvenor." Crown 8vo, 6*s.* .

KINGSTON (W. H. G.). See "Snow-Shoes," "Child of the Cavern," "Two Supercargoes," "With Axe and Rifle," "Begum's Fortune," "Heir of Kilfinnan," "Dick Cheveley." Each vol., with very numerous Illustrations, square crown 16mo, gilt edges, 7*s.* 6*d.*; plainer binding, plain edges, 5*s.*

LADY Silverdale's Sweetheart. 6*s. See* BLACK.

Lectures on Architecture. By E. VIOLLET-LE-DUC. Translated by BENJAMIN BUCKNALL, Architect. With 33 Steel Plates and 200 Wood Engravings. Super-royal 8vo, leather back, gilt top, with complete Index, 2 vols., 3*l.* 3*s.*

Lenten Meditations. In Two Series, each complete in itself. By the Rev. CLAUDE BOSANQUET, Author of "Blossoms from the King's Garden." 16mo, cloth, First Series, 1*s.* 6*d.* ; Second Series, 2*s.*

Library of Religious Poetry. A Collection of the Best Poems of all Ages and Tongues. With Biographical and Literary Notes. Edited by PHILIP SCHAFF, D.D., LL.D., and ARTHUR GILMAN, M.A. Royal 8vo, pp. 1036, cloth extra, gilt edges, 21*s.*

Lindsay (W. S.) History of Merchant Shipping and Ancient Commerce. Over 150 Illustrations, Maps, and Charts. In 4 vols., demy 8vo, cloth extra. Vols. 1 and 2, 21*s.* ; vols. 3 and 4, 24*s.* each.

Little Britain; together with *The Spectre Bridegroom,* and *A* Legend of Sleepy Hollow. By WASHINGTON IRVING. An entirely New *Edition de luxe,* specially suitable for Presentation. Illustrated by 120 very fine Engravings on Wood, by Mr. J. D. COOPER. Designed by Mr. CHARLES O. MURRAY. Square crown 8vo, cloth extra, gilt edges, 10*s.* 6*d.*

Low's Select Novelets. Small post 8vo, cloth extra, 3s. 6d. each.

Friends: a Duet. By E. S. PHELPS, Author of "The Gates Ajar."
"'Friends' is a graceful story . . . it loses nothing in the telling."—*Athenæum.*

Baby Rue: Her Adventures and Misadventures, her Friends and her Enemies. By CHARLES M. CLAY.

The Story of Helen Troy.
"A pleasant book."—*Truth.*

The Clients of Dr. Bernagius. From the French of LUCIEN BIART, by Mrs. CASHEL HOEY.

The Undiscovered Country. By W. D. HOWELLS.

A Gentleman of Leisure. By EDGAR FAWCETT.
"An amazingly clever book."—*Boston Transcript.*

Low's Standard Library of Travel and Adventure. Crown 8vo, bound uniformly in cloth extra, price 7s. 6d.

1. **The Great Lone Land.** By Major W. F. BUTLER, C.B.
2. **The Wild North Land.** By Major W. F. BUTLER, C.B.
   How I found Livingstone. By H. M. STANLEY.
4. **The Threshold of the Unknown Region.** By C. R. MARKHAM. (4th Edition, with Additional Chapters, 10s. 6d.)
5. **A Whaling Cruise to Baffin's Bay and the Gulf of Boothia.** By A. H. MARKHAM.
6. **Campaigning on the Oxus.** By J. A. MACGAHAN.
7. **Akim-foo: the History of a Failure.** By MAJOR W. F. BUTLER, C.B.
8. **Ocean to Ocean.** By the Rev. GEORGE M. GRANT. With Illustrations.
9. **Cruise of the Challenger.** By W. J. J. SPRY, R.N.
10. **Schweinfurth's Heart of Africa.** 2 vols., 15s.
11. **Through the Dark Continent.** By H. M. STANLEY. 1 vol., 12s. 6d.

Low's Standard Novels. Crown 8vo, 6s. each, cloth extra.

My Lady Greensleeves. By HELEN MATHERS, Authoress of "Comin' through the Rye," "Cherry Ripe," &c.

Three Feathers. By WILLIAM BLACK.

A Daughter of Heth. 13th Edition. By W. BLACK. With Frontispiece by F. WALKER, A.R.A.

Kilmeny. A Novel. By W. BLACK.

In Silk Attire. By W. BLACK.

Lady Silverdale's Sweetheart. By W. BLACK.

Sunrise. By W. BLACK.

The Trumpet Major. By THOMAS HARDY,

An English Squire. By Miss COLERIDGE.

Low's Standard Novels (*continued*):—

Mary Marston. By GEORGE MACDONALD.

Guild Court. By GEORGE MACDONALD.

The Vicar's Daughter. By GEORGE MACDONALD.

Out of Court. By Mrs. CASHEL HOEY.

History of a Crime: The Story of the Coup d'État. By VICTOR HUGO.

Alice Lorraine. By R. D. BLACKMORE.

Lorna Doone. By R. D. BLACKMORE. 18th Edition.

Cradock Nowell. By R. D. BLACKMORE.

Clara Vaughan. By R. D. BLACKMORE.

Cripps the Carrier. By R. D. BLACKMORE.

Erema; or, My Father's Sin. By R. D. BLACKMORE.

Mary Anerley. By R. D. BLACKMORE.

Innocent. By Mrs. OLIPHANT. Eight Illustrations.

Work. A Story of Experience. By LOUISA M. ALCOTT. Illustrations. *See also* Rose Library.

The Afghan Knife. By R. A. STERNDALE, Author of "Seonce."

A French Heiress in her own Chateau. By the Author of "One Only," "Constantia," &c. Six Illustrations.

Ninety-Three. By VICTOR HUGO. Numerous Illustrations.

My Wife and I. By Mrs. BEECHER STOWE.

Wreck of the Grosvenor. By W. CLARK RUSSELL.

John Holdsworth (Chief Mate). By W. CLARK RUSSELL.

A Sailor's Sweetheart. By W. CLARK RUSSELL.

Elinor Dryden. By Mrs. MACQUOID.

Diane. By Mrs. MACQUOID.

Poganuc People, Their Loves and Lives. By Mrs. BEECHER STOWE.

A Golden Sorrow. By Mrs. CASHEL HOEY.

A Story of the Dragonnades; or, Asylum Christi. By the Rev. E. GILLIAT, M.A.

Low's Handbook to the Charities of London. Edited and revised to date by C. MACKESON, F.S.S., Editor of "A Guide to the Churches of London and its Suburbs," &c. Paper, 1s.; cloth, 1s. 6d.

MACGREGOR (John) "Rob Roy" on the Baltic. 3rd Edition, small post 8vo, 2s. 6d.; cloth, gilt edges, 3s. 6d.

—— *A Thousand Miles in the "Rob Roy" Canoe.* 11th Edition, small post 8vo, 2s. 6d.; cloth, gilt edges, 3s. 6d.

Macgregor (John) Description of the " Rob Roy" Canoe, with Plans, &c., 1s.

—— *The Voyage Alone in the Yawl " Rob Roy."* New Edition, thoroughly revised, with additions, small post 8vo, 5s.; boards, 2s. 6d.

Macquoid (Mrs.) Elinor Dryden. Crown 8vo, cloth, 6s.

—— *Diane.* Crown 8vo, 6s.

Magazine. See Harper, Union Jack, The Etcher, Men of Mark.

Magyarland. A Narrative of Travels through the Snowy Car- pathians, and Great Alföld of the Magyár. By a Fellow of the Carpathian Society (Diploma of 1881), and Author of " The Indian Alps." 2 vols., 8vo, cloth extra, with about 120 Woodcuts from the Author's own sketches and drawings, 42s.

Manitoba : its History, Growth, and Present Position. By the Rev. Professor Bryce, Principal of Manitoba College, Winnipeg. Crown 8vo, with Illustrations and Maps, 7s. 6d.

Markham (C. R.) The Threshold of the Unknown Region. Crown 8vo, with Four Maps, 4th Edition. Cloth extra, 10s. 6d.

Maury (Commander) Physical Geography of the Sea, and its Meteorology. Being a Reconstruction and Enlargement of his former Work, with Charts and Diagrams. New Edition, crown 8vo, 6s.

Memoirs of Count Miot de Melito, Minister, Ambassador, Councillor of State, and Member of the Institute of France, between the years 1788 and 1815. Edited by General Fleischmann. From the French by Mrs. Cashel Hoey and Mr. John Lillie. 2 vols., demy 8vo, cloth extra, 36s.

Memoirs of Madame de Rémusat, 1802—1808. By her Grandson, M. Paul de Rémusat, Senator. Translated by Mrs. Cashel Hoey and Mr. John Lillie. 4th Edition, cloth extra. This work was written by Madame de Rémusat during the time she was living on the most intimate terms with the Empress Josephine, and is full of revelations respecting the private life of Bonaparte, and of men and politics of the first years of the century. Revelations which have already created a great sensation in Paris. 8vo, 2 vols., 32s.

—— *See also* " Selection."

Menus (366, one for each day of the year). Translated from the French of Count Brisse, by Mrs. Matthew Clarke. Crown 8vo, 10s. 6d.

Men of Mark : a Gallery of Contemporary Portraits of the most Eminent Men of the Day taken from Life, especially for this publication, price 1s. 6d. monthly. Vols. I. to VI., handsomely bound, cloth, gilt edges, 25s. each.

Mendelssohn Family (The), 1729—1847. From Letters and Journals. Translated from the German of SEBASTIAN HENSEL. 2 vols., demy 8vo, 30s.

Michael Strogoff. 10s. 6d. and 5s. *See* VERNE.

Mitford (Miss). *See* " Our Village."

Music. *See* " Great Musicians."

My Lady Greensleeves. By HELEN MATHERS, Authoress of "Comin' through the Rye," "Cherry Ripe," &c. 1 vol. edition, crown 8vo, cloth, 6s.

Mysterious Island. By JULES VERNE. 3 vols., imperial 16mo. 150 Illustrations, cloth gilt, 3s. 6d. each; elaborately bound, gilt edges, 7s. 6d. each. Cheap Edition, with some of the Illustrations, cloth, gilt, 2s.; paper, 1s. each.

NARRATIVES of State Trials in the Nineteenth Century. First Period: From the Union with Ireland to the Death of George IV., 1801—1830. By G. LATHOM BROWNE, of the Middle Temple, Barrister-at-Law. 2 vols., crown 8vo, cloth, 24s.

Nature and Functions of Art (The); and more especially of Architecture. By LEOPOLD EIDLITZ. Medium 8vo, cloth, 21s.

Naval Brigade in South Africa (The). By HENRY F. NORBURY, C.B., R.N. Crown 8vo, cloth extra, 10s. 6d.

New Child's Play (A). Sixteen Drawings by E. V. B. Beautifully printed in colours, 4to, cloth extra, 12s. 6d.

New Guinea: What I did and what I saw. By L. M. D'ALBERTIS, Officer of the Order of the Crown of Italy, Honorary Member and Gold Medallist of the I.R.G S., C.M.Z.S., &c., &c. In 2 vols., demy 8vo, cloth extra, with Maps, Coloured Plates, and numerous very fine Woodcut Illustrations, 42s.

New Ireland. By A. M. SULLIVAN, M.P. for Louth. 2 vols., demy 8vo, 30s. Cheaper Edition, 1 vol., crown 8vo, 8s. 6d.

New Novels. Crown 8vo, cloth, 10s. 6d. per vol. :—
Christowell: a Dartmoor Tale. By R. D. BLACKMORE. 3 vols.
The Braes of Yarrow. By CHAS. GIBBON. 3 vols.
A Laodicean. By THOMAS HARDY, Author of " Far from the Madding Crowd," "Trumpet Major," &c., &c. 3 vols.
Waiting. By Miss A. M. HOPKINSON. 3 vols.
Don John. By Miss JEAN INGELOW. 3 vols.
Warlock of Warlock. By GEORGE MACDONALD. 3 vols.
Riverside Papers. By J. D. HOPPUS. 2 vols., small post 8vo, 12s.
Cecily's Debt. By Mrs. A. B. CHURCH. 3 vols.

Nice and Her Neighbours. By the Rev. CANON HOLE, Author of " A Book about Roses," " A Little Tour in Ireland," &c. Small 4to, with numerous choice Illustrations, 12s. 6d.

Noah's Ark. A Contribution to the Study of Unnatural History.
By PHIL ROBINSON, Author of "In my Indian Garden," "Under
the Punkah," &c., &c.   2 vols.   Small post 8vo, 12s. 6d.

Noble Words and Noble Deeds.   From the French of E. MULLER.
Containing many Full-page Illustrations by PHILIPPOTEAUX.   Square
imperial 16mo, cloth extra, 7s. 6d. ; plainer binding, plain edges, 5s.

Nordenskiöld's Voyage around Asia and Europe. A Popular
Account of the North-East Passage of the "Vega." By Lieut. A.
HOVGAARD, of the Royal Danish Navy, and member of the "Vega"
Expedition.   Demy 8vo, cloth, with about 50 Illustrations and
3 Maps, 21s.

North American Review (The).   Monthly, price 2s. 6d.

Nothing to Wear ; and Two Millions.   By W. A. BUTLER.
New Edition.   Small post 8vo, in stiff coloured wrapper, 1s.

Nursery Playmates (Prince of).   217 Coloured Pictures for
Children by eminent Artists.   Folio, in coloured boards, 6s.

*O*FF *to the Wilds: A Story for Boys.*   By G. MANVILLE
FENN.   Most richly and profusely Illustrated.   Crown 8vo, cloth
extra, 7s. 6d.

Old-Fashioned Girl.   See ALCOTT.

On Horseback through Asia Minor.   By Capt. FRED BURNABY,
Royal Horse Guards, Author of "A Ride to Khiva."   2 vols.,
8vo, with three Maps and Portrait of Author, 6th Edition, 38s. ;
Cheaper Edition, crown 8vo, 10s. 6d.

Our Little Ones in Heaven.   Edited by the Rev. H. ROBBINS.
With Frontispiece after Sir JOSHUA REYNOLDS.   Fcap., cloth extra,
New Edition—the 3rd, with Illustrations, 5s.

Our Village.   By MARY RUSSELL MITFORD.   Illustrated with
Frontispiece Steel Engraving, and 12 full-page and 157 smaller Cuts.
Crown 4to, cloth, gilt edges, 21s.; cheaper binding, 10s. 6d.

Our Woodland Trees.   By F. G. HEATH.   Large post 8vo,
cloth, gilt edges, uniform with "Fern World" and "Fern Paradise,"
by the same Author.   8 Coloured Plates (showing leaves of every
British Tree) and 20 Woodcuts, cloth, gilt edges, 12s. 6d.   Third
Edition.   About 600 pages.

Outlines of Ornament in all Styles.   A Work of Reference for
the Architect, Art Manufacturer, Decorative Artist, and Practical
Painter.   By W. and G. A. AUDSLEY, Fellows of the Royal Institute
of British Architects.   Only a limited number have been printed and
the stones destroyed.   Small folio, 60 plates, with introductory text,
cloth gilt, 31s. 6d.

PAINTERS of All Schools. By LOUIS VIARDOT, and other Writers. 500 pp., super-royal 8vo, 20 Full-page and 70 smaller Engravings, cloth extra, 25s. A New Edition is issued in Half-crown parts, with fifty additional portraits, cloth, gilt edges, 31s. 6d.

Painting (A Short History of the British School of). By GEO. H. SHEPHERD. Post 8vo, cloth, 3s. 6d.

Palliser (Mrs.) A History of Lace, from the Earliest Period. A New and Revised Edition, with additional cuts and text, upwards of 100 Illustrations and coloured Designs. 1 vol., 8vo, 1l. 1s.

———— *Historic Devices, Badges, and War Cries.* 8vo, 1l. 1s.

———— *The China Collector's Pocket Companion.* With upwards of 1000 Illustrations of Marks and Monograms. 2nd Edition, with Additions. Small post 8vo, limp cloth, 5s.

Parliamentary History of the Irish Land Question (The). From 1829 to 1869, and the Origin and Results of the Ulster Custom. By R. BARRY O'BRIEN, Barrister-at-Law, Author of "The Irish Land Question and English Public Opinion." 3rd Edition, corrected and revised, with additional matter. Post 8vo, cloth extra, 6s.

Pathways of Palestine: a Descriptive Tour through the Holy Land. By the Rev. CANON TRISTRAM. Illustrated with 44 permanent Photographs. (The Photographs are large, and most perfect Specimens of the Art.) Published in 22 Monthly Parts, 4to, in Wrapper, 2s. 6d. each. Vol. I., containing 12 parts, 24 Illustrations, cloth, gilt edges, 31s. 6d.

Peasant Life in the West of England. By FRANCIS GEORGE HEATH, Author of "Sylvan Spring," "The Fern World." Crown 8vo, 400 pp. (with Autograph Letter of seven pages from Lord Beaconsfield to the Author, written December 28, 1880), 10s. 6d.

Petites Leçons de Conversation et de Grammaire: Oral and Conversational Method; being Lessons introducing the most Useful Topics of Conversation, upon an entirely new principle, &c. By F. JULIEN, French Master at King Edward the Sixth's School, Birmingham. Author of "The Student's French Examiner," "First Steps in Conversational French Grammar," which see.

Photography (History and Handbook of). See TISSANDIER.

Physical Treatise on Electricity and Magnetism. By J. E. H. GORDON, B.A. With about 200 coloured, full-page, and other Illustrations. In respect to the number and beauty of the Illustrations, the work is quite unique. 2 vols., 8vo, 36s.

Poems of the Inner Life. A New Edition, Revised, with many additional Poems. Small post 8vo, cloth, 5s.

Poganuc People: their Loves and Lives. By Mrs. BEECHER STOWE. Crown 8vo, cloth, 6s.

Polar Expeditions. *See* KOLDEWEY, MARKHAM, MacGAHAN, NARES, and NORDENSKIÖLD.

Poynter (Edward J., R.A.). *See* "Illustrated Text-books."

Publishers' Circular (The), and General Record of British and Foreign Literature. Published on the 1st and 15th of every Month, 3d.

Pyrenees (The). By HENRY BLACKBURN. With 100 Illustrations by GUSTAVE DORÉ, a New Map of Routes, and Information for Travellers, corrected to 1881. With a description of Lourdes in 1880. Crown 8vo, cloth extra, 7s. 6d.

RAMBAUD (Alfred). *History of Russia, from its Origin* to the Year 1877. With Six Maps. Translated by Mrs. L. B. LANE. 2 vols., demy 8vo, cloth extra, 38s.

Recollections of Writers. By CHARLES and MARY COWDEN CLARKE. Authors of "The Concordance to Shakespeare," &c.; with Letters of CHARLES LAMB, LEIGH HUNT, DOUGLAS JERROLD, and CHARLES DICKENS; and a Preface by MARY COWDEN CLARKE. Crown 8vo, cloth, 10s. 6d.

Rémusat (Madame de). *See* "Memoirs of," "Selection."

Richter (Jean Paul). *The Literary Works of Leonardo da* Vinci. Containing his Writings on Painting, Sculpture, and Architecture, his Philosophical Maxims, Humorous Writings, and Miscellaneous Notes on Personal Events, on his Contemporaries, on Literature, &c.; for the first time published from Autograph Manuscripts. By J. P. RICHTER, Ph.Dr., Hon. Member of the Royal and Imperial Academy of Rome, &c. 2 vols., imperial 8vo, containing about 200 Drawings in Autotype Reproductions, and numerous other Illustrations. Price Eight Guineas to Subscribers. After publication the price will be Ten Guineas.

Robinson (Phil). *See* "In my Indian Garden," "Under the Punkah," "Noah's Ark."

Rochefoucauld's Reflections. Bayard Series, 2s. 6d.

Rogers (S.) Pleasures of Memory. *See* "Choice Editions of Choice Books." 2s. 6d.

Rose in Bloom. *See* ALCOTT.

Rose Library (*The*). Popular Literature of all Countries. Each volume, 1s. ; cloth, 2s. 6d. Many of the Volumes are Illustrated —

1. **Sea-Gull Rook.** By JULES SANDEAU. Illustrated.
2. **Little Women.** By LOUISA M. ALCOTT.
3. **Little Women Wedded.** Forming a Sequel to "Little Women."
4. **The House on Wheels.** By MADAME DE STOLZ. Illustrated.
5. **Little Men.** By LOUISA M. ALCOTT. Dble. vol., 2s. ; cloth, 3s. 6d.
6. **The Old-Fashioned Girl.** By LOUISA M. ALCOTT. Double vol., 2s. ; cloth, 3s. 6d.
   . **The Mistress of the Manse.** By J. G. HOLLAND.
   . **Timothy Titcomb's Letters to Young People, Single and Married.**
7.
9. **Undine, and the Two Captains.** By Baron DE LA MOTTE FOUQUÉ. A New Translation by F. E. BUNNETT. Illustrated.
10. **Draxy Miller's Dowry, and the Elder's Wife.** By SAXE HOLM.
11. **The Four Gold Pieces.** By Madame GOURAUD. Numerous Illustrations.
12. **Work.** A Story of Experience. First Portion. By LOUISA M. ALCOTT.
13. **Beginning Again.** Being a Continuation of "Work." By LOUISA M. ALCOTT.
14. **Picciola; or, the Prison Flower.** By X. B. SAINTINE. Numerous graphic Illustrations.
15. **Robert's Holidays.** Illustrated.
16. **The Two Children of St. Domingo.** Numerous Illustrations.
17. **Aunt Jo's Scrap Bag.**
18. **Stowe (Mrs. H. B.) The Pearl of Orr's Island.**
19. —— **The Minister's Wooing.**
20. —— **Betty's Bright Idea.**
21. —— **The Ghost in the Mill.**
22. —— **Captain Kidd's Money.**
23. —— **We and our Neighbours.** Double vol., 2s.
24. —— **My Wife and I.** Double vol., 2s. ; cloth, gilt, 3s. 6d.
25. **Hans Brinker ; or, the Silver Skates.**
26. **Lowell's My Study Window.**
27. **Holmes (O. W.) The Guardian Angel.**
28. **Warner (C. D.) My Summer in a Garden.**
29. **Hitherto.** By the Author of "The Gayworthys." 2 vols., 1s. each.
30. **Helen's Babies.** By their Latest Victim.
31. **The Barton Experiment.** By the Author of "Helen's Babies."
32. **Dred.** By Mrs. BEECHER STOWE. Double vol., 2s. ; cloth gilt, 3s. 6d.
33. **Warner (C. D.) In the Wilderness.**
34. **Six to One.** A Seaside Story.
35. **Nothing to Wear, and Two Millions.**
36. **Farm Ballads.** By WILL CARLETON.
37. **Farm Festivals.** By WILL CARLETON.
38. **Farm Legends.** By WILL CARLETON.

Round the Yule Log: Norwegian Folk and Fairy Tales. Translated from the Norwegian of P. CHR. ASBJÖRNSEN. With 100 Illustrations. Imperial 16mo, cloth extra, gilt edges, 7s. 6d.

Russell (W. Clarke). See "A Sailor's Sweetheart," 3 vols., 31s. 6d.; "Wreck of the Grosvenor," 6s.; "John Holdsworth (Chief Mate)," 6s.

Russell (W. H., LL.D.) Hesperothen: Notes from the Western World. A Record of a Ramble through part of the United States, Canada, and the Far West, in the Spring and Summer of 1881. By W. H. RUSSELL, LL.D. 2 vols., crown 8vo, cloth, 24s.

—— *The Tour of the Prince of Wales in India.* By W. H. RUSSELL, LL.D. Fully Illustrated by SYDNEY P. HALL, M.A. Super-royal 8vo, cloth extra, gilt edges, 52s. 6d.; Large Paper Edition, 84s.

SAINTS and their Symbols: A Companion in the Churches and Picture Galleries of Europe. With Illustrations. Royal 16mo, cloth extra, 3s. 6d.

Science Ladders. Fcap. 8vo, stiff covers, 6d. each.

SERIES I.

No. I. Forms of Land and Water. With 15 Illustrations.
" **II. The Story of Early Exploration.**

SERIES II.

" **I. Vegetable Life.** With 35 Illustrations.
" **II. Flowerless Plants.**

SERIES III.

" **I. Lowest Forms of Water Animals.** With 22 Illustrations.
" **II. Lowly Mantle and Armour-Wearers.**

Schuyler (Eugène). The Life of Peter the Great. By EUGÈNE SCHUYLER, Author of "Turkestan." 2 vols., demy 8vo, cloth extra.

Selection from the Letters of Madame de Rémusat to her Husband and Son, from 1804 to 1813. From the French, by Mrs. CASHEL HOEY and Mr. JOHN LILLIE. In 1 vol., demy 8vo (uniform with the "Memoirs of Madame de Rémusat," 2 vols.), cloth extra, 16s.

Seonee: Sporting in the Satpura Range of Central India, and in the Valley of the Nerbudda. By R. A. STERNDALE, F.R.G.S. 8vo, with numerous Illustrations, 21s.

Seven Years in South Africa: Travels, Researches, and Hunting Adventures between the Diamond-Fields and the Zambesi (1872—1879). By Dr. EMIL HOLUB. With over 100 Original Illustrations and 4 Maps. In 2 vols., demy 8vo, cloth extra, 42s.

Serpent Charmer (The): a Tale of the Indian Mutiny. From the French of LOUIS ROUSSELET. Numerous Illustrations. Crown 8vo, cloth extra, gilt edges, 7s. 6d. ; plainer binding, 5s.

Shadbolt (S.) The Afghan Campaigns of 1878—1880. By SYDNEY SHADBOLT, Joint Author of "The South African Campaign of 1879." Dedicated by permission to Major-General Sir Frederick Roberts, G.C.B., V.C., &c. 2 vols., royal quarto, cloth extra ; to subscribers before publication, 2l. 10s. ; to non-subscribers, 3l.

Shooting: its Appliances, Practice, and Purpose. By JAMES DALZIEL DOUGALL, F.S.A., F.Z.A., Author of "Scottish Field Sports," &c. New Edition, revised with additions. Crown 8vo, cloth extra, 7s. 6d.

> "The book is admirable in every way. . . . . We wish it every success."—*Globe.*
> "A very complete treatise. . . . . Likely to take high rank as an authority on shooting."—*Daily News.*

Sikes (Wirt). Rambles and Studies in Old South Wales. With numerous Illustrations. Demy 8vo, cloth extra, 18s. By WIRT SIKES, Author of "British Goblins," which see.

Silent Hour (The). See "Gentle Life Series." .

Silver Sockets (The); and other Shadows of Redemption. Eighteen Sermons preached in Christ Church, Hampstead, by the Rev. C. H. WALLER. Small post 8vo, cloth, 6s.

Smith (G.) Assyrian Explorations and Discoveries. By the late GEORGE SMITH. Illustrated by Photographs and Woodcuts. Demy 8vo, 6th Edition, 18s.

———— *The Chaldean Account of · Genesis.* By the late G. SMITH, of the Department of Oriental Antiquities, British Museum. With many Illustrations. Demy 8vo, cloth extra, 6th Edition, 16s. An entirely New Edition, completely revised and re-written by the Rev. PROFESSOR SAYCE, Queen's College, Oxford. Demy 8vo, 18s.

Snow-Shoes and Canoes ; or, the Adventures of a Fur-Hunter in the Hudson's Bay Territory. By W. H. G. KINGSTON. 2nd Edition. With numerous Illustrations. Square crown 8vo, cloth extra, gilt edges, 7s. 6d. ; plainer binding, 5s.

South African Campaign, 1879 *(The).* Compiled by J. P. MACKINNON (formerly 72nd Highlanders), and S. H. SHADBOLT; and dedicated, by permission, to Field-Marshal H.R.H. The Duke of Cambridge. 4to, handsomely bound in cloth extra, 2l. 10s.

Stanley (H. M.) How I Found Livingstone. Crown 8vo, cloth extra, 7s. 6d. ; large Paper Edition, 10s. 6d.

Stanley (H. M.) "My Kalulu," Prince, King, and Slave. A Story from Central Africa. Crown 8vo, about 430 pp., with numerous graphic Illustrations, after Original Designs by the Author. Cloth, 7s. 6d.

—————— *Coomassie and Magdala.* A Story of Two British Campaigns in Africa. Demy 8vo, with Maps and Illustrations, 16s.

—————— *Through the Dark Continent,* which see.

Story without an End. From the German of Carové, by the late Mrs. SARAH T. AUSTIN. Crown 4to, with 15 Exquisite Drawings by E. V. B., printed in Colours in Fac-simile of the original Water Colours; and numerous other Illustrations. New Edition, 7s. 6d.

—————— square 4to, with Illustrations by HARVEY. 2s. 6d.

Stowe (Mrs. Beecher) Dred. Cheap Edition, boards, 2s. Cloth, gilt edges, 3s. 6d.

—————— *Footsteps of the Master.* With Illustrations and red borders. Small post 8vo, cloth extra, 6s.

—————— *Geography,* with 60 Illustrations. Square cloth, 4s. 6d.

—————— *Little Foxes.* Cheap Edition, 1s.; Library Edition, 4s. 6d.

—————— *Betty's Bright Idea.* 1s.

—————— *My Wife and I; or, Harry Henderson's History.* Small post 8vo, cloth extra, 6s.*

—————— *Minister's Wooing.* 5s; Copyright Series, 1s. 6d.; cl., 2s.*

—————— *Old Town Folk.* 6s.; Cheap Edition, 2s. 6d.

—————— *Old Town Fireside Stories.* Cloth extra, 3s. 6d.

—————— *Our Folks at Poganuc.* 6s.

—————— *We and our Neighbours.* 1 vol., small post 8vo, 6s. Sequel to "My Wife and I."*

—————— *Pink and White Tyranny.* Small post 8vo, 3s. 6d. Cheap Edition, 1s. 6d. and 2s.

* *See also* Rose Library.

Stowe (Mrs. Beecher) Queer Little People. 1s.; cloth, 2s.

────── *Chimney Corner.* 1s.; cloth, 1s. 6d.

────── *The Pearl of Orr's Island.* Crown 8vo, 5s.*

────── *Woman in Sacred History.* Illustrated with 15 Chromo-lithographs and about 200 pages of Letterpress. Demy 4to, cloth extra, gilt edges, 25s.

Student's French Examiner. By F. JULIEN, Author of "Petites Leçons de Conversation et de Grammaire." Square cr. 8vo, cloth, 2s.

Studies in the Theory of Descent. By Dr. AUG. WEISMANN, Professor in the University of Freiburg. Translated and edited by RAPHAEL MELDOLA, F.C.S., Secretary of the Entomological Society of London. Part I.—"On the Seasonal Dimorphism of Butterflies," containing Original Communications by Mr. W. H. EDWARDS, of Coalburgh. With two Coloured Plates. Price of Part. I. (to Sub-scribers for the whole work only), 8s; Part II. (6 coloured plates), 16s.; Part III., 6s.

Sunrise: A Story of These Times. By WILLIAM BLACK, Author of "A Daughter of Heth," &c. Crown 8vo, cloth, 6s.

Surgeon's Handbook on the Treatment of Wounded in War. By Dr. FRIEDRICH ESMARCH, Surgeon-General to the Prussian Army. Numerous Coloured Plates and Illustrations, 8vo, strongly bound, 1l. 8s.

Sylvan Spring. By FRANCIS GEORGE HEATH. Illustrated by 12 Coloured Plates, drawn by F. E. HULME, F.L.S., Artist and Author of "Familiar Wild Flowers;" by 16 full-page, and more than 100 other Wood Engravings. Large post 8vo, cloth, gilt edges, 12s. 6d.

TAINE (H. A.) "Les Origines de la France Contemporaine." Translated by JOHN DURAND.
    Vol. 1. **The Ancient Regime.** Demy 8vo, cloth, 16s.
    Vol. 2. **The French Revolution.** Vol. 1. do.
    Vol. 3. **Do.** do. Vol. 2. do.

Tauchnitz's English Editions of German Authors. Each volume, cloth flexible, 2s.; or sewed, 1s. 6d. (Catalogues post free on application.)

────── *(B.) German and English Dictionary.* Cloth, 1s. 6d.; roan, 2s.

───────────────

* *See also* Rose Library.

Tauchnitz's French and English Dictionary.   Paper, 1s. 6d.;
cloth, 2s.; roan, 2s. 6d.

———— *Italian and English Dictionary.*   Paper, 1s. 6d.; cloth,
2s.; roan, 2s. 6d.

———— *Spanish and English.*   Paper, 1s. 6d.; cloth, 2s.; roan,
2s. 6d.

Through America; or, Nine Months in the United States.   By
W. G. MARSHALL, M.A.   With nearly 100 Woodcuts of Views of
Utah country and the famous Yosemite Valley; The Giant Trees,
New York, Niagara, San Francisco, &c.; containing a full account
of Mormon Life, as noted by the Author during his visits to Salt Lake
City in 1878 and 1879.   Demy 8vo, 21s.; cheap edition, crown 8vo,
7s. 6d.

Through the Dark Continent: The Sources of the Nile; Around
the Great Lakes, and down the Congo.   By H. M. STANLEY.
Cheap Edition, crown 8vo, with some of the Illustrations and Maps,
12s. 6d.

Through Siberia.   By the Rev. HENRY LANSDELL.   Illustrated
with about 30 Engravings, 2 Route Maps, and Photograph of the
Author, in Fish-skin Costume of the Gilyaks on the Lower Amur.
2 vols., demy 8vo, 30s.

Tour of the Prince of Wales in India.   See RUSSELL.

Trees and Ferns.   By F. G. HEATH.   Crown 8vo, cloth, gilt
edges, with numerous Illustrations, 3s. 6d.
   " A charming little volume."—*Land and Water.*

Tristram (Rev. Canon) Pathways of Palestine: A Descriptive
Tour through the Holy Land.   First Series.   Illustrated by 22 Permanent Photographs.   Folio, cloth extra, gilt edges, 31s. 6d.

Two Friends.   By LUCIEN BIART, Author of " Adventures of
a Young Naturalist," " My Rambles in the New World," &c.   Small
post 8vo, numerous Illustrations, gilt edges, 7s. 6d.; plainer binding, 5s.

Two Supercargoes (The); or, Adventures in Savage Africa.
By W. H. G. KINGSTON.   Numerous Full-page Illustrations.   Square
imperial 16mo, cloth extra, gilt edges, 7s. 6d.; plainer binding, 5s.

UNDER the Punkah.   By PHIL ROBINSON, Author of "In
my Indian Garden."   Crown 8vo, limp cloth, 3s. 6d.

Union Jack (*The*). *Every Boy's Paper.* Edited by G. A. HENTY. One Penny Weekly, Monthly 6*d.* Vol. III. commences with the Part for November, 1881, and contains the first Chapters of Three Serial Stories by G. MANVILLE FENN, LOUIS ROUSSELET, and W. H. G. KINGSTON, from the French of "Landelle." Illustrated by the Best Artists. With the first Part is presented a Photograph of Jules Verne, and a Coloured Plate, "Rounding the Lightship," a Yachting Incident; and this Volume will also contain New Stories by Col. BUTLER, Author of "The Great Lone Land," JULES VERNE, an Historical Story by the Editor, &c., &c. Volume II. for 1881, beautifully bound in red cloth (royal 4to), 7*s.* 6*d.*, gilt edges, 8*s.* Beautifully Illustrated with over 400 Illustrations, including 52 full-page Engravings, 8 Steel ditto, 7 Coloured Plates, and Photograph of the Editor.

The Contents comprise:

The Cornet of Horse: a Tale of Marlborough's Wars. By the EDITOR.

The Young Franc-Tireurs: a Tale of the Franco-German War. By the EDITOR.

The Ensign and Middy: a Tale of the Malay Peninsula. By G. MANVILLE FENN.

The Steam House: THE DEMON OF CAWNPORE. A Tale of India. By JULES VERNE.

Rawdon School: a Tale of Schoolboy Life. By BERNARD HELDMANN.

Dorrincourt: a Story of a Term there. By BERNARD HELDMANN.

Peyton Phelps; or, Adventures among the Italian Carbonari. By G. STEBBING.

Gerald Rattlin: a Tale of Sea Life. By GEO. ELFORD.

A Fight in Freedom's Cause.

An Eventful Ride.

The Ghost of Leytonstone Manor.

An Editor's Yarns.

True Tales of Brave Actions.

And numerous other Articles of Interest and Instruction.

A few copies of Volume I., for 1880, still remain, price 6*s.*

Upolu; *or, A Paradise of the Gods;* being a Description of the Antiquities of the chief Island of the Samoan Group, with Remarks on the Topography, Ethnology, and History of the Polynesian Islands in general. By the late HANDLEY BATHURST STERNDALE. Edited and annotated by his brother, Author of "Seonee," "The Afghan Knife," &c. 2 vols., demy 8vo.

VICTOR *Hugo and his Times.* Translated from the French of A. BARBOU by ELLEN E. FREWER. 120 Illustrations, many of them from designs by Victor Hugo himself. Super-royal 8vo, cloth extra.

Vincent (*F.*) *Norsk, Lapp, and Finn.* By FRANK VINCENT, Jun., Author of "The Land of the White Elephant," "Through and Through the Tropics," &c. 8vo, cloth, with Frontispiece and Map, 12*s.*

LARGE CROWN 8vo . .	and from 50 to 100 full-page illustrations.			
WORKS.	In very handsome cloth binding, gilt edges.	In plainer binding, plain edges.	In cloth binding, gilt edges, smaller type.	
	s. d.	s. d.	s. d.	
Twenty Thousand Leagues under the Sea. Part I. Ditto Part II.	10 6	5 0	3 6	2 vols., 1s.
Hector Servadac . . .	10 6	5 0	3 6	2 vols., 1s.
The Fur Country . . .	10 6	5 0	3 6	2 vols., 1s.
From the Earth to the Moon and a Trip round it	10 6	5 0	2 vols., 2s. each.	2 vols., 1s.
Michael Strogoff, the Courier of the Czar . .	10 6	5 0	3 6	2 vols., 1s.
Dick Sands, the Boy Captain	10 6	5 0	3 6	2 vols., 1s.
Five Weeks in a Balloon .	7 6	3 6	2 0	1s. 0d.
Adventures of Three Englishmen and Three Russians	7 6	3 6	2 0	1 0
Around the World in Eighty Days	7 6	3 6	2 0	1 0
A Floating City . . .	7 6	3 6	2 0	1 0
The Blockade Runners .			2 0	1 0
Dr. Ox's Experiment . .			2 0	1 0
Master Zacharius . . .			2 0	1 0
A Drama in the Air . .	7 6	3 6		
A Winter amid the Ice .			2 0	1 0
The Survivors of the "Chancellor"	7 6	3 6	2 0	2 vols. 1s. e
Martin Paz			2 0	1 0
THE MYSTERIOUS ISLAND, 3 vols. :—	22 6	10 6	6 0	3 0
Vol. I. Dropped from the Clouds	7 6	3 6	2 0	1 0
Vol. II. Abandoned . .	7 6	3 6	2 0	1 0
Vol. III. Secret of the Island	7 6	3 6	2 0	1 0
The Child of the Cavern .	7 6	3 6	2 0	1 0
The Begum's Fortune . .	7 6	3 6		
The Tribulations of a Chinaman	7 6			
THE STEAM HOUSE, 2 vols.:—				
Vol. I. Demon of Cawnpore	7 6			
Vol. II. Tigers and Traitors	7 6			
THE GIANT RAFT, 2 vols.:—				
Vol. I. Eight Hundred Leagues on the Amazon.	7 6			
Vol. II. The Cryptogram	7 6			

WAITARUNA: A Story of New Zealand Life. By ALEXANDER BATHGATE, Author of "Colonial Experiences." Crown 8vo, cloth, 5s.

Waller (Rev. C. H.) The Names on the Gates of Pearl, and other Studies. By the Rev. C. H. WALLER, M.A. Second Edition. Crown 8vo, cloth extra, 6s.

—— *A Grammar and Analytical Vocabulary of the Words in* the Greek Testament. Compiled from Bruder's Concordance. For the use of Divinity Students and Greek Testament Classes. By the Rev. C. H. WALLER, M.A. Part I. The Grammar. Small post 8vo, cloth, 2s. 6d. Part II. The Vocabulary, 2s. 6d.

—— *Adoption and the Covenant.* Some Thoughts on Confirmation. Super-royal 16mo, cloth limp, 2s. 6d.

—— *See also* "Silver Sockets."

Wanderings South by East: a Descriptive Record of Four Years of Travel in the less known Countries and Islands of the Southern and Eastern Hemispheres. By WALTER COOTE. 8vo, with very numerous Illustrations and a Map, 21s.

Warner (C. D.) My Summer in a Garden. Rose Library, 1s.

—— *Back-log Studies.* Boards, 1s. 6d.; cloth, 2s.

—— *In the Wilderness.* Rose Library, 1s.

—— *Mummies and Moslems.* 8vo, cloth, 12s.

Weaving. See "History and Principles."

Where to Find Ferns. By F. G. HEATH, Author of "The Fern World," &c.; with a Special Chapter on the Ferns round London; Lists of Fern Stations, and Descriptions of Ferns and Fern Habitats throughout the British Isles. Crown 8vo, cloth, price 3s.

White (Rhoda E.) From Infancy to Womanhood. A Book of Instruction for Young Mothers. Crown 8vo, cloth, 10s. 6d.

Whittier (J. G.) The King's Missive, and later Poems. 18mo, choice parchment cover, 3s. 6d. This book contains all the Poems written by Mr. Whittier since the publication of "Hazel Blossoms."

—— *The Whittier Birthday Book.* Extracts from the Author's writings, with Portrait and numerous Illustrations. Uniform with the "Emerson Birthday Book." Square 16mo, very choice binding, 3s. 6d.

Wills, A Few Hints on Proving, without Professional Assistance.
By a PROBATE COURT OFFICIAL. 5th Edition, revised with Forms
of Wills, Residuary Accounts, &c. Fcap. 8vo, cloth limp, 1s.

With Axe and Rifle on the Western Prairies. By W. H. G.
KINGSTON. With numerous Illustrations, square crown 8vo, cloth
extra, gilt edges, 7s. 6d.; plainer binding, 5s.

Woolsey (C. D., LL.D.) Introduction to the Study of Inter-
national Law; designed as an Aid in Teaching and in Historical
Studies. 5th Edition, demy 8vo, 18s.

Words of Wellington: Maxims and Opinions, Sentences and
Reflections of the Great Duke, gathered from his Despatches, Letters,
and Speeches (Bayard Series). 2s. 6d.

Wreck of the Grosvenor. By W. CLARK RUSSELL, Author of
"John Holdsworth, Chief Mate," "A Sailor's Sweetheart," &c. 6s.
Third and Cheaper Edition.

Wright (the late Rev. Henry) Sermons. Crown 8vo, with
Biographical Preface, Portrait, &c. [*In the press.*

London:

SAMPSON LOW, MARSTON, SEARLE, & RIVINGTON,

CROWN BUILDINGS, 188, FLEET STREET, E.C.

GREAT ARTISTS.

"Few things in the way of small books upon great subjects, avowedly cheap necessarily brief, have been hitherto so well done as these biographies of the Great Ma in painting."—*Times.*

"A deserving series."—*Edinburgh Review.*

"Most thoroughly and tastefully edited."—*Spectator.*

"The scheme is a good one."—*The Pen.*

"This most interesting, and, we may add, attractive series."—*Liverpool Albion.*

"This excellent series of monographs on the *Great Artists* keeps rapidly adding t claims on public attention as a condensed library of fine-art history. Based on the h idea of bringing together, within small compass, the results of the most recent criticism investigation, the scheme has been admirably carried out by the writers entrusted with several biographies. Competent knowledge of the literature gradually accumulating r the work of famous artists has in each case been brought to bear, the reader being at placed in possession of the more material facts and put in the way of pursuing fu inquiries, if so minded."—*Scotsman.*

"It would not have been easy to find a writer better fitted than Mr. Austin Dobso treat Hogarth and to class him, and the task has been clearly a pleasure "—*Academy*

"Should do good service in extending knowledge on art subjects."—*Cambridge Revi*

Each Volume is illustrated with from Twelve to Twenty Full-page En vings, printed in the best manner, and bound in ornamental cloth cover, 3s.

The following Biographies are now ready:—

HOGARTH.	**LEONARDO DA VINCI.**
TURNER.	**FIGURE PAINTERS**
RUBENS.	**HOLLAND.**
HOLBEIN.	**MICHELANGELO.**
TINTORETTO.	**DELAROCHE** and **VERNE**
LITTLE MASTERS OF GER-	**FRA ANGELICO.**
MANY.	**FRA BARTOLOMMEO.**
RAPHAEL.	**LANDSEER.**
VAN DYCK and **HALS.**	**GIOTTO.**
TITIAN.	**REYNOLDS.**
REMBRANDT.	

GAINSBOROUGH and **CONSTABLE.** By GEORGE BROCK-ARNO M.A. Illustrated with 17 Engravings after their most popular works, including "The Duchess of Devonshire," and "The Blue-boy," GAINSBOROUGH; and "The Valley Farm," and "The Cornfield," CONSTABLE.

SIR DAVID WILKIE. By JOHN W. MOLLETT, B.A. Illustrated w numerous Engravings,—including double-paged pictures of "Bli Man's-Buff," "The Rent Day," "The Penny Wedding," "Dunc Gray," and many other popular works.

*** Other Volumes are in preparation.